"Everyone can learn something about courage and self-discovery from *Becoming a Man*."

—*San Francisco Chronicle*

"One of the most complex, moral, personal, and political books to have been written about gay life."

—*L.A. Weekly*

"Fiercely committed to bequeathing a map of his psychic terrain to spare others the pain of his solitary journey, [Monette's] fine memoir is affirmative and ultimately celebratory."

—*New York Times Book Review*

"Monette writes sentences so good that reading them to distant friends over the phone, whole paragraphs at a time, hardly seems compliment enough."

—*Washington Post Book World*

"Remarkable . . . unsparingly observed and beautifully written. . . . The power of this riveting book is in part the application of Monette's acute intelligence, his ceaseless observation, and his cagey wit to a simple, impossible problem. American culture demanded of Paul—as it still demands of lesbian and gay youth—that he be the one thing he could not be: straight. . . . Thrilling and painful for those of us who know firsthand what he is talking about. For those who have been unaware, this is a necessary book."

—*Los Angeles Times Book Review*

"This memoir, which begins with rage and ends with a breath of belated counterculture hopefulness, suggests that the age of AIDS is still the age of discoveries. . . . Monette writes with verve and bitter wit and an elegance made brittle by so much controlled anger. . . . No one has written more honestly about the sexual revolution and why we had to have it."
                                                  —*New York Newsday*

"A daring and heartbreaking memoir. Facing the truth about himself may not, in the end, have saved Monette's life, but it did set him free, and in the society he describes, that is triumph enough."
                                                  —*Boston Globe*

"Should open many closet doors. . . . Regardless of your sexual orientation, you can't read *Becoming a Man* without more fully appreciating the emotional minefield awaiting gay youth—and the courage required to negotiate it."
                                                  —*Seattle Times*

"Monette understands that the journey from boy to man is a dangerous one for all men. . . . The best lesson of this exceptional autobiography is that we as men can transcend repression."
                                                  —*Village Voice*

"From the opening page, with its stunningly apt observation that the closet feels as if you have 'no story at all,' . . . Monette takes his readers on a roller coaster of an odyssey. . . . One of the most impressive achievements of this superb memoir is Monette's success at crafting his narrative so that it is at once his unique story, with all the excruciating particularity of his situation, and, at the same time, the story of an entire generation of gay men."
                                                  —*Lambda Book Report*

"Beautifully written. . . . A heartfelt illumination of how a gay person overcame the self-reproach that societal condemnation enacts."   —*Publishers Weekly*

"A poignant, bittersweet memoir. . . . Each stage of [Monette's] personal journey is described at an intimate, insightful, human level."   —*Library Journal*

"Maybe one of the great American autobiographies. . . . A book in which virtually every gay man will see himself; with which virtually every lesbian and bisexual will empathize; which will powerfully move the parents, siblings, and friends of gays. . . . As witty as it is anguished and as full of understanding as of anger, this is Monette's best book."   —*Booklist*

"A deep, clear lake of recollection as tranquil on its surface as it is intensely passionate in the subterranean rills that feed it. . . . Stands as a talisman for the millions of queer lives it so clearly parallels."   —*The Advocate*

Becoming
a Man

Paul Monette

Becoming
a Man

Half a Life Story

PERENNIAL ■ CLASSICS

"Lux Et Veritas" from *Sixty Poems of Martial Translation*, copyright © 1967 by Dudley Fitts, reprinted by permission of Harcourt Brace Jovanovich, Inc.

"Do What You Gotta Do" by Jim Webb © 1967 Charles Koppelman Music / Martin Bandier Music / Jonathan Three Music Co. All rights reserved. International copyright secured. Used by permission.

A hardcover edition of this book was published in 1992 by Harcourt Brace Jovanovich, Inc. It is here reprinted by arrangement with Harcourt Brace Jovanovich, Inc.

HarperCollins books may be purchased for educational, business, or sales promotional use. For information please write: Special Markets Department, HarperCollins Publishers Inc., 10 East 53rd Street, New York, NY 10022.

First HarperSanFrancisco paperback edition published 1993.

First Perennial Classics edition published 2004. Perennial Classics are published by Perennial, an imprint of HarperCollins Publishers.

Designed by Lydia D'moch

Library of Congress Cataloging-in-Publication Data is available.

ISBN 0-06-059564-7

06 07 08 ❖/RRD 10 9 8 7 6 5 4 3

For my brother
    who's walked the tallest of us all
And for Winston
    who keeps me dancing even in the dark

I hear it was charged against me that I sought to destroy institutions,
But really I am neither for nor against institutions,
(What indeed have I in common with them? or what with the
   destruction of them?)
Only I will establish in the Manahatta and in every city of these
   States inland and seaboard,
And in the fields and woods, and above every keel little or large that
   dents the water,
Without edifices or rules or trustees or any argument,
The institution of the dear love of comrades.

— Walt Whitman

Foreword

TOWARD THE END OF HIS life, Paul Monette spoke of *Becoming a Man* with the hope that his book would continue, in his absence, to provide solace and meaning for gay men and women who, like himself, grew up closeted and horribly alone. Monette came of age in the 1950s, when cultural reference points such as *Father Knows Best* served to both illustrate and cement American society's expectation that men and women be heterosexual and together create the only acceptable lifestyle, that of the nuclear family. Having spent the early part of his career on novels and poems that in his estimation "meant nothing," Monette was galvanized by the death of his lover, Roger Horwitz, from AIDS and by the persecution of homosexuals that continued to draw strength from the epidemic spread of that disease. He was ready to bear witness to his life as a man who loved men.

Borrowed Time, published in 1988, described Monette's last years with Horwitz, a relationship that seemed to have been perfect, even transcendent, as many of his readers wrote to tell him. Uncomfortable with the idealized, increasingly iconic image his admirers wanted and that he'd unwittingly helped them create, Monette, who had arrived at happiness only after years of secrecy and self-loathing, was inspired to correct—or at least complicate—the picture. After all, if his partnership with Horwitz were construed as representing the antithesis to manhood as it was conceived in *Father Knows Best*, then as a model it was necessarily reductive, limiting, and dangerous, with the capacity to nourish further misunderstanding and persecution. In 1990, Monette embarked on what was in effect a prequel to *Borrowed Time*: an honest, acute, enraged, polemical, witty, ultimately triumphant, and sometimes very unhappy story of one man's long struggle to accept his homosexuality.

Becoming a Man was published in 1992, when Monette was forty-six and dying of AIDS. Robbed of a future, robbed of his prime, a man whose youth had been sacrificed to prejudice and whose discovery of love came only after he'd managed to separate himself from self-hatred and from a society that (at best) marginalized gay men as designers, hairdressers, and charming dinner guests, Monette's vision of an audience was—as it would have to have been—compromised by his circumstances. Many writers dismiss their work in gestures of false humility. Having long suffered as a liar, Monette had become honest even to a fault. His underestimation of the appeal and the value of his last book wasn't a pose. His politics, which insisted on social equality, had shown him how democracy could inspire divisiveness rather than respect; his cultural vantage had been long narrowed by his particular entrapment, whittled down to the proverbial keyhole; together these must have made it impossible—presumptuous—for him to imagine himself in the role of Everyman. By the time he was writing what he subtitled his *Half a Life Story*, he was so surrounded—at last protected and insulated—by apologists and friends that we can forgive him for losing sight of all the many who, no matter their gender, date of birth, sexual orientation, or politics, were people very like the person he had been: people with dire secrets.

The closet isn't a province exclusive to homosexuals. There are as many closets as there are things to hide, and it would be a shame to allow Paul Monette to present his work to only a fraction of his potential readership. Great books transcend the specificity of their characters and settings and times; they speak truths about all human beings, everywhere, during every age. *Madame Bovary* is a great book because, in revealing the ravenousness of one woman, Gustave Flaubert allows his readers to glimpse the terrible hunger at the center of every mortal life, a maw into which limitless gowns and jewels and lovers may be thrown without quieting its clamor for more. *Ariel* is a great book because Sylvia Plath wields poetry like a knife, using it to vivisect herself, but in the process cutting everyone, allowing us to recognize our wounds in her spilled blood. *The Drowned and the Saved* is a great book because Primo Levi's unflinching, lifelong contemplation of the very thing he could not stand to consider—the Holocaust—becomes an imperative that we make human sense especially of those acts that defy our humanity and our reason.

And *Becoming a Man* is a great book because by showing his readers the extraordinary cost of living his secret life as a gay man, Paul Monette reacquaints all of us with our own secrets and the prices they exact. Secrecy protects; it sets apart. For these reasons, it's often confused with privacy, which also limits access to identity, property, and intimacy. But privacy, though it requires barriers and silences, doesn't inspire deceit; it need not imply conflict or hostility between what is guarded and what is public; nor does it presuppose guilt and innocence. To conceal a thing automatically makes the thing interesting, and thus both privacy and secrecy have the capacity to transform—to grant power and desirability to what is hidden. To protect privacy we might say to a prying individual, "That's none of your business." To shore up a secret we usually lie; we attempt to present a misleading, often contradictory, mask for the truth. The distinction is not absolute, but privacy is essentially benign, while it's hard to maintain the idea of secrecy as neutral, morally speaking.

When Paul Monette was nine and a half, and "primed for the sort of guilt that seals off all exits," his mother caught him and another boy with their pants unzipped and asked him what they were doing. "Nothing," he lied, and in that moment his life changed. His mother's suspicions, in no way alleviated by the lie, and his instinctive need to hide what he'd only just begun to understand as a pivotal—and disgraceful—difference between him and other boys predicted an alienation that would grow beyond his mother, ultimately separating Monette not only from most of the people with whom he came into contact but also, and much more destructively, from himself.

Religion, race, sexual identity, sexual partner, habit, philosophy, addiction, taste, even something as silly as dying one's hair: what is hidden may be of little or no consequence to anyone but the person hiding it, but the purgatory of the closet proceeds from the closeted's conviction that if anyone were to perceive who he or she really is, that person would revile and reject him or her. Conceived to protect, secrets have an insidious power. Within the keeper of a secret, the mandate to contain and guard cannot be limited to one subject or even one region of the psyche. Instead, the habit of secrecy, constantly reinforced to protect the hidden information, infects the whole person, who becomes not merely the keeper of a secret, but a secretive person, a person increasingly unavailable to human contact, a person who has lost the potential for intimacy and for love, a person who is fatally alone, and, worst of all, a person whose psyche is fragmented into a true, unexpressed self and however many personae he invents to obscure that withering, starved, despised essence. The closet is not so much a place in which a person may choose to hide as it is both requirement and symptom of a damaged soul.

The stakes are high in *Becoming a Man*. It's a peculiarly suspenseful book, one that reads like a thriller with a life hanging in the balance. It wouldn't be misleading to compare it, for example, to a novel like *Looking for Mr. Goodbar* by Judith Rossner. In that book a young woman, suffering the psychological blight of a girl whose self-regard has been forever diminished by her physical deformity, courts death in the shape of a demon lover. In *Becoming a Man*, Paul Monette, suffering the psychological blight of a boy whose self-regard has been destroyed by the shame and fear of being gay in a world of murderously intolerant straights, attempts to amputate his soul while sparing whatever of his body and intellect remains. What will become of the boy who began by hiding from his mother? Will he continue to hide throughout his life? Will he love and be loved? Will he live before he dies?

"Everybody else had a childhood." These are the opening words of *Becoming a Man*. After his years as a student at Phillips Academy and Yale University, followed by an aborted career as a prep school teacher—a career distinguished more by the terrors of a year-long affair with a student than by any academic conquest; after one unrequited crush after another, a handful of desperate, furtive, and ultimately dispiriting assignations; after suffering "the prison of twelve to twenty-five"; after all these trials, will Paul Monette find redemption, happiness, love? As readers we witness his evolution as a liar and are made increasingly anxious by our deepening conviction that

Monette's closet might become something more like a casket.

Written at the end of his life, written as he was dying of a disease that must have seemed the physical manifestation of the prejudice gay men have always recognized as murderous, *Becoming a Man* is a cri de coeur, not a simple scream but an articulate, lucid, and sustained howl. A cry distinguished by art, interrupted by anger and grief, tempered by humor, elevated by hope. A cry that can only be quieted by being heard.

And yet, as readers, we're an incidental audience. *Becoming a Man* has the integrity of having been written—lived—for the sake of its author. It's the one story Paul Monette had to tell himself, the one he stayed alive to finish.

Admit. Accept. Allow. Own. The language of confession flows not outward but inward. It is language that reveals confession's impact on the self rather than on the listener. When the closet door first opens, it's not so much that someone rushes immediately out as that so much flows in: the life that was denied.

—KATHRYN HARRISON

Becoming
a Man

One

EVERYBODY ELSE HAD A CHILDHOOD, for one thing — where they were coaxed and coached and taught all the shorthand. Or that's how it always seemed to me, eavesdropping my way through twenty-five years, filling in the stories of straight men's lives. First they had their shining boyhood, which made them strong and psyched them up for the leap across the chasm to adolescence, where the real rites of manhood began. I grilled them about it whenever I could, slipping the casual question in while I did their Latin homework for them, sprawled on the lawn at Andover under the reeling elms.

And every year they leaped further ahead, leaving me in the dust with all my doors closed, and each with a new and better deadbolt. Until I was twenty-five, I was the only man I knew who had no story at all. I'd long since accepted the fact that nothing had ever happened to me and nothing ever would. That's how the closet feels, once you've made your nest in it and learned to call it home. Self-pity becomes your oxygen.

I speak for no one else here, if only because I don't want to saddle the women and men of my tribe with the lead weight of my self-hatred, the particular doorless room of my internal exile. Yet I've come to learn that all our stories add up to the same imprisonment. The self-delusion of uniqueness. The festering pretense that we are the same as they are. The gutting of all our passions till we are a bunch of eunuchs, our zones of pleasure in enemy hands. Most of all, the ventriloquism, the learning how to pass for straight. Such obedient slaves we make, with such very tidy rooms.

Forty-six now and dying by inches, I finally see how our lives align at the core, if not in the sorry details. I still shiver with a kind of astonished delight when a gay brother or sister tells of that narrow escape from the coffin world of the closet. *Yes yes yes*, goes a voice in my head, *it was just like that for me*. When we laugh together then and dance in the giddy circle of freedom, we are children for real at last, because we have finally grown up. And every time we dance, our enemies writhe like the Witch in *Oz*, melting, melting — the Nazi Popes and all their brocaded minions, the rat-brain politicians, the wacko fundamentalists and their Book of Lies.

We may not win in the end, of course. Genocide is still the national sport of straight men, especially in this century of nightmares. And death by AIDS is everywhere around me, seething through the streets of this broken land. Last September I buried another lover, Stephen Kolzak — died of homophobia, murdered by barbaric priests and petty bureaucrats. So whether or not I was ever a child is a matter of very small moment. But every memoir now is a kind of manifesto, as we piece together the tale of the tribe. Our stories have died with us long enough. We mean to leave behind some map, some key, for the gay and lesbian people who follow — that they may not drown in the lies, in the hate that pools and foams like pus on the carcass of America.

I don't come from the past, I come from now, here in the cauldron of plague. When the doors to the camps were finally beaten down, the Jews of Europe no longer came from Poland and Holland and France. They came from Auschwitz and Buchenwald. But I will never understand how the straights could have let us die like this — year after year after year, collaborating by indifference — except by sifting through the evidence of my queer journey.

Why do they hate us? Why do they fear us? Why do they want us invisible?

I don't trust my own answers anymore. I'm too twisted up with rage, too hooked on the millennium. But I find myself combing the past these days, dreaming dreams without sleep, puzzling over my guys, the gay and the straight and the in-between. Somewhere in there is a horror of love, and to try to kill the beast in them, they take it out on us. Which is not to say I don't chastise myself for halving the world into *us* and *them*. I know that the good guys aren't all gay, or the bad all straight. That is what I am sifting for, to know what a man is finally, no matter the tribe or gender.

Put it this way. A month after Stevie died, running from grief, I drove three days through Normandy. In the crystalline October light I walked the beach at Omaha, scoped the landing from a German bunker, then headed up the pasture bluff to the white field of American crosses. American soil in fact, this ocean graveyard, unpolluted even by the SS visit of Reagan in '84, who couldn't tell the difference between the dead here and the dead at Bitburg. You can't do Normandy without D-Day. After Omaha, the carnage and heroism shimmer across the pastureland, ghosts of the soldiers who freed the world of evil for a while.

Two days later I fetched up in Caen, where they've built a Museum of Peace on the site of an eighty-day battle fought by three million men. Newsreel footage and camp uniforms, ration books, code breakers, yellow star and pink triangle. You watch it all happen like a slow bomb, from the end of World War I, the dementia of power, till the smithereens are in smithereens. You walk numbly from year to year, country to country, helpless as a Jew or a Gypsy or a queer.

And in the belly of the place there's this extraordinary room lined with pictures on either side. On the right are the collaborators, men — all men, of course — who ran the puppet governments for the Nazis. Vichy and Belgium and Denmark, the whole of Europe ruled by fawning men with dead eyes and fat ties, grins that show the gristle between their teeth. On the left wall, opposite, are the leaders of the Resistance — several women here — and they're lean and defiant and *alive*. Europe is in prison and the world is imploding, and these people are smiling because they can't lose.

So that is what I am doing in the past, figuring out who goes on the left wall and who on the right. For that is the choice, it seems to me: collaborate or resist. The left wall is not all gay and lesbian, and not everyone is out of the closet. I can't judge the world of my first twenty years by the laws of freedom that followed Stonewall. No man was the same after that. And I understand that every ethics — the gods I don't believe in and the wise men I do — tells me to forgive. But if that is what I have to do, I will have to learn not to forget first; to let in the light on the last attic room, the bones of a buried life.

It isn't all mine anyway — neither the lost years nor the victory — this tale of a boy who made it out of the woods. For I am the final gleam of Roger and Stephen as well, the two men I am surest of, who willed their stories to me. We couldn't have met each other anywhere but out in the open. As to whether being in the closet puts you on the wrong wall, with the collaborators, that is for men and women to judge themselves. I can't conceive the hidden life anymore, don't think of it as life. When you finally come out, there's a pain that stops, and you know it will never hurt like that again, no matter how much you lose or how bad you die. This I know: Those who are still in the closet will get the tale wrong, however I tell it. Get it as wrong as a cardinal would, or a shit-eating bachelor Republican. Knowing how they will get it wrong will be one of the things that keeps me going.

It's my word against the pictures, in any case — the 40's Brownie snapshots with scalloped edges. I look like a kid, I'm even laughing. In the front yard on Elm Street, five minutes' walk from the village, pulling the ears of a Saint Bernard called See-Soo. I am two or three, and the dog has a snappish attitude, except with me. I can do what I like, poke him and ride him and pull at his fur, and he takes it like a giant teddy bear.

This is the era as well of my singing and dancing on the dining room table, set there by my favorite aunt, Grace — later simply Auntie Mame. To whom I am ever grateful, though she cringes to recall it, for taking me when I was fourteen to see *Suddenly Last Summer* — from which I emerged dazzled and strangely sophisticated, if not quite sure what happened to Sebastian.

That was at the Andover Playhouse, two doors up from the Catholic church, which was cheek by jowl with the Boston & Maine depot. The story where nothing happens takes place here for twenty years, in Andover Massachusetts, a country town then, now a suburb of Boston. Founded in 1646 by whey-faced Puritans, all of whom seem to have ancestors down to the present age, cheeks hollow from sucking pennies. The only thrill they allowed themselves was the chafe of the woolens they wore, winter and summer.

Pretty in its way, Andover, with those arching trees vaulting the white-picket streets, Elm and Maple and Chestnut. The country around was still a patchwork of orchards and bedroom-sized Colonial burial grounds. And always the woods at the end of every street, the silent echo of the red man's footfalls, all the way out to Lake Cochicowick. On the windowsill in a kid's bedroom you'd find a row of stone arrowheads picked up in the woods behind his house.

It's ten miles west of Salem, where they burned a half-century of witches, mostly gay and lesbian. And four miles north of Reading, where Charles Stuart plotted the imperfect crime, the ritual slaughter of his pregnant wife. There's a Lizzie Borden in every town in Massachusetts, biding her time and her axe. Mostly the bodies are buried behind the barn. A good fifteen miles north of Boston, thus light years away. People in Andover talked about going to Boston as if it were a three-day trek by oxcart. You only went to the city for a Red Sox game, or a red-light tumble in Scollay Square.

No memory whatsoever of the life on Elm Street, though the house is still there, the roofline of the horse barn sagging close to the breaking point. We lived upstairs from my Grandmother Lamb, who'd capped her own long widowhood with a second husband—unheard of in those parts, scandalous as divorce. A widow was meant to be half-dead and look it.

This Robert Lamb had sailed over from England after the War to deliver a Rolls Royce to Andover's mythically rich mill owner, whose stone-gated estate was a woods of its own, reported to have a theater and a bowling alley, and a children's playhouse complete with its own china pattern. Robert Lamb was only meant to instruct the ham-fisted chauffeur in the care and handling of that yacht of a car, but the mill owner's wife decided she needed a proper Brit accent to go with it. So Lamb stayed and drove the car, refined as a landed duke himself, while the mill owner's wife rode in the back, looking lost and a little embalmed.

But that is the story passed down, not mine at all. It might as well be the *eighteen*-forties. Except my father has just returned from the War, nine missions over Japan, the navigator. He and my mother have been Air Force gypsies—South Carolina, Texas, New Mexico—aching to get back to New England, where the seasons come in the right order. I am born the day after they move into Elm Street. They're both twenty-three, married four years, high-school sweethearts before. Paul and Jackie—in the pictures he looks like John Wayne in *Stagecoach*, and she's Irene Dunne in *The Awful Truth*. Or are those their favorite movies?

I don't remember. And I never really cared to ask, either, because it had nothing to do with me. If the dog had mauled me, perhaps, or if I'd fallen off the table and split my head, there might have been a glimmer. Then the baby's years would have been a proper shadow of what came later. Instead there is just this rumor of joy, a stunt baby singing his head off, riding a pony, paddling the shallows at Old Orchard Beach. Not me.

By 1950 we have our own house, at 116 High Street. Prefab, knocked together by my father and uncles. Big Paul is driving a truck for the Cross Coal Company, and Little Paul ought to be in kindergarten—except I'm not. Nobody's ever explained it to my satisfaction. I'm born in October, so I didn't turn five till the school year had already started, and four-year-olds couldn't go. But then why did they put me not in kindergarten but first grade a year later, still just five? I don't care, except it leaves my fifth year high and dry, extending the blur of amnesia. Still I'm no one.

Was it then that my mother went in to have her appendix out? This, too, is all secondhand, but my father tells me sheepishly how he was driving me over to my grandmother's house so he could go up to the hospital. We passed a hilltop cemetery, and I pointed and said, "She's in there, isn't she?" That's the first sentence I recognize — that's me. Someone forgot to tell me everything was fine. Notice the bleak fatalism, the boy waiting to toss off his awful knowledge: *Oh by the way, Dad, I know she's dead.*

The only thing new about 116 High Street was the television, a four-inch screen of snow in a lumbering cabinet, the first TV in the world, it seemed, given the crowd of relatives and neighbors who gathered in awe. Even through the snow I recall the images clearer than my family: Kate Smith and Howdy Doody, and Dinah Shore for Chevrolet. The lurid banality of the 50's was all there in incubation, the postwar slumber of the soul, tuned to whatever felt easy. Now that the radio had an eye, it would do all the seeing for us.

Was there news? If so, we didn't watch it. I don't remember Truman, or Eisenhower later, but maybe they hadn't perfected the White House hookup yet, the uranium shine of Oval Office doubletalk. Besides, all the news that would define me twenty years later went unreported. The two sick queens who hunted us down when I was too young to know — Roy Cohn and J. Edgar Hoover — were given free rein by the Red Scare delirium; they flushed out queers and wrecked lives to throw the scent off their own ravening desire. Cardinal Spellman being the third member of the homo death squad, postwar division. Three little closeted mama's boys, ensuring that the Aryan dream of elimination would continue.

Mama's boy. The evidence of 116 High Street suggests as much, but it's still all hearsay. The cemetery remark aches with Oedipal static — *How dare you die on me?* Then the first day of school: I stood at the classroom window, unconsolable, learning nothing, waiting for Mother to come pick me up. Would kindergarten have helped? Did my mother and I spend year five together instead, in a school of our own, where I learned the fear of abandonment? Much much later, when I was forty and she was sixty, on oxygen now, she shook her head ruefully, taunted by ghosts: "I wish we'd watched more sunsets together."

But isn't that what we did instead of kindergarten?

Right after that — it had to be before November of '51 — she was walking me across the parking lot to the school, and she fell. Stumbled on something and sat down hard on the pavement. I really do remember this, remember standing beside her helplessly, her face level with mine, a twist of pain. She couldn't get up, and I wasn't strong enough. Then two grownups trotted over to help us. Now I was embarrassed that we had caused a scene, my mother and I. And yet she rose from the ground, in their arms, with a certain grace and laughed it off. I remember the laugh.

I never mentioned this for thirty years. It didn't seem much to tell, connected to nothing. But one winter day we were sitting in the dining room, my mother's place to think. I was in from California, weekending in the old country. I laughed when I said it. "Remember the day you fell outside the school? I was so embarrassed."

A wrinkled half-smile as her eyebrows lifted, always loving a chance to set the record straight. "I was pregnant with Bobby," she replied softly. "That could've been very serious."

Could've been? I felt this tilt in my gut, to see how half-blind memory was. Pregnant with my brother, so if we were walking to school, it had to be that autumn of first grade, and before November 6. There must be a reason why a man can only recall two things from his first six years — a ride past a graveyard, his mother falling. Guilt, I suppose, or a piercing sense of inadequacy that will course through the boy like an underground river, eroding from within. Like those kids who take the blame for their parents' divorce, or the daily beatings, or the nightly rape. The looming cave of emptiness where the past ought to be, for the river has cut a channel a mile deep through solid rock, fed by a single wrong idea. The idea that what was about to happen to us was nobody's fault but mine.

I suppose there must have been some moment when they told me my brother was born. Probably Nana Lamb — that's where I stayed. She and Bob were living by then in Shawsheen, in a bungalow at the edge of the mill owner's kingdom. A boy, they must have said, and he would be called Robert Lamb Monette — after the Englishman himself, so you see what a fine impression he'd made on the family. So when could I see the baby? And why wasn't everyone happy?

The rest I would have to learn by inadvertence, for this was the week I became invisible, the spy whose cover was being a child. None of the medical stuff was intelligible, of course, except for "crippled." From here I see how the word is rotten with judgment, obscenely Biblical, hissing curses. *Your brother will never walk. He will forfeit his boyhood shuttling back and forth to a hospital for crippled children, where they will break his legs and try to reassemble them, over and over in a jigsaw of pain. Damn you all.*

Spina bifida was the technical term, but it took a lifetime before my brother and I could speak it plain. When they brought him home and I saw him first in his bassinet, I thought they must have made a mistake, or I'd heard it wrong. Because he was lovely. The thinness of his legs, the frozen knees and ankles, were irrelevant. Babies didn't need to walk, anyway. They rode in strollers and carriages. For a while at least we could put it all off, and no one would know unless we told them. I wasn't telling.

I understand now how brave my parents were to bring him home at all. Some people didn't. The family porn that passes for Christian rectitude has always funded nicely the putting away of the not-quite-perfect. Homes and farms, Special Care, Blue-Cross-covered. Kin to the children abandoned by the millions in the Middle Ages, foundlings put out to die. Baby girls snuffed in China, immolated in India. Suffer the little children, indeed.

And so they embarked on this journey, Paul and Jackie. How prepared, by what clichés of fortitude, I can't imagine. Apparently they were given to understand that Bobby would likely die before he was five, then ten, fifteen — on and on, an everpresent shadow never quite disappearing, all the time on its side. But here was the remarkable thing: They went at it as if there were nothing wrong, as if we were normal. No complaints, no tears I ever saw. Yankee tough. I don't blame them for this anymore. Grit is an ethics all its own. Except, I needed to talk to somebody about it, so I could stop being invisible.

We moved again, to Florence Street, a bare stone's throw from the center of town. In second grade at Central, I got all A's. *Paul is perfect*, it says on one of Mrs. Rumfield's blue report cards. Me against the evidence yet again. I even blended in with a neighborhood gang of thugs, though never straying any further out of line than Mr. Krinsky's junkyard, where I was forbidden to play. I loved that Caligari junglegym of rusty bedsprings and dead appliances. I knew the rules: the slightest cut, and you'd end up with lockjaw, and never hide in an icebox. *Memento mori*. When you opened an old Amana in Krinsky's yard, you always held your breath in case there was a smothered kid inside.

Already I'd started to flirt with genderfuck. I clumped up and down on the hardwood floors in my mother's heels, prancing even, right in front of the grownups. And I had a thing for paper dolls. I almost remember the tail end of a flareup between my parents, over the issue of my inappropriate fascinations. No word like *sissy* yet, and the only subtext I picked up was the pleasure of being fretted over. Because otherwise, *Paul is perfect* left no room for anything, sealed like a box at Krinsky's.

Possessive mother? Absent father? Not especially. I thought they were both quite nice, and beautiful as movie stars. If anyone was distant, I was. Secretive and isolated, conscious of being a cool observer, all those A's a kind of shield. Besides, my brother was the one who had to be taken care of—literally, carried. That's the most vivid image I have of my father's strength, bearing Bobby in his arms whenever we all went out, long after the infant years. If it made me jealous or left me out, I can't summon the feeling.

I remember the moment in art history at Andover, when the terra-cotta image flashed onscreen, Zeus carrying Ganymede away, the boy in his arms. It was my father and my brother. But I put the lid on the memory right away, vaguely aghast, because the statue was about lust, the hunger of the god for mortal youth. It didn't bear too much thinking, wrapped as I was by then in the bodiless cocoon of my own adolescence. I got an A in art history anyway.

My father's efforts to redirect me from paper dolls to right field were half-hearted enough, and I bless him now for not forcing the issue. Happily, within a few years my brother was as mad for sports as Big Paul, and that took the heat off me. I admit there's a boggling irony here — that my brother turned into a sandlot star of sorts, batting from a seated position and crawling around the bases, dragging those atrophied legs behind. For me it proved an unutterable relief; I put away my Wilson fielder, never quite broken in. Let *them* be the male-bonded unit. They still are — swapping ball scores, crowing over the Celtics as they sit down to a killer game of cards. Me, I can't tell the plays from the players even with a program. And ask either my father or brother: I play the dumbest cards of anyone in the family, so passive when it comes to bidding that I am barely there.

A little theory here, or anti-theory. A debate is brawling these days among the gender scholars, between the "essentialists" and the "constructivists." The essentialist argues that there is a genetic predisposition to being gay and lesbian. Thus gay people have always existed, "different" from the mainstream but crucial to the health of the race. This separate kind has always been a class of nurturers and teachers, healers and shamans — consciously so, and cherished, even, by tribes from Arizona to Tahiti. In the formulation of sociobiologist E. O. Wilson, "Homosexuals may be the genetic carriers of mankind's rare altruistic impulses."[1]

---

1. I am indebted here, as throughout, to Richard Isay's groundbreaking work in *Being Homosexual: Gay Men and Their Development*, where Wilson is quoted at greater length. Also to Mark Thompson, whose *Gay Spirit* and subsequent work have dared to envision a unified field theory of essentialist and constructivist.

The constructivists would have it that gender and sexual identity are wholly modern ideas, that nobody in the deep past could have thought of himself as "gay" because there was no such thing. Gender is a social construct of a post-agrarian age, or post-industrial, or post-something. I admit my own sympathies lie with the essentialists — though it's clear enough that a modern queer, his brothers and sisters no longer hidden, engages a larger identity than his mute ancestors ever could. A self among others.

The anti-theory involves the repudiation of so-called classical analytic theory, where the homosexual is "deviant" because he never resolves the Oedipal riddle. It turns out not to be so classical after all. Freud himself, in his famous letter to a gay man's mother, suggested that being queer was inborn and healthy. More to the point, as Dr. Isay argues, it was the immigrant psychoanalysts after the War who pumped up the deviant model when they settled in America. For purely political reasons: they saw the drift of McCarthyism and made their second-best bed with rigid conservatism, betraying the radical, antibourgeois thrust of psychiatry in Europe. Conformity became the only truth.

Which isn't to say we weren't as dysfunctional as any other nuclear meltdown family in the 50's. Still, my family didn't make me queer. The deviant is the homophobe, but you've already thrown your youth away by the time you've learned that. As for denial, the Monettes were registering off the graph by 1953. We'd moved yet again, to 37 High Street — 37R, the house in the rear. My father, who'd been promoted from the truck to the office of the coal company, had scraped together the down payment on a pair of two-family houses.

My brother was two years old and still riding in a stroller, otherwise carried by Zeus. In other words, no wheelchair — as if that would be somehow admitting defeat. In the house my brother crawled around — *creeping*, we called it, unaware that it sounded like the way ghouls moved in horror movies. Bobby's condition didn't seem strange at all to us; it was simply a fact of life. Until we went out, and strangers stared, and everyone seemed to know.

My brother has swallowed a lot of bitterness about the absence of that wheelchair, for which he says his body was *designed*. They were holding out, I expect, for a proper March of Dimes sort of miracle. The glowing grin of a kid on crutches, one step short of dancing. And eventually that's what the cripple doctors pushed for, too, the sentiment of the poster child: *The lame shall walk.*

In her last years, my mother was passionately outspoken about the lack of guidance and resources, especially when I'd tell her about all the AIDS support groups. Paul and Jackie had had to go it alone. No place to process their own suffering, psychiatry being out of the question, not for the working class in a country town. Just the church, in our case Christ Episcopal, a Richardsonian brownstone Romanesque tucked between the white-spired Congregational and the third-hand Greek revival of the Baptists.

The rector of Christ was one John Moses — a booming Old Testament voice worthy of his name, and a heartiness so visceral, he took your breath away. My father taught sixth-grade Sunday school, my Aunt Grace fourth. Nana Lamb went to eight A.M. communion, "because they get you in and get you out." Fond of the prophet Moses as all the rest of the parish ladies, Nana was never big on sermons. She also worked the Saturday shift at the church thrift shop, practically a fixture there, dressed to the nines with her upswept steel-gray hair, an unmistakable air of *noblesse oblige*. She took to the Anglican edge of it all like a duchess, though without the icy permanent sneer and fish handshake of a Brahmin.

And the invisible boy? Well, I almost never missed a Sunday all the way through sixth grade, and got confirmed besides. I like to think I was always a closet atheist, but for a while at least I went along with the others. I hadn't started having it out with Catholics yet, except for a small encounter with Maidie Lynch. A budding moron in third grade, somehow Maidie had missed the cut for parochial school, and she came to us instead at Central, offering up novenas with delirious abandon. Apprised by some little inquisitor, Maidie discovered that my father had converted from the R.C.'s when he married my mother. Stalking up to me in the cafeteria, Maidie pounced.

"You're going to go to hell, Paul Monette," she informed me with glittering eyes. "Conversion's a mortal sin! You'll burn forever — and your brother's the proof!"

My first acquaintance with the sins of the father, how they passed down and damned his issue. I laughed in Maidie's face. And though I continued my perfect attendance on Sundays, the eight-year-old had had his first real lesson in religion. God didn't come out on top.

Sunday afternoons we'd go over to Lawrence in the '51 Buick, to visit the other side. The Monette grandparents were as stubbornly French as my mother's people were English. They lived in a great peeling pile of a gingerbread Victorian, where Grandpa Joe still had his shingle out, though he was well into his eighties when I knew him. An awesome presence, who ate onions raw like apples and stilled his own liquor in a bathtub. The parlor walls were chockablock with glass-fronted bookcases, leather-bound sets of authors, mostly French immortals. If his learned gravity was unapproachable, he was kind enough to us kids and always gave us quarters. Invariably Bobby and I stayed meekly at floor level, eye to eye with the black gryphons that held up the library table.

Joe was a totem figure in Lawrence, lawyer and general sage to masses of immigrants from Quebec, the broken-French mill-workers who kept the hum going in the vast brick textile engines along the Merrimack. He'd made and lost a couple of fortunes, and apparently drunk his fair share of champagne from chorus girls' slippers. Decidedly anticlerical, but that was nothing compared to his animus toward the Irish. Hardly alone in that: where I come from, Micks and Canucks are the Hatfields and McCoys, with so much hate to spew about one another that they hardly had any left over for blacks and other exotic types.

The only son among four sisters, Joe had taken his entrance

exams to Harvard Law in classical Greek, because his English was still shaky. And told us once — even at eight I remember being appalled at the arbitrariness — that he'd added the last two letters to the family name because he got so tired of his Harvard profs mispronouncing Monet with a hard T. The single truly outsize figure in the family, always held up to me for the value of having a profession. Twenty years later I'd still run into the occasional elderly frog whose eyes would mist and voice choke when he heard I was Joe Monette's grandson.

The four sisters meanwhile stayed in Montreal, becoming nuns. There's a single sepia photograph of these gaunt and basset-faced ladies in wimples. Too ugly to find husbands, my French grandmother used to remark with scathing disdain. Ubaldine, she was called, and no slouch or fading violet despite the aura of gravitas that clung about her husband. She rented three floors of upstairs rooms in the big house, to boarders who seemed like Damon Runyon characters to me — traveling men and oddly fallen women with too much rouge and fumigant perfume.

Ubaldine was pencil-thin and caustic, and fearless at evicting. Her culinary specialty was head cheese, a sort of grainy pâté that tasted wondrous but didn't bear too much scrutiny of the pig scraps that went into it. A couple of summers we stayed with her in her boarding house at Hampton Beach, over the border in New Hampshire. The clientele was even more fly-by-night — guys who ran the carnival rides over at Salisbury, or the ring-toss booths and skeeball alleys in the faded Hampton casino.

She made her own money and tucked it away, having learned the hard way not to trust the ups and downs of the old lawyer's fortunes, and having no desire to subsidize the bubbly for the chorus girls. Years after Joe died — Ubaldine lived to be ninety, too, despite a half century of diabetes — her usual remark about the man she'd lived with sixty years was a sort of French harrumph. Sounded like good riddance. But she made damn sure she had a priest and two nuns at his wake, droning a rosary on and on, thus having the last word on his violent antipopery.

That Sunday world of the ancients was my only regular foray

into the urban stew of Lawrence, already half-dead in the 50's as the textile baronies fled to the South in droves. It always had the feel of a ghost city, mined out and long passed by. Where Andover had those woods at the end of every street, Lawrence always seemed to lead to slag heaps, the tailings and derelict factories like a Krinsky's junkyard for giants.

Maybe once a month my father would take me over to Cross Coal with him on a Saturday morning, an irresistible time together that didn't require me to throw a pass or bat four hundred. The sheds and coalyard on Railroad Street were a moonscape of the raw and brutal. Conic piles of anthracite three stories high, a fleet of grimy dumptrucks, and coal drivers out of a chimney sweep's tale, bulked like aging linebackers and grinning through the soot.

Big Paul was the main dispatcher, boss of a crew of drivers and mechanics whose blue trucks seemed to fuel the whole of Merrimack Valley, the industrial revolution on wheels. More and more it was oil rather than coal, my father sending out teams in the summer to refit old houses with oil burners. The company had been around since the mid-nineteenth century, delivering firewood and coal off horse wagons.

I don't know how much I've romanticized all this, since I did it from the beginning. I thrilled to the rough and tumble of the men, the purple streams of profanity, the cowboy moves as they loaded and weighed the trucks. Mostly Canuck, with names like Gus and Fat. They treated me like a prince, letting me trail after them into the shed where their lockers were, strewn with tabloids and cartons of doughnuts. I wasn't conscious ever of eroticizing the place, but it was definitely a world of men, and I loved it.

Fearfully proud of my father too, how he knew every cellar in Christendom, knew who the deadbeats were and who called only when the bin was empty. The main event of Saturday morning was eating, big stevedore breakfasts at railroad diners, a ladle of beans and salt pork running into the eggs and brown bread. They all knew Dad in Lawrence — the cops, the dolly waitresses, the bib-apron shopkeepers on Essex Street.

I stayed back in his shadow, the kid with all A's, not shy exactly but out of my league and keeping my own counsel. And when we went back to the office, I'd play with the adding machines and a stone-age Royal typewriter, its butterfly tiers of letters slapping the paper so hard, they punched right through. I don't know what I wrote, but I practiced it like a musical instrument — two fingers, same as today.

I figure we were at 37 High Street from '52 to '55, third grade to fifth. The neighborhood was decidedly downscale, mostly two-family and blue-collar. A couple of streets running off High were unpaved; clusters of millworker cottages with chickens running wild. The gang of kids had the run of the backyards, some not even mowed, the derelict barns and stables fabulous places to hide. Outside our bedroom window was a yellow cherry tree, the Queen Anne variety, and something stirs yet when these appear at my upscale market in Hollywood at seven dollars a pound, the taste of being young.

Next door was a girl my age, Joyce, whose family was French and Indian, some long-assimilated clan of the Massachusetts nation. Joyce was also in my class, crash-landing with D's and F's on every report card. For a while it didn't keep us apart, and we collaborated in fantasy games in western gear. She was the scout and I the cowboy hero, so *The Lone Ranger* must've been our jumping-off point. From my present vantage I have no doubt that her deep-seated tomboy nature was incubating a lesbian. By sixth grade the F's had driven her crazy, and Joyce became a duck-tailed hood in junior high, hell-raising and much expelled. Dyslexic, I suppose, but we had no word for it then. And long gone from my life, though I've always wondered what kind of chance Joyce had to come out. Our differentness from the rest was so similar in the cowboy days, despite our opposite grades. Both loners, both out scouting.

But my main playmate was Toby, the second of three boys who lived with their mother in an achingly tidy white bungalow four doors down from us. Toby's father had died of cancer a couple of years before I knew him — the first death I ever took in on a conscious level, or at least the empty space it left behind. Not that we ever talked about it, but there was a muted quality to Toby, a wound that had grown inexpressible. It connected us under the skin.

We tramped the yards after school in various psychic disguises, from Tarzan to *Wagon Train*, Joyce joining in if we thought we'd encounter hostile Indians. We were the first generation to enact its myths from the tube. I was already addicted to reading, and so demanded equal time for the Hardy Boys and Robin Hood, but it was no contest. I sat glued to the TV in the den — by now twelve inches and the snow just flurries — from six till nine every night of the week, drinking up stories for after school.

As it happened, Toby was the only kid I knew who wasn't allowed to watch at all. Also not permitted candy or Coca-Cola — these bleak austerities somehow connected to the fate of being fatherless. So I was always the yarn spinner, recapping each week's episodes and using the thread to play out our own adventures. Hands down, the show that provided the most vivid terrain was *Lassie*. Tommy Rettig as Jeff, Jan Clayton as Mom, George Cleveland as Gramps — I can see the credits rolling even now, the names more real than the faded ghosts of High Street, cousins and classmates both.

A thousand times we played these parts, Toby and I. As story editor, I would always get to be Jeff, leaving Toby the role of Porky — second banana, without a question. Porky lived on the next farm down the road, and besides his girth and slovenly appetite, he was notable for his breathless running and dogged loyalty to Jeff. But since Toby never actually saw the show and carried no extra weight himself, his stage name never bothered him. The canine role was given by default to our golden cocker, Skipper, no hunter and surely no warrior, so we all had to do a little stretching.

What is it, girl? I think she wants us to follow her. And with that we'd be off through the fields and woods, rescuing children from wells and corralling runaway palominos. No dark edges, as I remember, good family viewing, every crisis wrapped before the last commercial. It would be soon enough that I'd want to be doing dirty things with Tommy Rettig, but that would come after my own blood initiation into the carnal. Meanwhile, the inseparable afternoons with Toby were the last to have the gone-fishin' texture of *Boy's Life*. Before Toby joined the Cub Scouts, with those sugar-free teeth of his, and before I became a wanton slut.

Jump-cut to 1990, two days after Thanksgiving. Still black-and-blue from Stevie dying, hardly back a week from Normandy, I drove up the coast past Zuma, then headed inland up the old Mulholland Highway. The Radical Faeries were having their annual gathering in the coastal mountains, once the sacred ground of the Chumash. So far this patch of hills has escaped the predations of the land eaters, nothing but chaparral on either side of the twisting road. I hooked a right into Camp Shalom, a Jewish summer camp that had gritted its liberal teeth and agreed to let the Faeries rent the place for a week.

I parked at the edge of a dry stream bed and walked through a grove of sycamore, out to a beaten field where the group was having its circle. I found the man who'd invited me — now my lover — and sat by him, catching the tail end of a legend being told by a figure in the circle's center. When he'd finished, another man came up to take his place, and a talisman necklace was passed to the new speaker. "From the heart," admonished several voices on the perimeter.

The ritual proceeded deep into the afternoon, drawing the tribe together. Some men were naked, some half-clothed in leather and feathers. Tattoos and piercings decorated several bodies, and here and there a catheter coiled in a patch of gauze on a chest, for the plague has ravaged the tribe. A curious mix of grief and exultation, the atmosphere not sexual, just free. All seven ages of man had come, it seemed, from callow boys in cutoffs to a white-bearded sage in a caftan. Whitman would have been right at home: "A man, yet by these tears a little boy again."

When the sun had sunk behind the trees, Winston and I went straggling away through the sycamores to find some food.

In a clearing still pooled with sun stood a small white ranch house with a porch, the camp's administration building. He pointed toward it and said, "That's where they used to shoot *Lassie*."

I stood transfixed in a hollow of time, recalling in a cascading rush all I have set down here of High Street and how we played. I'm a child of Hollywood, no doubt about it, full of B-plots and Bette Davis lines, but this was something more. Because it wasn't just the old footage rolling — Mom calling Jeff to supper from the porch — but the world out there beyond the sycamores, rife with open spaces and runaway palominos. Who ever thought about where they filmed it?

I looked around at the dusty trees, the brush-covered hill and the rocky pass beyond leading out of the canyon along the dry stream bed. And I thought, *This is why I came here*. Meaning the whole move to California, this rough terrain I couldn't get out of my head since the first day I saw it in '64. Not ever quite understanding that I'd seen it before, how many seasons on CBS, running headlong with Toby a breath behind me.

I was nine and a half when everything changed. I left behind the boys' stories, because they didn't make sense anymore, and felt no regret except for the loss of the wild country they happened in. The backyards ceased to be badlands, a rattler under every rock, and the woods no longer promised to spirit me away. The town became just a town again, with no escape except to grow up and flee it. And the bleached frontier where boys ran free, circled overhead by wheeling hawks, was shut away in a toy box. Till the Faeries brought me full circle.

The sea-change came in the shape of a ruffian called Kite. I no longer know what the nickname stood for. He lived on one of those rutted dirt lanes with chickens, his father a red-faced drunk who worked at Tyer Rubber. I knew Kite from the corner of my eye, but only to keep my distance. At nine he was already famous for picking fights and for a mouth like a sewer. All I really remember of what he looked like was the pugnacious jut of his chin. He always seemed to be snarling and showing his crooked teeth. Millworkers' kids didn't get braces.

It was rumored among us softer types that Kite and his brothers were whipped by their dad with a razor strop whenever he was drunk, which was all the time. If it hurt, you'd never have known by looking at Kite, the most dry-eyed kid in the neighborhood. But what really shocked us was to hear how Kite rode his bike to Pomp's Pond every day in the summer — to *swim*. This was defiance bordering on madness, for Pomp's was the local Polio Pit. A single wrong swallow in those days, and you'd end up in an iron lung, or so our spooked parents believed. No swimming except in the ocean.

I knew how Kite saw me — half awe and half contempt, on account of those endless A's. It was strange and a little dangerous to be talking to him at all, but I couldn't find anyone else that day. The yards were silent, as if a piper had lured the children away. I was standing perplexed in somebody's driveway, feeling deserted, when Kite was suddenly there on his bike, wheeling around me in slow circles. Did I know where everyone was? he asked, taunting me with the secret. I gave him back an imperious shrug, as if I couldn't have cared less.

"They're in the Thompson barn," he said, veering off in a lazy figure eight and doubling back. "Ruthie showed us between her legs." My face went hot with shame. "There's nothing there."

I'd never thought about what was there. I stood frozen, straining for nonchalance, even as the circles of his ride seemed to bind me like a spider web. "You wanna go over and see?" he asked.

"No," I retorted, a little too loud, and turned away. But not before I caught the last twist of a smile on his face, patient and almost bored, so certain was he of his prey. And — what was most disturbing — as if he knew me better than I knew myself.

How long before it came to a head? Days or weeks, I can't be sure, but I thought about Kite incessantly. Not about Ruthie, or even the naughty spectacle of the neighborhood kids turning the

Thompson barn into a strip joint. It was all Kite, his unstated dare riddling my mind. So when I trotted through the yards one winter afternoon and came around the side of Naylor's toolshed, what followed was as inevitable as falling out of a tree from climbing too high, drunk on cherries.

Kite was taking a leak in the bushes. His eyes locked on mine, that superior patient smile again, and I was lost. The stream dribbled to drops, and he shook it, but didn't put it back in his pants. Ducked instead through the broken window of the toolshed. I followed, shedding my A's like a chrysalis. He yanked my pants down, and we rubbed our two hard weenies together. Neither of us any bigger than the first joint of my little finger, hairless and nothing to shoot. But I was hooked on pleasure from that day on.

And hooked on Kite, more than anything because he was a bad boy. That was the turn-on — the twist of his dirty mouth, the punk veneer, the boot-camp father, like an urchin in *Oliver Twist*. Next to Kite I was so Protestant upright, insufferably well-mannered and self-effaced. And bodiless for the three years since my brother was born, because the body was too upsetting to think about, let alone play with. Till Kite I was on a neat monastic track, junior division, rising above the flesh. A Puritan choirboy and a prig, already sucking pennies. I honestly can't recall a single thought about sex before Kite. But now that I'd had a taste of sweet damnation, it was hard to think of anything else.

The guilt may have been there right along, but I was too hungry to notice at first. I don't know how many times it happened between us, maybe only a dozen, but it felt like the main subject of fifth grade, way ahead of long division. Never a planned thing: Kite and I would see each other on the street and go off behind a barn, or up in the attic of our garage. We'd have pissing contests — once in a can of white paint, a kinky thrill afterwards to watch my father brush it onto a fence.

By June we were sleeping outside in a tent, putting it together like a couple of scouts, though the merit badge we were going for wasn't for camping. Finally we could get naked and really go to town, sticking those little gumdrop members between each other's legs for some simulated fucking, taking turns on top. As for Miss Noyes's class that year, I breezed right through, but distracted and on automatic — like Lady Chatterley pouring tea, squeezing her knees at the memory of the gamekeeper humping her from behind.

D. H. Lawrence is right on target, because *he* would've seen — Forster, too — that this first fire in my loins was all about class. *Paul is perfect* was slumming. Odd, because I never thought of my family as being any class at all, certainly not moneyed. In Andover the rich lived elsewhere — up on the hill by Phillips Academy, in country settings out of Currier & Ives, on streets like Crabapple Lane. My turmoil over all that still waited a few bends further ahead, an ambush that would cut my balls off.

Yet there was something more subtle at work in my family than money; call it an instinct for gentility that was equal parts Episcopal and English. Something to do with upstairs/downstairs too, the butler's self-esteem more highly evolved than a landed duke's, except in our case it was the chauffeur. Not that Nana Lamb and Bob had airs, exactly, but they lived with a certain well-born grace of manners in that bungalow just inside the west gate of the wooded estate.

Most Friday nights, I'd stay over with them, and be served my egg in a Spode eggcup, the salt in a dish with a tiny silver spoon, good ironed linen napkins. For my mother's people the move from Lawrence to Andover was a move up, and quickly led to a transfer of allegiance from Methodist to Episcopal — a difference of intangibles. More high-toned, somehow. They were definitely out to better themselves, staunch Republicans, with always a special loathing for Roosevelt. Poor Republican seemed like an oxymoron to me, once I'd got the parties straight, but my parents clearly believed they'd cast their lot with a better class.

I don't know what filtered down to me, beyond the oft-repeated notion that education led only one way — up — and thus

I had an ace in the hole. I certainly understood I was meant to end up somewhere else than High Street. An uncle used to ask me, "Are you going to be a doctor or a lawyer or a dentist?" No other choice, it seemed.

Maybe Kite was a way of getting out from under the weight of gentility. I've always had a thing for men from unpaved places, not too polished, definitely not English. Lust and the English make no sense to me, Constance Chatterley's lover notwithstanding. In that Lawrentian phoenix-fire of me and Kite, the boundaries of my good boy's life were all erased. I had no notion it couldn't last, even though it made me more secretive than ever. No guilt or shame as yet, but a sense of having a life to hide, which only made it more exciting.

I don't believe I'd ever heard of "queers" or "homos" — the scorch of that disdain waited over the border of adolescence. Thus the illicit play with Kite was no more wrong or out of place than any other kind of sex, the whole subject of which was un-genteel. And I never thought I *loved* him, exactly, or ever wanted to kiss him. It was all penis to penis. But that is not to belittle it, or dismiss it as boys being boys, something to be grown out of. That's how straight men shrug off the brief encounters of their youth, the excess of hormones forcing them to make do with each other until they can nail a woman. For all I know, it's how Kite himself put the whole thing out of his head, assuming he ended up straight.

I took it all in deadly earnest, and even began to see beyond Kite, dimly perceiving the future as a meeting-ground for boys like us. Nine is not too young to feel the tribal call. Stevie used to say he'd go to confession at nine or ten, good Irish Catholic stock, and mumble that he'd been impure "in thought, word, and deed." By which prissy circumlocution he meant he was dragging half the neighborhood boys and various cousins besides into the brambles of West Hartford. But even as the punishment purred through the grille — fifty Hail Marys, a thousand — Stevie could smell the garlic stink of hypocrisy. Because what the priest was slapping his hand for was going to be Stevie's life, no matter how much it was called a sin. And with a radar honed by all those violations in the brambles, he also knew the priest was hungry for him.

Nine and a half is old enough. For me at least, it was a victory of innocence over a world of oppression I didn't even know was out there. Not that such a pitch of wildness didn't have its costs. After Kite in the toolshed, things were never the same with Toby — never the same unbounded best-friend status. Because if a boy was going to be my fuck buddy, then where did that leave the boy who was just my friend? Without any role models out there, in the utter silence that surrounded being queer, how would I ever figure out that there was a way to put Kite and Toby together? That as long as I kept them apart, love would be sexless and sex loveless, endlessly repeating its cycle of self-denial and self-abuse. The process by which we become our own jailers, swallowing the key.

The project of our enemies is to keep us from falling in love. It has always been thus, the history writ by straight boys who render us invisible, as if we were never there. Left and right, fascists and communists, they loathe us in equal measure. Then the Holy Fathers of every religion, their sick equation of pleasure and sin. If you isolate us long enough and keep us ignorant of each other, the solitary confinement will extinguish any hope we have of finding our other half. But for once, it turns out, history was on our side. We know now that World War II mobilized so many men and women, the queer ones finally met one another — below deck, in barracks, in off-base bars.[2] And when you are no longer the only one, the tide of history turns.

So in 1954, while I was rutting with Kite in the barns of High Street, the first groping organizations of us "invisibles" began to take shape: Harry Hay and the Mattachine Society in California being the most intrepid. The ravings of Joe McCarthy were fi-

---

2. See Allen Berube, *Coming Out Under Fire*.

nally coming to naught, but only after leaving a twister's path of wreckage, where "homosexual" and "Red" were virtual synonyms. I remember watching the Army-McCarthy trials in the TV room on High Street, understanding nothing but the gravity. In any case, to a budding queer the neutralizing of McCarthy was a small triumph, given that Hoover's FBI and Spellman's castrating dogma were alive and well, dancing the pro-America goose-step. It would be twenty years before the inevitability of history caught up with Little Paul. Till then, all I would have to go on was my dick.

As for the call of wildness, I have one gaudy memory of the world catching up with me and Kite, the equal of any wind and rain that ever beat down on Lawrence's lovers. In September of '55 we were swamped by a pair of hurricanes, back to back—Carol and Edna, I think they were called. I remember the literal eye of the first, crouched behind the green sofa with Bobby, the sudden eerie silence. Half the trees on High Street were downed, roofs blown off and torrents of water flooding the cellars. We had no lights for a week after, and a block of ice in the gray tin sink was all our refrigeration.

The kids loved it—no school for a week—and our hearts quickened with excitement, or mine did, anyway, when the doom warnings began to sound that a second storm was coming. As the wind picked up and the sky moiled with pewter and yellow clouds, I slipped out of the house and made my way across the wrack-strewn yards, loving the feel of apocalypse. Circling around as the rain began to pelt, I was coming through Joyce's back field when I saw Kite. He was standing in the doorway of Joyce's tree house, a place so jerry-built and full of holes, it had somehow ridden out the first storm, bending like a reed.

I called Kite's name and ran to shinny up the apple tree, ravenous. We stripped naked and wrestled on the plank floor, rain coming in on us, roof tarpaper flapping above us like a sail. I think that was the day we discovered sixty-nine, though here I am probably editing memory shamelessly. Surely we'd contorted ourselves to double-suck before, in the pup tents of summer or

26

somebody's barn. Yet here in the tree, in our animal coupling, it was the two of us who seemed to generate the rising wind and rain. Or maybe everything up to meeting Kite had been the opposite of a storm — all eye — and now that its force had been unleashed, it would shake our tidy neighborhood to bits.

Eventually we stopped — still too young to come, even in the whirlwind. Racing home through puddles, I managed to slip back into the house unmissed. I got away with certain things in those days because I'd built up such a fund of acting sensibly, mature beyond my years. My parents wouldn't have dreamed I could walk out into a hurricane, or have one in my head. I stowed my soaking clothes in a ball in the closet and got into my Hopalong Cassidy pajamas. I wanted that storm to go on forever, wreaking havoc and keeping the timid indoors.

I thought one could live on wildness. More and more I couldn't wait to grow up and be rid of childhood, and not so I could start filling cavities. But how could I have overlooked that Kite and I were headed for a showdown with the world? We took no special precautions not to be caught. And if Kite could so casually spread the story of Ruthie's show in the Thompson barn, then what did he say about me? We were hardly playmates otherwise, and he hated school. We'd pass each other in the hallways, barely nodding. There was nowhere else to go. How long can you count on hurricanes?

Bob Lamb died that fall, just before Christmas, leaving Nana widowed a second time — something I share with her now. At the time I noticed how much she didn't cry, which the family probably chalked up to Yankee backbone and a Brit upper lip. Thirty-five years later, I understand that a second grief is marked by deafening silence rather than keening, the ashy taste of anticlimax.

Which finally throws some light on the other mute grief I witnessed that winter. Toby's mother, killed in a freak accident in Boston traffic, a heart attack that slammed her foot on the gas pedal and sent her careening into a truck. My mother cried out in horror as my father read the details from the *Eagle-Tribune*. I went right down to Toby's house—maybe my parents sent me—to say I was sorry. I remember he opened the door but didn't come out, the screen door latched between us. I blurted out some dumb condolence, and Toby shrugged. At the time I felt his numbness as rejection, repaying me in kind for withdrawing the best-friend bond we'd had. Too late to apologize for that, and within a few weeks he and his brothers had gone away to live with distant family, no goodbye for me. Somehow I'd failed him, trading him off for my secret life with Kite.

I was primed, in other words, for the sort of guilt that seals off all the exits. Yet the moment itself was minimal enough, hardly the stuff of a hurricane fire. Kite was over to play at my house, a dank cold day, and just as the winter dusk was falling, the two of us were kneeling by the bedroom window, the one that looked out on the cherry tree. When Kite announced he had a boner, we unzipped our flies and waggled our weenies, snickering. No big deal. I had enough self-control not to break out the *Kama Sutra* with parents in earshot. But I left the light off and the door open.

"What're you boys doing?"

The scald of my mother's querulous voice seared the dwindling day with judgment. In an instant our two flies were zipped, and I swung around and said, "Nothing." She stood there silent, making me squirm, but neither of us spoke another word.

In the next two days, the squirm became a way of life, as I filled up every silence in the household with bright chatter. My mother and I avoided being alone together, but I could feel the edge of her preoccupation. My nervous happy-talk was a frantic attempt to make an unspoken deal, that we both forget the whole thing. Was she torturing me by letting me swing by my own grinning rope? Did she even remotely understand that her damning silence was turning sex into something strangely private, just between her and me?

On the third day, I came home from school and found her brooding at the kitchen table, smoking a cigarette. Right away I started to talk, changing the unspoken subject, strewing the table before her with A's. She finally looked at me grimly and upped the ante: "What were you doing with Kite?"

No deal. "I told you — nothing," I flung back, skittering away to the living room door. Then tossed it again, with bitter emphasis. *"Nothing."*

She looked down at the cigarette in her hand, tapping it into the ash tray, and said no more.

I was right, of course — it *had* been nothing. Yet I knew as I walked lead-footed to my bedroom that the high-wire act of passion was over, because it was somehow wrong. Even if I'd had the wherewithal to challenge her confusion, it wasn't worth the fight. There had already been enough damage to our family, more than enough of the pain of being different. The last thing they needed was something weird from me. Thus did the subtext of my growing-up get set in stone: *I had to be the normal one.* To compensate for the family curse, my brother, whose laughing demeanor and scrappiness were already at odds with the tragic whispering of neighbors and gawkers.

So I told myself I would give it up, even prayed at night for it to be taken away, not knowing that "it" was love. *Forgive me for what I did with Kite, and don't let it happen again.*

No moment of my first twenty years is more indelible than the kitchen inquisition of my mother. All the ambiguity of sex reduced to a single question, the implication crystal clear that something very bad had happened — unnatural, even. The flinching of my heart from that point on would ensure our brief exchange a central place in therapy, fifteen years later. Eventually I would come to see that it wasn't the crime of homosex so much as sex itself that had so overwhelmed my mother.

Oh, we finally had it out, she and I, combing it over like ancient myth in those dialogues of the dining room table, the oxygen hissing softly from the tank that followed her everywhere now. She swore she'd put the entire incident out of her mind, but that, I think, was wishful thinking. She should have told my father, she said, and let *him* have it out with me. Poor lady — how many mothers hide the first queer evidence from the fathers, compounding the distance all around? And how exactly would it have come out any better if my father had asked the question? My answer would have been just the same — *Nothing* — and I still would've ended up gritting my teeth to be normal.

I think she just felt helpless, out of her depth. When she came upon me and Kite in the winter dusk, it was one more thing she couldn't handle. The last straw of who knows how many disappointments and humiliations she and my father faced, defying the world that thought of us as anything but normal. We were all victims of the peculiarly American obsession that everyone be the same, once the pot has melted down. A sameness decreed by the advertisers, and the white-bread fantasies of the tube. Little did we know that being different was our only hope, my brother's as much as mine.

I've long since forgiven my mother and me. But it used to bother her terribly to hear how unbearable my growing up felt, worse and worse through the minefields of adolescence, on account of the shame of being queer. How fervently she wanted me to remember the happy childhood she swore had taken place. She had all the scalloped pictures to prove it. But I wouldn't budge: the pictures were lies. I had only one small consolation for her, as she battered herself with the very guilt she'd laid on me in the hurricane season on High Street. I told her she and my father must've done it all right in the end, because Bobby and I both managed to find great love. If she'd really fucked up, I'd be all alone.

I'm not sure it was ever enough for her, who never stopped wishing the leatherbound album and life had been the same. I'd exonerate her as best I could, telling her she had a right to be happy in the past, even if I wasn't. But I also know that once she'd made her peace with me being gay, she realized how much time she'd wasted. Those were the sunsets she came to regret, the years when she dreaded the terrible knowledge of what she'd walked in on, that watershed day in '55. Her closet became as airless as mine. And her and my father's coming out would be as needlessly protracted, like raising a family all over again.

For years after—this I didn't tell her—a rainy day at dusk would render me almost suicidal. And later on, that violet hour would find me out cruising to fill the void, fucking on the cusp of nightfall. I never saw Kite again, or never more than a stiff walk home from school together, both acting as if our year of wildfire had been all a mirage. I heard he ended up in reform school — or was it prison? — or is it a trick of my memory that has invented a punishing fate for him? Just the sort of comeuppance I would've relished in my closet years, when I was my people's enemy.

In the spring I learned we were moving away from High Street, and I was punchy with relief. There was nothing left for me there. The frontier country of Jeff and Porky had faded into the common light of day. The backyard barns and sheds had changed before my guilty eyes into the rooms of hell. Not only would sixth grade be a new slate, I would start all over in a new neighborhood — a chance to be normal, without a past.

As for my longing to be an adult, master of all the storms, in the end I got half my wish. A twist on the fate of Tithonis in the Trojan legend, who asked the goddess Aurora for immortality, but neglected to specify immortally *young*. Older and older forever, that was Tithonis's curse. In the case of Little Paul, the raging loss of innocence with Kite had rid me of the invisibility of childhood. (Good riddance, as my French grandmother would've harrumphed.) But it also left me stuck in the amber of wrong desire—kneeling by my bedroom window, looking out on a leafless cherry tree. In a twilight world where no one is ever a child again, and where no one ever grows up.

TWO

I DON'T KNOW WHEN hate starts. Bigotry has to be taught, that much is clear, because babies and small children don't think in vicious epithets. On the other hand, it certainly doesn't take much to find yourself a scapegoat. We only had one black family in Andover, but by the fourth grade all the nigger jokes were in place. I remember this quite vividly, because that was the year the oldest boy of that family was hit by a train and decapitated, crossing the Boston & Maine tracks to the poorest pocket of town. Nobody cried at school or observed a moment of silence. They told nigger jokes instead, kicking around that severed head like a football.

I suppose there must have been more than one Jewish family. It happened that I was friends at school with Peter Goodman, the other kid in the class with straight A's. And therefore I was more attuned to the kike jokes whispered behind his back — though rather than protest them I pretended not to hear them. My first collaboration with the enemy. The most I could summon up was a cluck of disdain when Maidie Lynch or one of her pious ilk came out with the hissing judgment that the Jews had killed Our Lord.

She learned that in church. Organized religion is the school of hate, and never more exultant in its righteous indignation than when it talks about gay and lesbian. In America the unholy alliance between the know-nothing fundamentalists and the

Catholic hierarchy keeps the faithful whipped up to a frenzy of witch-hunting and fag-bashing. We "stand as a proxy for all that is evil," according to one researcher of homophobia, such that "hating gay men and lesbians is a litmus test for being a moral person."[3]

The "Roman problem," as a priest once put it to me ruefully, goes all the way back to Aquinas — a thirteenth-century barbarian of the Church whose seething nonsense about women and gays has passed into Holy Writ. It's worth recalling that the Church was a welcoming place for gays and lesbians in its first millennium, as open to them as it was to married priests. I also recognize that there was a moment, in the benign reign of John XXIII, when the warp and the bigotry could have been confronted. It's no accident that Vatican II was letting in the light at the same time that feminism and the Stonewall revolution threw down the gauntlet before the patriarchy.

But Vatican II castrated itself, and the rosy 60's are no more. A new Inquisition is in full cry, led by the rabid dog in brocade, Cardinal Ratzinger of the Curia, the malevolent divine who laid down the law that loving gay was a matter of "intrinsic evil." In the decade of the AIDS calamity I've come to see the church of the Polish pope as a sort of Greenwich Mean of moral rot — thus in my small way returning the compliment of Sturmführer Ratzinger. Hardly a week goes by that we don't hear from the pope's minions in the colonies — O'Connor in New York, Mahony in L.A. — spewing their misogyny and homophobia, delirious with triumph that sex finally equals death.

But I try not to hate Catholics, even so. In this I take my cue from the Holy Fathers themselves, who assure us God hates the sin and not the sinner. So I bite my tongue for the little old ladies who go to Mass, the yearning ethnic poor who somehow manage to see God through all the brocade, and even the wincing priests who write to me that the present reign of terror will pass.

---

3. Interview with Dr. Gregory Herek, *New York Times*, July 10, 1990.

They are welcome to their deity, and whatever ceremonies get them there. But I and my brothers and sisters are the victims of a pogrom, cold-bloodedly orchestrated in the situation rooms of the Vatican. The Roman problem is political, not religious. And the parameters were set for the modern age by Pius XII, who washed his hands like Pilate because Jews weren't a Catholic charity, and anyway they killed Our Lord. Pius — the absent defendant at Nuremburg.

Nevertheless, it makes me sick inside, to hate the way my enemies hate. I understand that I'll never get around my rage at the tyranny of religion to see if there's anything Higher out there. The Bible is still the only dirty book I've ever read, at least in its current incarnation as a weapon of the homophobes. Bible scholarship keeps trying to catch up, proving that all the hatred of gay is just stupid translation, though the snake-oil preachers don't want to hear it. But perhaps I'm just as stuck as they are — with the acquired prejudices of Grandpa Joe, to whom the Irish and their priests were a subhuman species.

"You're so angry at God," my mother used to say, maddeningly countering my unbelief. Is it as simple as that: my mother with her rock-steady faith, and me the atheist throwing it in her face? The children of atheists, they say, are always first at the altar for Communion — presumably because they sit in the front pew. As a friend of mine lamented after she read *Women Who Love Too Much*: "It's so depressing to be a cliché."

Yet if my Roman prejudice is intense, I still saw what I saw, and can't unsee it. Sixth grade at Central: the Irish toughs led by Vinnie O'Connor, a bully's bully, huge and hulking with a blood-lust sneer that made even Kite look like a choirboy. It happened in the basement corridor, just outside the boys' lavatory, where the sixth grade had its lockers. Vinnie and a group of three or four others had somebody pinned in a corner. Vinnie was snarling and shoving.

"Yeah, you're a homo, ain't ya? Little fairy homo. Ain't that right?"

Then he shot out a fist and slammed his victim's head against the wall. A bustle of students streamed past to their lockers, eyes front and pretending not to see. But my locker was just a few feet away; I couldn't help but hear it all if I wanted to get my lunchbox. Besides, I was drawn to it now, as to a wreck on the freeway.

"Homo, homo, homo," Vinnie kept repeating, accompanying each taunt with a savage rabbit punch. The victim pleaded, terrified but trying not to cry. It was Austin Singer, a meek, nervous kid who was always working too hard to make friends; the son of a math teacher at Phillips Academy. He vigorously denied the homo charge, choking it out between punches, which only made Vinnie angrier. He growled at two of his mick henchboys, who pinned poor Austin's face to the wall.

Vinnie made a hawking sound and spit a glob of phlegm on the brick beside Austin's face. "Come on, homo — lick that off." Austin whimpered and tried to pull back. Vinnie brought up his knee into Austin's kidney, making him cry out. Where were the teachers? All old maids, two floors away in the teachers' room, eating their own bird lunches. "Lick it, homo," Vinnie hissed.

One of the brute lieutenants pushed Austin's face along the brick, scraping it raw. And now Austin, broken, surrendered whatever dignity was left. His tongue lolled out, and he licked up the phlegm while the bullies cheered. "Swallow it!" Vinnie commanded. From where I stood, by my locker, I saw in a daze of horror, the self-disgust in Austin's face as he got it down without retching.

Vinnie and his boys sprang away, shrieking with laughter. Instantly I busied myself with my lunchbox, terrified they would notice me. As they swaggered away, neither I nor anyone else made a move toward Austin — slumped in the corner as if it would have been easier to die than survive this thing. We all went hurrying away to eat our waxed-paper lunches. I never, never talked to Austin again. But, as I hastened to assure myself, we hadn't been friends anyway.

The cold truth I took from the scene of Austin Singer's humiliation was this: *At least I could still pass.* I never even gave a thought to the evil of what Vinnie had done, how sick with confused desire, the carnal thrill of degradation. The only reality lesson in it for me was not to be recognizably Other. At all costs I would discipline myself to appear as regular as Vinnie's boys, lest he suspect me and pin me to the wall. I'd see those Irish hoods sauntering up the hill to town from St. Augustine's after Mass, and I'd grin and fawn and try to walk with the same bow-legged swagger.

What did it have to do with their being Catholic? I wondered about that even then, how it was they got away with bullying and torture. It seemed to be all mixed up with confessing and getting absolved — we were studying sacraments in confirmation class, the Romans versus us. I suppose I can't blame Ratzinger for Vinnie O'Connor, a rotten apple in any barrel. But why was it they seemed the very same guys, a decade later on the evening news, mobbing the streets of Boston against forced busing? The nigger jokes of the Irish toughs were translated into a murderous fight for turf. Nobody black was safe in Southie after dark, when the locals began to drink in earnest.

And nobody gay. One night, in my twenties, I watched a red-faced drunk — the spitting image of Vinnie O'Connor, but full-grown now and twice as lethal — chase two men down Boylston Street for holding hands. He roared that he would shred their faces with the broken bottle he wielded. How much of that did he learn in church, along with his catechism dose of "intrinsic evil"?

My prejudice in these matters is manifest, even to me, but, then, I'm not seeking rapprochement with the powers of Rome. I leave that task to the outraged nuns, the muzzled theologians, the Dignity groups who are barred the sacraments because they persist in the sin of love. It would be another thirty years before I married an Irishman myself — well, half an Irishman anyway. Stevie's other half was Polish, like the smiling pope himself, another race with a spotless record for snuffing queers. Lech Walesa — talk about choirboys — promised during his summer campaign for the presidency that he would *rid* Poland of homosexuals. He didn't say how, but the death camps are still right there.

So I have one mixed Catholic marriage and four great-aunts who were nuns, and I'm going to hell anyway on account of my father's transfer. But I had no idea till I started talking out the Catholic stuff with Stevie — so deliciously lapsed himself — how very effectively Vinnie O'Connor had bashed my head the day he broke Austin Singer's spirit. We are creatures of the cruelties we witness.

Happily, the move to Stratford Road in '56 was a move up the blue-collar scale, away from kids like Kite and Vinnie, from the hardened lives of the millworkers, an underclass ahead of its time. Though still only four blocks east of town, Stratford Road was a suburb compared to High Street: two neat rows of postwar bungalows facing each other, ten on either side. The frontyard trees were still mostly saplings — in front of number 11, a pair of Japanese plums snowed with blossoms every May but more notable for their summer swarms of beetles than for their fruit. It was a bare hundred-yard dash from one end of Stratford Road to the other, a tract builder's shortcut between Chestnut and Summer streets, substantial thoroughfares both, old as the horse days.

A much more manicured world, most of the houses as white as the people who lived in them. On Stratford Road we had five schoolteachers — four of whom live there still — and otherwise a cozy mix of local businessmen and the rare commuter to Boston. For a while we even had a state senator with a crinkly Kennedy smile and telegenic silver hair, but they moved away quite suddenly, trailed by rumors of a mistress, graft, and kickbacks. The denizens of Stratford Road had no more use for Boston politicians than for Boston itself. Our own form of government was Town Meeting, still manageable enough to hold in the auditorium at Punchard High, every new stoplight the subject of excruciating debate.

The neighborhood kids were mid-50's wholesome with a vengeance. Play was much more organized than on High Street: twilight games of hide-and-seek, croquet and badminton in the yards. Though we all had bikes, we never seemed to ride them any farther than school or one another's house. If there was anything slightly askew about my presence among this butter-melt species of nice kids, it was my being a couple of years older. Eleven now and pushing the envelope of adolescence, I consciously avoided boys my own age.

In part this was due to the Ball Problem: too many of my peers in the thick of Little League and peewee football, while I couldn't hit the side of a barn. But more than that I recall it as a deliberate shying from the brink of growing up. At school I was already straining to laugh when one of the sixth- or seventh-graders told a dirty joke. I never got the punch line.

"This guy's fucking a girl name Snow, and he leaves the bathtub running." Ronnie Carew regaled us boys as we waited our turn at the jigsaw. It was fifth-period Shop, and we were cutting out leaf-shaped nut trays. "Guy downstairs bangs on the ceiling and yells, 'Hey asshole, we got three inches of water down here!' 'Oh yeah?' says the other guy, 'Well, I got you beat then, 'cause I'm six inches in Snow.'"

I literally hadn't a clue what was meant: why did he leave the water running in the first place? Not even the basic physiology of intercourse had filtered down to me. I was still wrestling with *Ruthie's got nothing down there*, though admittedly I'd made great strides with Kite in the penis department. But I wouldn't have dreamed of asking anyone in my class to explain the joke, because they all seemed to know already. I had to pretend I understood. The slightest hint of naiveté, and I could find myself lapping spit off the wall. I was already starting to be more open with girls than boys, but not too much, not so anyone like Vinnie would notice. The gulf, after all, was widening, as surely as the girls split off to Home Ec while the guys did Shop.

My nut dish, incidentally, was a travesty. Also my desk lamp, a short circuit waiting to happen. The two ways in which I was bodiless — a dweeb at sports, and closed off to the male bond of sexual misinformation — somehow reinforced each other, leaving me almost spastic, at war with my physical self. I stubbed my toes and slammed my fingers in doors. No finesse, no body English. Already there were boys at school advancing through the portals of manhood — muscling up, shaving already, even sporting hair *down there*, though this was only speculation till the first shower of seventh-grade gym.

The only thing I recall about my body in those middle years was being allergic to bees and wasps. This curious aberration began in my twelfth summer, at first just a run of bad luck, it seemed. Every week or so I'd be mowing the lawn or picking blackberries, and I'd swat at the buzzing around my head, thinking it was a fly, and *pow*, I'd be stung. Wailing and tears and local swelling were all it amounted to at first, my mother plastering the spot with a paste of baking soda "to draw out the fire."

Until August, when we caravaned the family to Hampton Beach, a rental cottage in a piney grove. These yearly two-week jaunts were happy times, even to one whose memories of childhood are so unrelentingly blank. I remember I was sitting on the porch swing after a swim, my baggy suit still wet and dripping. I caught sight of a bee in the morning-glory trellis, watched him doze from flower to flower. Then, as if in response to some bad karma I was giving off, he made straight for me, dive-bombing before I could move, and stung my thigh.

It didn't hurt any worse than the others, but now I was convinced I had the whole species after me. That none of the summer's stings had been an accident, after all. A week later came the *coup de grâce*. I was hanging up that same wet bathing suit on the clothesline — was the color too bright? — when a wasp swooped down without warning and stung the crown of my head. My shrieks this time were as much from the paranoia as the pain.

Within a half-hour I started to swell — all of me. The memory is quite specific still, the feeling of my pudgy fingers rubbing numbly against each other as my parents raced me to a doctor. My head was swollen round as the moon, and I could hardly breathe. The doctor gave me a shot of adrenaline fast. I remember him and my parents gaping at me, waiting for me to unballoon. I was calm as you please by then, comforted, I think, by all the fuss, and being so vividly noninvisible.

What has stayed with me from that emergency, however, has

nothing to do with bees or even pain. The swollen sensation, fingers puffed and doughy, somehow stands in for the moment I turned adolescent. Changing like an alien, my bloated body near to bursting. From twelve to fourteen I played with myself almost every day but never came — so stupid, I didn't know what coming was. I'd take myself to the edge a thousand times and stop short, terrified I would explode. The throb of panic obliterated the pleasure. Suddenly the engorgement of my penis was freakish and unnatural, out of control like my body the day of the almost mortal sting. And, as with the sting, a sort of paranoia gripped me: that if I didn't keep my pleasure in check, it would drive me over an edge of no return. As if that one stroke too many would unleash a swarm that would devour me — like Sebastian on the beach.

Can you fear orgasm before you know what it is? Apparently so. The guilt and ignorance about sex had been accumulating like scar tissue ever since the confrontation with my mother over Kite. No wonder I turned the bees into Furies. For how many summers afterwards, just to find myself in a field of flowers would bring the phobia on. I ran at the sound of anything that buzzed — ran into traffic more than once, an eruption of horns and screeching brakes. I still run. In autumn the bees in the chaparral above my house are crazy with thirst, and they skim the pool. If they buzz too close, I dart away flailing, causing even the dog to perk his ears at this St. Vitus's Dance of mine. (*Runs like a girl*, I can hear them sneer from the edge of the track at prep school.)

But my bodilessness wasn't only a recoil from adolescence. The sixth grade also marks my brother's first extended hospitalization. We were all supposed to be thrilled, as it was considered an honor and a privilege to be accepted by the Shriners' Hospital for Crippled Children. Three hours away in Springfield, down Route 9 and out Route 20, the weekly pilgrimage for a two-hour Sunday visit would bring my parents home looking hollow-eyed and defeated. The poor kid was only six, and he'd sob to be taken home when the Sunday visits were over. Nobody seemed in the least thrilled.

I think he was there for three months — almost surely over Christmas, because I remember my parents bringing home a virtual carload of toys that the Shriners' Santa had lavished on him. There was also the provocative news that Roy Rogers and Dale Evans had paid a Christmas visit to the kids, in full buckskin. Already star-struck, I burned with frustration not to have been there for the show. But I wasn't allowed to visit at all, nobody under sixteen was. Except once, when I drove out there with my parents through a driving rain, only to stand outside, waving through the hospital window to Bobby, the glass too thick for us to talk.

For a while he had casts on both legs, so the reset bones could heal straight and let him stand on crutches. After that were the braces welded into special shoes. I don't recall how long it took him, months I suppose, actually to walk with the crutches across a room. Our small March of Dimes miracle, though soon enough the crutches would be only for certain public occasions, going to school and church, visiting relatives. My brother's face a ferocious study in concentration as he swung himself forward, legs as stiff and wooden as the crutches.

Most of the time, he used what we called his "cart." This one-of-a-kind vehicle was cobbled together by Gus and Abbot, the pair of mechanics who kept the trucks running at Cross Coal. In their spare time they fashioned a bare-bones iron chassis out of scrap, with four spoked wheels. It was driven by a double lever that Bobby gripped like a crane operator, sawing back and forth to propel himself forward. Once he had his cart, he was finally free to move, and there wasn't anyone in town who didn't know the sight of him pumping his way along the sidewalks. Independent, no longer carried by Zeus.

In time he could ride it as fast as a bicycle, his upper body brawny as a power lifter. That was much later, of course, but even in his hospital years I don't recall ever treating him fragile. When he was still in casts, we'd wrestle on the floor in front of the television, usually after remorseless teasing from me. And I mean wrestle. I was twice as big, but Bobby was strong and lightning quick and fearless. That was the first thing you noticed, watching him negotiate the obstacle course of the walking world. You never had any sense he was afraid for himself. He lunged at life, whether it was playing baseball sitting on the ground or trundling after his running friends in his cart. Self-pity never entered into it.

I don't think I understood this at the time. And if I did, the daily evidence of his pluck and fortitude did nothing to assuage my buried guilt about being able to walk when he couldn't. Or the helpless emptiness of being alone in the house with my parents while Bobby was in the hospital. Time suspended: nothing happened and nobody moved. I had no power to lighten the gloom, no matter how normal I acted. The string of A's continued, but I could do that one-handed now. I never lost my temper, never raised my voice. A bland insipid smile glazed my face instead, twin to the sexless vanilla of my body.

Admittedly, I'm fighting against the evidence yet again. No snapshots this time, but a grisly poll taken in seventh grade names me "Most Popular" boy in school. Not exactly a scientific sample. And the other gargoyle categories — "Best Hair," "Best Shoes" — reveal the taste of 1957 at its kitsch peak. My popularity had to do with my driven personality, distinguished in those days by grinning verbal skills and a desire to be nice to absolutely everyone. In practice this amounted to a certain desperate chattiness, just like the days when I filled the silence around my mother's brooding judgment of me and Kite. I became a comedian and a charmer, breathlessly smart and witty, the Noel Coward of the junior division. My gawkiness and pratfalls — even my flinching wimpiness in gym class — I managed to give it all a spin of endearing self-deprecation. I could make anyone laugh, a relentless gossip, but the jokes were the polar opposite of being six inches in Snow.

How I expected to hide being gay in the role of the clown sophisticate I can't imagine — but it seemed to work. I think even Vinnie O'Connor and his boys probably voted for me. I also understood instinctively that my eunuch's charm, utterly sexless and thus unthreatening, gave me the power to talk to all the prettiest girls. Cilla Fitzgerald for one, the Elizabeth Taylor of seventh grade, with her haughty gaze and the body of death poured into angora sweaters through which you could read the cup size of her bra. She turned the sullen young men to inarticulate jelly, so hungry were they for her delights. While I, who wanted nothing from her, would have her in gales of laughter as we sat on the stone bridge in the park that fronted the school.

The courtier's role. I learned it early, substituting my oh-so-worldly banter for the hetero rites of passage. The safety zone of that persona would be abruptly obliterated once I got tossed into the brute arena of an all-boys school. But the courtier skills were always there, ready to tap into when I'd find myself with interesting women. A dozen years later, it would be my stock in trade, when I spent two years as the world's first color-blind decorator. The ladies of the suburbs could live without color, as long as they had their regular fix of my laser wit and gossip over cappuccino.

I loathe and detest the courtier boy, so busy being popular he doesn't know how to come. I understand that he gained me entry to myriad places, and not just to the four-bedroom ranch houses of the almost divorced, who hoped that new drapes in the dining room might hold things together a little while longer. The courtier's capering dances would stand me in good stead in Hollywood too, especially with the chronically single who supervise "development," mostly young women and closeted men. As a world-weary producer friend of mine often tells the eager youths who want a piece of the business: "You don't need to go to film school. You need to go to charm school."

There are men who live the role of emasculated courtier without the least self-doubt. The perks of being a "walker" to a rich and stylish lady are considerable, after all. The hot-lunch program at Mortimer's and Trumps is filling enough that a man could live on toast and tea otherwise. The perfect extra man for a dinner party or a country-house weekend. It goes without saying that the husbands of stylish ladies can't abide all those charity balls and special events, for which the eunuch escort was practically invented. I came so close to being a eunuch escort full-time that I can almost taste the crystalized sugar passed with the after-dinner coffee. For men who like that sort of thing — as Miss Brodie used to tell her special girls — that is the sort of thing they like.

I should have been finding a boy of my own instead of talking to Cilla Fitzgerald about which one of her many suitors for the Junior Prom she ought to accept. That was the most sinister aspect of my courtier's self-denial: the sizing up of straight men for a mating dance I had no part in. And then later to be a shoulder for Cilla to cry on, after she'd dumped the beast in question. A sort of Cyrano without portfolio, too frightened to admit to myself that I wanted the very men Cilla cast off. The better you get at being just a shoulder, the more unsexed you become. It's hard to know what to aspire to, unless it's Truman sitting beside the pool with Babe Paley, carping with her about Bill's mistresses as the butler brings out yet another Long Island iced tea.

Once at least it landed me in trouble — shortly after that Junior Prom, with its swags of crepe paper and a mirrored ball twirling from the ceiling in the center of the boys' gym. The theme was a sort of Elvis luau by way of *American Bandstand*, suffused with the bowling-trophy glamour of the mid-late 50's. And Connie Dufault, in a smoldering strapless and wrist corsage of speckled carnations, was elected Queen, which made her unnervingly good-looking boyfriend King. By the end of the night, they were dancing so close in their double tin crowns, mouths clamped together and pelvises rubbing, they might as well have been in bed.

I don't recall which girls I was gossiping with on the Monday morning after, or what put it into my head, but I told them I'd heard a rumor that Connie and the King were fucking. A total fabrication, besides which I hadn't a clue what fucking looked like. But worse than the lie and the ignorance, I remember, was the prissy disdain in my voice, the huff of wounded standards. *Going all the way* was doubtless how I put it, producing a satisfying gasp from the "good" girls, who never went further than second base, swear to God.

Idle gossip. Not a pretty way to be popular, but a sexless boy can't help it, spellbound as he is by the carnal moves of royalty. I couldn't tell my claque of girls how riveted I'd been on the Prom King's grinding hips — his football hands stroking Connie's bare back up and down, even cradling her buttocks, to the strains of Tommy Edwards crooning "It's All in the Game." In the absence of porn or the TV jiggle and cock-tease of a later age, the groping makeout of Connie and her King was the closest I'd ever come to the raw thing, man and woman. It seemed such a small invention, to say they did it for real.

A couple of weeks later — out of school for the summer by then — the four Monettes were eating supper on the back porch when the doorbell rang. My father went to answer, thinking it was the paper boy, and came back nodding at me: "It's one of your friends from school."

I sauntered through the kitchen, wondering who it could be, but pretty sure that whoever it was had been drawn by my voluble charm. I couldn't make out the half-turned figure through the rusty screen, except to see he was big. Then I swung the screen door ajar, and the Prom King stepped into the breach, glaring daggers at me: "You Paul Monette?" I nodded in dumb horror. To a ninth-grade football jock a seventh-grade peasant like me did not exist. "You and I need to have a little talk," he declared with a grim smile.

He beckoned me outside. Even in my pounding panic I knew that if I left the house he'd beat me to the ground. Instead, with strained politeness I asked him in, which disconcerted him, then led the way upstairs so the family wouldn't hear us. I took us into Bobby's room, because my room was just above the back porch, and started pleading before he could lift a finger. He'd got it all wrong — I'd been misquoted — the last thing I'd ever do was insult my King and Queen. I was like a prisoner who spills all the secrets as soon as he sees the torture room, before the first whip is cracked. I think I even begged: *Please don't hurt me.*

He looked at me with huge disgust, his eyes darting to the crutches and shoe braces. He later told somebody — I don't remember whom, any more than I do the King's name — that I had been too pathetic to beat to a pulp. He couldn't bear to touch me, I was so slimy. His only rough demand was that I call Connie and apologize, there and then. Nearly whimpering with relief, I led him into my parents' room and made the call — fawning on Connie and praising her virgin beauty while she listened, aloof and strapless.

As I hung up the phone, the King turned away without another word, clumped down the stairs and out of the house. And I walked back to supper in a daze of self-loathing, summoning up a soulless nonchalance, and a dumb excuse to throw the family off. But the terror and debasement stayed with me for years, twisting me up with the thousand deaths a coward dies. I knew I would do anything not to fight, betray whole armies if I had to. And understood obscurely that a wheedling tone of self-effacement — apologizing for my very being — was the only way to neutralize the force of a real man.

Later I would learn that being a eunuch courtier to a man required a different sort of groveling, more of a flatterer than a jester. I learned to gossip more carefully, more subtly. During those middle school years I also went to dancing school at the November Club, where all the jocks were tongue-tied and stepped on their feet while I soaked up the ballroom moves and dazzled the chaperone mothers. I had no friends to speak of, certainly no other boy, but I was a whiz at a party, dancing as fast as I could.

My brother meanwhile was going to a school out of *David Copperfield*. Miss Marland's it was called, a single schoolroom behind a rickety gift shop on Main Street, across from the November Club. There were three Miss Marlands, staunch Episcopalian spinsters all, but only Edna ran the little school. Not much in the way of lessons, my brother says, but everyone gathered around the organ in the mornings to sing hymns. Underfoot were enough dogs to fill a Booth cartoon, and a couple of old men boarders as well, stinking of stale urine and padding about in their p.j.'s.

Edna was a marvel of entrepreneurship, leaving no stone unturned in the cottage industry of her life. She sold mail-order dresses from catalogues, as well as a most obscure line of perfume and beauty products. My brother says he doesn't recall a single customer in the gift shop, whose curios sat beneath decades of dust, and in any case the stench of uncollected dogshit lay over the whole place like a miasma. Bobby would sometimes escape the chaos by ducking into one of the boarders' rooms, where he'd watch the Red Sox with Mr. Milnes, who stank a little bit less than the rest of the Marland emporium.

Well-meaning was written all over it. The public schools were wholly undesigned for the handicapped, and everyone decided my brother needed the special care of Miss Marland. I think the town of Andover even paid the tuition. Nobody saw, in the segregation of the disabled, anything wrong, that it was a guilty attempt to put out of mind and sight the savagery of fate. And indeed Miss Marland couldn't have been more fiercely dedicated to her brood, those stalwart morning hymns proof, if anyone needed proof, of her zeal. The problem was, most of the other students were retarded to one degree or another. Year after year they all read at the second-grade level, while my brother, his brain untapped, whiled away the time trading ball scores with Mr. Milnes.

I remember the yearly Christmas pageants of the Marland School, presented on the stage in the parish house of Christ Episcopal. The Marland sisters were pillars of the church, the last surviving members of one of Andover's textile dynasties. The Marland Mill was long since shuttered, its boisterous looms grown quiet in the brick factory on the Shawsheen River. I don't know where all the money went, but the aging sisters stood their ground—their name resonating still in the town's collective memory and on a prominent hillside in the Christ Church graveyard, shaded by ancient firs.

My brother was always the star of the pageant, mainly because he was the only student who could think in sequence and remember lines. So he'd stand center stage, hanging on his crutches, reciting some god-awful uplifting poem—*Abou Ben*

Adhem, may his tribe increase — then lead his slower classmates in the carol singing.

It was no education at all in the formal sense, but a sort of survival test, to see if the mind could triumph over a total lack of matter. Somehow Bobby made it through eight years of hymns and dogshit, on to high school and college, but he's always spoken about the Marlands with toxic irony — day care in a madhouse. It was nobody's fault but the times', I suppose, that "special education" lumped together the crippled and the retarded, apples and oranges, teaching nothing. But he's not a bitter man, my brother. Last winter, when our mother was buried in the churchyard, Bobby noticed the Marland headstone listed only two of the sisters. When Charlotte died, the last of the line, there had been no one left to remember her and cut her name in stone. So my brother had it done, completing the trio.

Somewhere in there, between seventh and eighth grade, I finished confirmation class and took my first communion. The assistant to the rector — the aforementioned Moses who boomed the good news of Jesus like a trumpet — was a mild-spoken curate named Wolfe. Though he did an energetic job of ushering us kids into the mysteries of faith, I couldn't help but feel a certain impatience in him as he rattled off the dogma — virgin mother, God and man in one, rose from the dead. Or was it I who'd grown impatient with the string of miracles that followed Our Lord across Judea? *He threw down his crutch and walked; the Master touched his eyes and he saw.* Not in our house, pal. The lame stayed lame.

This despite the growing passion of my mother's faith. She'd begun to read Scripture with a Christian Science lady from up the street, a kindly blue-haired type whose roses were flower-show perfect, and who always brought a couple of riotous blooms when she came to call. All morning Sunday, the hi-fi swayed to Tennessee Ernie Ford singing gospel. We also had a subscription to *Guideposts*, a monthly magazine of "little miracles" — strength through prayer and heart-tugging tales of pious children who wondered why they couldn't say grace in a coffee shop. Why not indeed? When everyone at the counter put down their forks and folded their callused hands, I flung the magazine aside with a grimace of disgust.

This is all just a fairy tale, I remember thinking when Mr. Wolfe explained the transubstantiation of bread and wine. The whole thing was a made-up story, Jesus and his miracles — though the story was nice enough, and harmless. I don't think I would have dared at that point not to believe in big-G God the Father, but the whole Christian pageant was just that, pomp and pretty allegory. I didn't feel especially jaded or empty about my unbelief, and managed to shrug my shoulders philosophically and go along for the ride. I liked the grownup drama of communion, the sense of initiation. Sometimes Wolfe would choose me to douse the candles at the end of a service, and I'd swagger up proudly with the pole snuffer, putting them out one by one as the congregation watched.

I hadn't yet come into contact with anyone "born again," or the ranting ministries of evangelism. Nobody really *talked* God in the infinitely discreet world of a small New England town. God was a given, like the Puritan moral code, but it would have been just as vulgar to speak of Jesus outside church as to speak of sex in any form. Mostly they taught us to live and let live, that we all believed in the same God. I wouldn't have dreamed of revealing my agnosticism. That would've been like asking to be thrown out of the country club, in a world where golf was the only way a civilized man walked outdoors.

I don't know what drew me back to the woods. Perhaps my break with Jesus took the guts out of that nightly prayer of mine: *Forgive me for what I did with Kite*. But all through the summer of '58 — after my confirmation in June, and the Prom King's menacing visit — the neighborhood play on Stratford Road felt tepid and unoriginal. "There's nothing to *do*," I'd whine as I moped around the house, then dutifully set off for another armload of library books or a muggy game of hide-and-seek. But I'd already read the whole four-foot shelf of the Hardy Boys, and there was no place new to hide.

Then one afternoon, I pedaled my English bike to the end of Summer Street, barely a quarter mile from home but still unbuilt and thick with trees. A big white house with a sprawling verandah stood at the top of the rise, surrounded by an orchard. This was the Denning house, whose shades were always drawn tight and whose apples fell unharvested, rotting in the soft unmown grass. The Denning place was the closest we had to a haunted house, and nobody trespassed — except in the dead of winter. Then, by some unspoken agreement, the children from miles around were allowed to cross the orchard into the wooded vale beyond, when Denning's pond was frozen solid.

I'd skated there for a couple of winters, toasting marshmallows at the crackling fires that the big kids lit on the mossy shore. Nobody ever went to Denning's pond in the summer — too many mosquitoes, and far too brackish for swimming, let alone the toes you'd lose to the snapping turtles. Nevertheless I made my way through the orchard and poked about on the spongy banks, stirring up the polliwogs with a stick. Already I liked the feel of wildness, the disconnect from suburban life — free to imagine myself on a desert island, living off the land. And yes, falling in love with my rippling image in the black water, more Narcissus than Crusoe.

A branch snapped, and I turned. Another boy was trolling the shallows nearby. We stared at each other like a pair of startled deer. I knew him vaguely from school, a year behind me, Richie something. He said he was looking for arrowheads; I said I was looking for frogs. We made our way back through the orchard to the road. I wasn't aware of any sixth sense of the carnal in our meeting, but as I retrieved my bike, he tossed out where he lived, beyond the woods, and said he had a clubhouse where he and his friends had meetings. I should come some time.

Oh, I knew right away that my second occasion of sin had arrived. I don't recall how we put it together, whether by phone or radar, but I found my way to Richie's house a few days later to meet the guys in the club. I don't even remember feeling threatened that Richie had pegged me for a fellow queer — a paranoid terror that would come to define me later, whenever another man came on to me, however vaguely. The fear that I had ceased to pass. For the boys in Richie's club, it had nothing to do with queer. There were five of them, including a pair of twin brothers, and all were Little League jocks. They'd waggle their dicks at each other, yet always under the guise of talking about girls.

The clubhouse was more a lean-to huddled against a split-rail fence. The game they played was called "I dare you," each of us taking a turn to dare the boy beside him. *I dare you to go take a leak in the mailbox. To lay a turd on the Dennings' doorstep. To take Richie's dick in your mouth.* By keeping it kinky and slapstick, they somehow avoided perceiving it as sex. We all had boners, but nobody ever came. It was mostly raunchy talk, all very tough-guy, an indoor sport that only lacked a ball.

I went there three or four times, trying to sound exactly like the rest, talking butch and doing my dares with the proper swagger. Then one time I showed up for a meeting, and Richie was there alone. He invited me into his house, because his parents both worked — unheard of on Stratford Road, where the mothers all stayed home, sainted as Jane Wyatt on *Father Knows Best*. The illicit feel of the empty house was heady as we stripped naked and chased each other around the doily-covered tables, the Bar-caloungers and Ethan Allen repro of a staid white-collar ranch.

My erotic technique, I fear, hadn't improved much since the hurricane days with Kite. We took turns lying on the floor, the one on top poking his dick between the bottom one's legs and getting some friction going. That and a lot of sucking. I think I was probably old enough to shoot, if I'd only known how, but Richie was still a few paces behind, not quite to the border of adolescence. Thus he was fascinated by the wispy bush of hair that had started in my crotch, as well as by the veiny straight-up member I was sporting, three times the size of his, in my thir-teenth summer. Barely twelve, Richie's own equipment was still a little boy's, poking straight out with its gumdrop head, not yet able to lift and flare like a cobra.

Richie would grill me about the glandular changes of the previous year, all the while squeezing and milking me, studying the pre-cum as it drooled out. "Lookit all your juice," he'd murmur in awe, so that a weird rooster pride warred with the awkwardness I felt, leaking this substance that had no name.

The animal hunger was the same I felt with Kite, except for one thing. I wanted to kiss Richie. I never came close to verbalizing that, let alone acting on it, because I understood that all romance was forbidden. We could dick around as much as we liked, but a kiss would have bordered on love. And yet I was aware of feeling tender as well as carnal. I would summon up Richie's face in my mind when I wasn't with him. The one crooked tooth in his lopsided grin, the porcupine brush of his waxed crewcut. He was a couple of inches shorter than I, bursting with energy and a raucous smutty laugh. Half Armenian, half black Irish, a mongrel just like me.

We kept up our sporadic meetings all through the next school year — I in the eighth grade, he in the seventh. I enjoyed our wrestling bad-boy sex throughout, but now I see I was only half there. For the sense of being "different" was all on my side. To this day I think he was queer too, and our sessions together never required a smokescreen of pretending we were getting ready to put it to women. But Richie kept me at a distance all the same, no intimacy of any sort, substituting instead a comrade's heartiness. I'd arrive at his house, and we'd get right down to it, no preliminaries. I guess I was learning the difference between a boyfriend and a "fuck buddy," though the latter term wouldn't come into vogue for another twenty years. Half my generation of gay men would go after that kind only, willing to try almost anything once — but no kissing.

Because it was very confusing, I tried not to think about it. I went on my courtier's rounds with redoubled frantic energy, working to keep everyone happy. A larger change was brewing all that year, as various forces decided I should pool my A's and run for daylight. I filled out an application to Phillips Academy, supported by letters from Mrs. DeCesare, my English teacher, and the prophet Moses of Christ Episcopal. I was given to understand throughout this process that here was my chance to make it into lawyering or dentistry, a class jump that no one in the family had had a shot at since Grandpa Joe at Harvard Law.

I did as I was told, though I was frightened as much as anything by that brick utopia on the hill, with its lofty porticoes and endless carpets of lawn. Phillips, as the townspeople called it — unable to nickname it "Andover" the way its boarding students did, as if the town at the foot of the hill had given up all rights to the name. The school reeked of privilege and separateness. In the years to come, I would learn the code of the ruling class, how a man with the proper credentials *went* to Andover but didn't *come* from there. For a local boy to pass through its wrought-iron portals — emblazoned with the beehive crest and motto in Latin, NON SIBI, *Not for himself* — meant that ever afterwards he would lose his citizen status in the village.

I took the entrance exams. I applied for a scholarship. I labored over the mandatory essay — "What I Expect to Get from My Four Years at the Academy," five hundred words or less — tossing off the requisite bull, unable to articulate the short answer, "Out of here." Because what was really left for me in the town, as my courtier's dance grew more frenetic, the boys and girls increasingly distinct from each other, no whisper of androgyny allowed? How long could I pass for straight among these kids who'd known me since first grade?

Assuming I passed at all anymore. My brother tells an excruciating story from this era. He was pumping his cart up Chestnut Street and suddenly found himself surrounded by a pack of thugs, probably from the housing project across the way. "His brother's a queer," announced their leader, the rest baring their teeth as they grunted in disgust. Bobby quaked in fear that he was about to be pulverized. Then the whole thing turned around. "We know *you're* okay," said the leader. "And if anyone tries to hurt you, you just tell us. 'Cause we'll wipe the street with 'em."

The circle of wolves parted, and Bobby wheeled away in relief. He didn't understand the curious way in which he had become a sort of mascot for the town, bringing out the protective best, even in wolves. But more important than that to him was the savage slur on his brother's name, which he understood not at all. As soon as he got home, he gave my mother a broken account, asking in earnest anguish what the boys had meant.

"Nothing," she told him — the same nothing that Kite and I had been guilty of on High Street. Then the kicker. "Bobby, why don't we let this be just between you and me."

Secrets upon secrets. Thus by inexorable degrees does the love that dares not speak its name build walls instead, till a house is nothing but closets.

I was oblivious. With three years gone since the crisis over Kite, I figured it was long forgotten between my mother and me. She seemed happy enough. I remember her laughing at Christmas, excited as a girl from Thanksgiving on, baking and wrapping, a blizzard of cards to everyone we knew. In addition, she had lately attained a place of high fashion and chic — at least in my eyes — by becoming an Avon lady. She covered the whole neighborhood for two or three years, new colors and perfumes every spring and fall. Bobby remembers her sample case as vividly as I do, fat as a weekend valise and with a hundred pockets. Late at night, while the rest were in bed, I'd come downstairs and unpack it, studying all the Siena blushes. My favorite scent was *Topaze*. Then I'd carefully pack it all back together, leaving no trace.

Except I guess she knew my secret anyway, no matter how well I'd hidden my tracks to Richie's house. And my father? He seemed happy too in those middle-school years on Stratford Road. He'd managed to buy an apartment house at Elm and Florence, six units in an old Queen Anne that bristled with porches and cornices. I used to help him paint and wallpaper whenever a place was between tenants. I liked laboring beside him, and eventually got very adept at doing trim — a steady hand with mullions and the intricate rosettes and scrolls along the moldings.

Did we three have a good relationship? I think so. Really, I had no expectations, and wouldn't have answered truthfully if either my mother or father had asked me how I was or what went on in my head. Had I let them get any closer, they might have seen the carnal truth, so I was the one who maintained the fences. When I received the news in the spring that I'd been accepted at the Academy, I was glad for them because they seemed so proud. Myself, I felt sick, not knowing if I had the right mask to wear in such an unknown world, or whether my courtier's moves would work. I was practically hoarse from ventriloquism already.

In fact, what stuns me the most about my brother's story of the thugs is the pang it still gives me today. To think that my elaborate show of obsequious patter didn't hide a thing. They all *knew*. And isn't that pang another name for the hollow stab of shame — the realization, this many years later, that I failed to pass after all? As if some unaccepting part of me still wants to go back and work at it harder, till no one will ever guess. Something that still can't laugh at the budding queen poring over the makeup case, whose hobby for the next four years will be his Liz Taylor scrapbook. Something that still winces that I wasn't enough of a man.

You think you've put all the self-hatred behind you, the long reach of sick religions, and then some memory cuts you down, reducing you once again to the only different boy in the world. But it isn't just my brother's recollection coming back to haunt me. I have a memory all my own which mocks the puny camouflage of the courtier/jester, searing me with the certainty that nobody can be trusted with the truth. That betrayal is the way of things, and always the end of love.

It was late in the spring, close to the finish of school. I was heading home by cutting across the playing fields, where every summer a carnival pitched its tents and filled the town with tawdry lights. Instinctively I'd stay away from the bleachers, beneath which the ninth-grade hoods usually gathered after school for a smoke. But the fields were so marshy from heavy spring rain that I had to skirt them, and pass close to the green-painted tiers of seats.

I turned at the sound of laughter, recognizing Richie even before I saw him. He was sitting hunched a few rows up, talking to a couple of kids I didn't know. I grinned and said hello, because Richie was looking straight at me. Our naked wrestling and smutty play in his parents' house had not prevented us from being friendly at school, if not exactly chummy. For me anyway, the casual nods in the halls set off a kind of illicit thrill, to think we shared a secret other life. I took a tentative step toward the bleachers — then stopped, noticing Richie was smoking a cig. I never saw him smoke before, and suddenly felt I was intruding.

"Hi, Paul," he said, flashing his crooked smile, but the words came out in a mocking tone that threw me. I glanced at the others, trying to pick up on the joke. Both of them wore an identical smirk, superior and arch. Whatever the joke might be, I was pointedly excluded.

I don't know what I said to get away, some inanity about homework — addressing myself to Richie. I waved a curt goodbye and headed off across the field, with as much nonchalance as I could muster. Before I'd gone three paces, a conspiratorial snicker stung my ears. One of them grunted "Homo," making no attempt to whisper. I like to think it wasn't Richie who actually spoke the word.

I had to trudge a hundred yards across the muddy ballfield, water seeping through my loafers, before I reached the cover of trees and was out of their line of sight. Every step a pathetic attempt at the bow-legged swagger of Vinnie's boys, somehow trying to show my tormentors that they were wrong. The pain in my chest was as sharp as the flush of red that burned my face, as I grappled to understand the Judas betrayal of my comrade in pleasure. I'd never been able to tell him I loved him, because I knew the least declaration would drive him away. Now all I had left was my pride, to try to show him when next our paths crossed how much I didn't care.

The pain was my heart closing. I knew now what a delusion it had been to think I passed for normal. But instead of freeing me — if you can't hide it, you might as well live it — the betrayal made me more bleakly determined than ever that no one would tempt me again. The determination didn't happen overnight, but the seed was planted. To avoid the sudden cut of a boy like Richie, I would remain barren for the next ten years, unseducible and impassive, defying anyone to prove that Paul Monette was queer.

My bridges were burned in Andover, that much was certain. I dutifully finished the last few weeks of school, nodding and pleasant as ever, even to Richie — especially to Richie. If anyone noticed a difference in me, it was in the courtier department. The Noel Coward breeziness, the fawning attentions on pretty girls, the standup routines at dancing school — all of it started to mute and dissipate. My prattling subdued, my eyes cast down, I attracted as little notice as I could. In a word, I turned invisible again, but even more invisible than when my brother was born, for this time I chose it.

So I had come up with the right mask after all, to see me through the journey up the hill to prep school. In the process I thought I could leave behind forever the pagan world of the woods beyond Denning's pond. My new face — meek, colorless — was almost a kind of relief, hardly worth a second look in the mirror, because hardly there at all. I would learn to be the person everyone saw through, walked through. Not worth mocking.

That summer provided me with the perfect stage to try it on. Somehow my father managed to land me the plummest job in town: clerk/cashier at the Andover Spa. This combination grocery store and soda fountain, a stone's throw from the triple intersection of Main and Elm and High streets, was the true magnetic center of the town. A convenience store ahead of its time, long before the numbing takeover by 7-Eleven of all the Mom-and-Pop traffic. Open till 10:30 every night, including all day Sunday, a feat of unheard-of daring in a state with such strict blue laws.

The Spa was famous for homemade ice cream — including an actual cup of brandy in every five-gallon drum of peach, thus sticking it twice to the blue laws. There was a vast humidified cigar case, stocked with everything from two-dollar Cubans to nickel stogies fit for souses and hobos. Plus the only full-scale magazine stand for miles around, leaning heavily toward the girlie peekaboo and *Police Gazette*, no law against browsing. By the storeroom stood a mahogany phone booth with a chair inside. The Spa was sole purveyor to the town of goods by S. S. Pierce, the Brahmins' high-toned brand name, pronounced *purse* unless you were lower class. In December a Christmas tree lot was set up in back, two dollars or three apiece, depending on the height. And always in the front window were laid out white-pine crates of pristine fruit, each piece wrapped in green tissue, the very best in town.

The fruit was a sort of immigrant's link, since the Spa had started out as a two-man fruit store, cobbled together at the bottom of the Depression by a pair of Greek brothers just off the boat. Nikos, the surviving brother, still ran the whole operation with a fiercely patriarchal hand, and indeed the Spa was never called by its proper name at all. The whole town knew it as "Nick's." Though Nick himself had grown a bit rickety by the time of my tenure there, he could still stand up to any hood from the high school who lingered too long at the fountain or littered the sidewalk in front.

The bane of Nick's life was his nephew Stavros, whose father's will had made him fifty-fifty partners with his uncle. Colorful didn't begin to describe Stavros. Possessed of the naughty good looks of a Greek Sinatra, as well as a pilot's license, he was a shopkeeper waiting to be a playboy millionaire. His manner was as brusque and confrontational as Zorba, his sneering parodies of Andover's high and low bourgeoisie always dead-on. Nick thought Stavros far too noisy and full of himself, and they disagreed about absolutely everything in the running of the store. Both had terrible tempers and stewed for days, barely speaking. Then various cousins and brothers-in-law would bustle in and drag them into the storeroom, hammering out a truce worthy of the *Iliad*.

To me they were both unfailingly kind and protective. I started at eighty-five cents an hour, a princely sum, joining a motley crew of regulars. Behind the counter I bagged for Joanne, the day cashier — a bad girl who cracked her gum and was rumored to have pulled the train for the varsity football team. I went back and forth from stockboy to soda jerk, throwing down sawdust to sweep the floors, squeegeeing the front windows. We were four doors up from the Town Grille, so there wasn't a drunk in town I didn't know by summer's end, including the red-faced Irish priest from St. Augustine's.

It was all such a gaudy new world, as if I'd signed on with a traveling carnival, except that this one stayed in one place. I would probably spend more time at Nick's than anywhere else in the next four years, certainly as much as I would in the tweedy halls of the Academy. In a way, it saved my life, otherwise so confused and closeted, by forcing me to mix it up with people of every stripe, high and low. At Nick's, *Peyton Place* met *The Dead-End Kids*. The Norman Rockwell burnish was all on the surface. And I who was such a model worker, infinitely well-mannered and unobtrusive, never missed a trick as to who was sleeping with whom and who got beat up at home after the Town Grille closed at night. A fly on the wall, so insignificant nobody saw how observant I was.

All summer long they swaggered in and out, the high-school boys in their chinos and white bucks, a pack of Luckies curled in the sleeve of their tee-shirts. Sporting ducktail haircuts, they huddled with Stavros by the ice-cream maker, buying rubbers for a buck apiece, no other place in town to get them. These were the older brothers of Vinnie O'Connor and his boys, a ceaseless flood of invective spewing out of the side of their mouths, a misanthropic loathing of everything different, especially blacks and Jews. Hate was their compass, these Irish toughs, bitter to think they'd end up in the same factory jobs as their fathers, and no place to go at night but the Grille.

I realized with a shudder that if I stayed in public school, these were the boys who would terrorize me. The tortures they could devise were surely more exquisite than the phlegm that Austin had to lick. In the meantime I was on neutral ground by working at the Spa, saved by my proximity to Nick and Stavros, the town's unofficial Greek chorus. For someone who already hated himself as much as I did — a weakling's body, an outcast in love, nothing like a man — I'd stumbled onto a sanctuary. Nick's was the town marketplace and school of life rolled into one, a concept old as the *agora*.

Even so, I kept my mouth shut, constructing hot-fudge sundaes for the portly burghers, serving up Alka-Seltzer to the morning-after crowd. The racial and ethnic slurs never stopped, till I wondered even then if hate was genetic, an instinct like fear. Without it ever being said, I knew that queer was close to the top of the enemies list. And allowed myself to hope that the new world I would enter in the fall was somehow more civilized, not so quick to break the spirit of the different. Because there was no looking back anymore. If I stayed here in this pretty town, I'd be torn apart by beasts.

Three

I WAS SUCH A CIPHER in prep school, so out of my league in every way, that it seems a pouting evasion of my personal nothingness to say it was all *their* fault. Yet that's how it felt for years and years — that Andover ground me beneath the heel of its Bass Weejuns because it needed losers to make its golden Adonises shine ever brighter. I wandered through so lost and sad, I can't believe nobody ever asked me what was wrong. *Nothing*, I would have said, by which I would've meant *Everything*. When Dorothy landed in Oz, the world burst into Technicolor. My ascent into the rarefied air of Andover proved to be the exact reverse, leaching every hue, till all I could distinguish were a thousand shades of gray.

The very first morning, as we filed into assembly, the hundred and fifty boarders in my class were already fast friends, their hearty alliances set. Doubtless they were overwhelmed in their own way, but a glittering self-confidence appeared to be their birthright, even if it was all show. Whole squads of them were stunningly fit and poised, an aristocracy of the chosen, none of the sallow features and bad teeth that stalked the halls of the junior high I'd left behind. And the first exclusion was there from the very beginning: Day students were second-class.

The headmaster had the ramrod bearing of a West Pointer, which he was, and an Olympian profile fit to be stamped on a silver dollar. George Washington himself had attended the first graduation. A plaque still marked the place where he'd planted a Washington elm, though the tree, succumbing to Dutch elm blight, proved less stalwart than the bronze. Our first pep talk laid it on very thick about the responsibilities of privilege, our duty to go out there and lead the charge for God and country. It felt almost as if we were being inducted into an army, albeit in the officers' corps. I wasn't sure what we were fighting yet.

The second mark of caste was tattooed on the foreheads of those of us on scholarship. *Nothing to be ashamed of, men*, not being rich to begin with. The unstated promise of the system, after all, was to make sure every last one of us made it into the moneyed gentry. Meanwhile, the sturdy ethics of the place dictated that nothing was ever free, and so there was a Bureau of Self-Help which assigned all the scholarship lads a menial four hours a week. I drew library duty and Saturday switchboard — nothing so gross as Commons duty, serving swill and scraping garbage, nor as titillating as running towels at the gym.

The gym was the third and final strike that proved I was a loser going in. For at Andover a strong body was the vessel of a strong mind, and two hours of teaming occupied the center of every afternoon. At the first muster of new recruits, the Neanderthal-browed Director of Athletics went through the rigors of every fall sport, from football to cross-country. Words cannot even approximate the bone-zero dread I felt, who had only played the outermost outfield, cringing at every fly ball.

I elected soccer, seeing that the drift of the meek and the chubby was in that direction. Below varsity and JV were four intramural teams — Gauls, Greeks, Romans, and Saxons, as I remember. We chose by lot, and I became Greek for the next four years. Tortured afternoons beneath the pewter skies of autumn, running at half-speed so as never to catch up with the ball, let alone score. Scared of getting hurt but scared more of doing it wrong, in a constant state of humiliation. The real Greeks would have stoned me as a coward and sent me into slavery.

It's true that the triple skein of fate that marked me as an outsider — day student, nonathlete, on scholarship — was borne by many others without any obvious burden. The challenges only toughened them. But it's also true that before the first week was out, the class had divided itself, by a sort of unspoken agreement, into three parts. Brains had nothing to do with it, since all of us had come in with a lifetime glut of A's. First were the Apollo athletes, effortless on any field but primed for special glory one high season a year, in hockey perhaps or lacrosse. Equal to these in loftiness were the Dionysus boys — gentleman athletes with gentleman grades, unique by virtue of worldliness and suavity. Some had got that way by being well-heeled, others by early conquest of women. They shared with the athlete-kings what Joan Didion calls the conviction that the lights would always turn green, wherever they traveled.

Which left a ragtag bunch of misfits, oddballs, and eccentrics. Among them, a pair of inseparable fat boys, called Tweedledee and Tweedledum as soon as we all read *Alice* in freshman English. Also a scowling stork of a boy with a green bookbag slung over his shoulder, defiantly peculiar and seeming to thrive on the snickers and finger-pointing. Then the various Holden Caulfields who found the rigor and uplift of the place embarrassing and contemptible, their bad attitude worn like a badge.

But most of us in the lower orders were simply gray and characterless, like the mystery meat they served in Commons. Running at full clip just to stay in one place. Grinding our way through twelve-hour daily schedules, scaling Himalayas of homework, unremarkable throughout. But that was all right, because even the lowly nerds and doofuses were on the ship bound for the yachted harbor of privilege, where the dweebiest among us would come under the protection of the old boys' network. Thereupon would follow, as the night the day, a slot in the Ivy League, and after that a berth on Wall Street — entitlements as old as the Washington elm.

I must add here that I understand that being a nerd in prep school doesn't rank high on the scale of human suffering. I didn't have to look any further than my brother to know what a life of struggle was. There's a whine in every memory I call up from the prep school years that is so deeply unappealing, even to me, that I find myself wanting to slap the faceless boy I was. As if to become my own Vinnie O'Connor, Jekyll-and-Hyde, and force that cowering fourteen-year-old to eat some spit and get a life. But how else to explain the closet I built except to describe the unrelieved perception of being *less than?* My failure to achieve the school's idea of manhood proved to me I was no man at all. For there was no other kind.

I wish I could say I hated it as Holden Caulfield hated it, because everyone was a phony. But they were not phony, they were all too real, Apollo and Dionysus both, so real they proved I wasn't. And it does me no good to wonder how it might have been easier had I only been able to come out. It's disorienting, to say the least, discovering that Andover now supports a Gay/Straight Alliance. The lesbian adviser called me last summer to request an interview for the alumni bulletin. I gritted my teeth and agreed, not just so I could fulminate against the one-way manhood taught by the prigs and strutting egoists of thirty years ago. No, it was also because I knew the captive audience of alumni still constituted the ruling class — from the current gibbering fool in the White House to sundry captains of finance. All the conspirators of silence whose straight hegemony has gone unchallenged because their gay roommates stayed in the closet. Coming out in the alumni rag seemed better than never.

Not that I was friendless, even in that first year. I hung around almost exclusively with two other day students, Francis and Gene. Both had come straight to Andover from eight years of parochial school. They had to study double-time because their previous A's were softer than most, despite the S/M flogging of the nuns. Francis was as gentle a boy as ever walked the bosky paths of Andover. The only son of old Irish parents, strict and lace-curtain proud; his long face was always dimly lit by a melancholy smile. I think he was sadder even than I, more defeated by life already. His years of playing piano led to organ lessons at school, solitary afternoons practicing on the vast pipe organ in the chapel. I can still feel an ache, like an old broken bone, that I wasn't a good enough friend to him — not kind enough or true enough.

But that is to get ahead of myself, to the place where two closets are like a pair of adjoining tombs. We laughed at least in the first year, studying in the cemetery with Gene. Eugene was much drier and altogether more aloof than Francis and I, with a bug up his ass about genealogy and the Social Register. He was obsessed by the Mayflower succession of the ancient Brahmin families of Boston, and so the graveyard was the perfect place for him, constructing family trees in the back of his algebra book.

I don't know what we found so congenial about the graveyard, but we studied there every afternoon between soccer practice and Math I, the last class of the day. A hillside cemetery behind the main classroom building, bordered by a crumbling stone wall and with graves that went back to the 1820's. Unless I have transposed her from some other plot of my life, Miss Harriet Beecher Stowe was buried there. The three of us would sit on Harriet's granite steps, the last glinting light of October filtering through the yellow maples, teasing one another when we should have been factoring x.

They were both queer, of course. I suppose I knew that then as well as I know it now. But since none of us could say it aloud, especially to ourselves, we fell into infantile parody and silly in-jokes. We never spoke of sex, *ever*, not even in puns. The world in which we didn't exist as sexual beings was so in control, it succeeded in making us eunuchs even among our own. And though Francis and Gene would rib me mercilessly about my Liz Taylor fetish, none of us seemed to understand how clearly it marked me as a budding queen. We invented a kind of camp out of whole cloth — bizarre TV references, mixing up idiot advertising slogans as we riffed on the pedantries of our teachers. To send up the straight-arrow earnestness fed to us every day in morning chapel, we resorted to everything short of drag. We were definitely peculiar-queer, but with an edge of desperation always. If the silliness ever stopped, somehow, we'd be left with the awful truth of being homo-queer.

As for me and Liz, it was a weird concatenation of forces that brought us together. Her trio of bad-girl performances — *Cat on a Hot Tin Roof*, *Suddenly Last Summer*, *Butterfield 8* — happened to coincide with the bee-swollen alienhood of my early adolescence. Meanwhile, Francis's parents were such good Catholics that they posted the Church's monthly sin list of movies on the kitchen bulletin board. All Liz's movies were branded with a C, for CONDEMNED. This only made me wilder to see them, thus my cajoling of Aunt Grace to take me, sharing a box of Milk Duds while the beach hustlers cannibalized Sebastian. The others I saw on my own, afternoon matinees in Lawrence at the Warner and the Broadway, gilded palaces in the old style, *putti*-carved boxes for the royal family.

I was ravished by the sight of Liz in a slip, tossing her raven hair as she hissed some Tennessee shocker of a line. I loved the brazen adulthood of the themes, the dangerous vulnerability of those *National Velvet* eyes staring out of a hooker's face. I'm not quite sure what I identified with, but it seemed to amount to a kind of *emotional* drag — trying on those steamy, gaudy feelings as if I were sitting in the dark wearing Maggie the Cat's lingerie. Which fit me better than the soccer drag at school — the shin pads, the steel-plate jock, the gray and maroon Greek jersey. Ever perverse, of course, I would soon enough go the other way in spades, so enamored of gym drag I could hardly put on a jock without getting hard.

Still, I probably would've left Liz in the bijou dark of the theater, returning to my doggy life, if she hadn't exploded into the headlines. My father brought home every night from Nick's the green-stripe edition of the Boston *Record*, the Hearst rag. Dad liked it because it carried the late ball scores, while I would take a break from my homework and read *Dear Abby* and the funnies. When Liz was rushed to the hospital with pneumonia, then underwent an emergency tracheotomy, the tabloid banners of the *Record* trumpeted the news full-volume. LIZ NEAR DEATH, etc., day after day of lurid updates.

I started cutting out the stories, as fascinated by the churning flood of publicity as I was worried about the lady herself. I wonder now if it wasn't a sort of symbolic ritual; if I didn't archive all that noise and drama because it was so opposite in character to my brother's hospitalizations — which by comparison seemed almost secret. And then the Liz publicity acquired a life of its own, as the *Cleopatra* scandal erupted. Liz and Eddie and Richard and Sybil, every day a new revelation. I can't remember a single thing I studied in ninth grade French or science, but I still recall how much it cost to fly chili from Chasen's in Beverly Hills to the *Cleopatra* set in Rome.

So began the white leatherette scrapbook. Doubtless I was the only student at Andover who faithfully read *Photoplay*. I still worked Sunday afternoons at Nick's, and one of my jobs was to weed the outdated magazines before the new shipment came on Monday. I'd tear out picture spreads of Liz from all the fanzines, till I had duplicates of certain shots, like baseball cards. I got so I could recognize her jewels — I always liked the emerald set.

Don't ask me why. Nobody ever talked Hollywood gossip around me, especially at school. Even Francis and Gene would roll their eyes at my "hobby," and they were the only ones permitted so much as a glance between the leatherette covers. Anyway, it wasn't just Liz. When Marilyn died in '62, I wore a black crepe-paper armband all that Sunday at Nick's, the customers looking at me as if I was deranged. I watched *The Late Show* every night on weekends — anything black-and-white with Deco sets — then told the plots to Francis and Gene in the graveyard: from the cocktail repartee of Nick and Nora Charles to the saucer-eyed bride's first sight of Frankenstein. Little did I know there were men out there, in the cities, who could quote whole Bette Davis scenes to one another, shrieking with laughter, though her movies were not exactly comedies. If someone had told me I was exhibiting a sensibility, I probably would've frozen in horror, terrified my wrists were going limp. I certainly couldn't have told you what Hollywood had to do with going to bed with men.

One day we were laughing, the three of us in a row on Harriet's grave, when suddenly a shadow fell on the marble, and we looked up into the white-lipped visage of Mr. Brownlee, who was standing on the path with grimly folded arms. "What're you boys doing?" he demanded — but surely I've misremembered it, giving him my mother's exact line from the day of the Kite ambush. And yet there was the same tone of shocked disgust. Mumbling sheepishly, the three of us slunk away, banished to the library.

It must have been spring then, by which time Brownlee was a three-headed misery in my life. He taught us freshmen Ancient History with ancient pastel-shaded maps, making it all sound rather like a football game that lasted several thousand years. Just out of college himself, as fatuous as he was earnest, Brownlee was bound and determined to shape us up. Compounding all that classroom rah-rah, he was one of the coaches for spring track — thus stood witness day after day to my panting last-place finishes in the warmup sprints. "*Move*, Monette!" he'd bark at me as I staggered past, clutching the baton, the weak link in every relay.

And if all that wasn't enough, he was also my freshman adviser — necessitating a squirming series of meetings on both sides, he sitting beneath a grinning wall of team pictures from his glory days at Cornell. Hard to say which of us floundered more, but he certainly never asked me how or who I was. Yet the trump card proved to be his: a written report that went out with my spring grades, delivered three weeks into the summer and thus avoiding a face-to-face.

Paul spends too much time acting silly with his day student playmates. It's not healthy. He's got a lot of growing up to do if he wants to be a man.

I knew what the reference was — that laughing day in the cemetery — and the not-so-subtle implication too. He'd pegged me as a fairy, though holding out a certain chilly hope that I could still snatch the baton and get on with the race. I don't recall my parents being troubled by the report, too coded perhaps, and anyway my B/B– grades were respectable enough. As for Brownlee's plea that I show a little more gumption in athletics, he allowed as how maybe I hadn't found my sport yet.

Oh, but I had. Without any formal instruction I'd finally figured how to bring myself all the way off. It happened at my desk one winter Sunday night; I was stroking my meat when I should have been studying Alexander's march through Asia Minor. Maybe I was pricked by one of the naked marble gods who decorated the text. In any case I finally went too far, and my long-muted instrument reared and shot. Ropes of foam splashed across the coast of Asia Minor like a tidal wave. I hadn't a clue what cum was, and in the ensuing panic thought I had somehow discharged bone marrow, the only white stuff I could imagine.

For a week I left myself entirely alone, convinced I'd be pissing blood next. When no further strangeness ensued, I knew I was home free. My soon obsessive riding of my joystick was surely no different from anyone else's at school. Despite the coaches' fervid belief that two hours' daily combat on the playing field would cool our hormones, boys would be boys and pull their puds. But I had no way of knowing anyone else's autoerotic scorecard, and in any case my superheated fantasies seemed to me entirely and painfully unique.

For I had become the possessed voyeur of the locker room, dumbstruck by the Parthenon frieze of heroic male flesh parading to the showers after practice. Upperclass men, the varsity Olympians, strutted and feinted with liquid ease as they flicked their towels at one another's butts. It wasn't just their bobbing members I was fixed on, or indeed a specific carnal hunger that left me dazed in their presence, the wind knocked out of me. This went far beyond wanting to suck. Such roaring self-assurance and aching good health they glistened with, these warriors of the afternoon, proportioned like Renaissance bronzes. A musculature as effortless and natural as the structure of a flower — none of that built and studied look, the overdetermined bodywork of the Nautilus age.

These were pagan demigods instead. In old Greece they would've been worshiped, and one day I would come to see how the closeted teachers did just that, bending the rules and even the grades for the right kind of smile from a jock. Not that the straight teachers weren't susceptible too, living as they did in a dewy nostalgia for the days when they ran like the wind themselves. Thus was manly beauty rewarded from every side. And the manly beauties received their due and tribute with a coy half smile of modesty, no less coquettish for being unconscious.

In Delphi and Thera, the gymnasiums where the heroes trained and worked out naked stand in the shadow of the Delphic temples, for the athlete in his prime was as close to Apollo as the oracle. But this was not the Greece in Brownlee's book. Brownlee's Greece took a long cold shower between battles, a fig leaf firmly in place to cover the privates. The pagan had no place in a world of clean-living men, who owed their fealty to the gray and buttoned-up God of morning chapel.

Totally inappropriate, then, my fleshly worship in the locker room. How small I felt beside them. This intersect would never have happened in a public high school, where a wimp like me would've had no business being in the gym at all. It was Andover's stubborn insistence that every one of us have a go at the ball — wimp and Olympian alike — that dragged me wincing into the showers, me who hated the soft androgyny of my body, which somehow managed to be both scrawny and plump at once.

Add to that my fear, eyes fixed on the tile floor, not to be caught staring. Then jerking off every night in the dark thinking about them, summoning them in their nakedness, but without the least desire to fuck with them. That's the oddest thing — that none of my Kite and Richie acrobatics had any relevance here. The gods were too far above me for me even to think of touching. I lay cocooned beneath the covers and whacked my meat in solitude, running the video over and over in my head, that antic frieze of demigods at play. This was like saying my prayers before bed, a lowly and humble offering to their greatness. Then, by way of *Amen*, I'd wipe up the marrow with a Kleenex.

Basically that's where my sexuality stayed for the next twelve years, locked in the locker room of my brain. Talk about arrested development. At twenty-six, when I finally staggered into therapy, I was still able to picture in stupefying detail a hundred different naked bodies from Andover — my pantheon, unchanged by time, like Keats's urn.

I never wanted to fuck them, because I wanted to *be* them. Had he known this, I wonder how choked poor dim Brownlee would've been as he typed my freshman report. Actually, I'd learned the lesson of manhood, Andover-style, all too well. You either had it or you didn't — and I didn't. What was "it"? Good white genes, ramrod posture, a hearty comradeship on the field of honor, and no bees like Furies to plague your summers. I admit quite freely that I got it all wrong — that a basic decency was there on the elm-covered hill as well, trying to make room in the circle of men for more than the athlete heroes. It's not as if anyone ever acted brutish like Vinnie O'Connor. But that went right by me. I was already too far gone in being different, the hiding of which was turning into a full-time job.

At Nick's that summer I worked four days and three nights a week, including a marathon thirteen hours on Sundays. Nick and Stavros trusted me now to cash out the registers at closing time, laying the banded bills in a canvas bank pouch for the morning deposit. Everyone in town knew me more or less from Nick's, and also that I went to school "up the Academy," as they would say in that flat laconic townsman's voice, swallowing half their words and all their R's.

And the curious thing was, I didn't really mind the distance it put between me and the town, being identified with the world of privilege. Though I lived a wholly disembodied life at school, no self to speak of at all, nobody seemed to know that in the village. At Nick's therefore I could hold myself slightly aloof, as if my real life were somewhere else. When in truth my life wasn't real anymore in either place, uphill or down.

My brother says he thought of me as being away from home from the moment I started Andover. He'd already be in bed when I came home late — from the library during the school year, from Nick's in the summer. He'd hear me go into my parents' bedroom to check in for the night, tossing off the

G-rated version of the day's events. Thus Bob remembers it better than I, who can't recall a single occasion with the Monettes in those first two Andover years. I say that strangely without regret, relieved to learn how well I passed for normal, at least on the home front.

I'd outgrown going to the office with my father on Saturday mornings, and anyway we had a half-day of Saturday classes. But I'd still spend Friday nights at Nana Lamb's whenever I was on vacation, always a morning walk through the woodland paths of the mill owner's estate. My Uncle Don had moved in with her when he came home from the Air Force — stationed in Barrow, Alaska with the polar bears, the coldest front in the Cold War. Don would usually be out with his poker buddies on Fridays, then sleep in till almost noon on Saturday. So she and I would have each other to ourselves, and she was the one I was closest to in the family, more even than when I was little.

She'd make me tell her what I learned in school, would nod thoughtfully, seeming to learn it herself as I relayed half-baked chunks. She set great store by education, having been forced out of school and into the mills at ten, too many Cowperthwaite mouths to feed at home. Now in her eighth decade she wasn't about to deny herself, and always had her hat on, figuratively speaking, ready to go. Because she couldn't drive, she ran up delirious bills with the two-hack taxi service of bone-thin Mr. Morissey — whom I always thought of as her personal chauffeur, even when he was carting home stiffs from the Town Grille.

The things she didn't deny herself were 8 A.M. Communion, white-filtered Kents in a gold-mesh case, Manhattans with double maraschinos, a proper salon wash and set, and lunch out. Any relative would do who'd run her up to Thompson's on 114 or the Howard Johnson's on Reading Road, with usually a detour to pick me up, since I was her favorite. She loved a laugh and could be quite risqué, though it never undercut her lofty dignity — what seemed a kind of patrician grandeur, though her means were modest enough. Decked out in her stylish sets of costume jewelry, she was the one who taught me how to order. I don't recall a word of the chitchat anymore, but it felt most devastatingly civilized, till the blue-and-orange formica of Howard Johnson's glittered like the Ritz. Out on the town with Nana, I was worldly, and didn't have to watch my every gesture to see if I was man enough. I felt that I was born for talking in restaurants.

The story I never tired of hearing, pumping for more and more details, was her trip to California the previous winter. She'd gone out with Don to visit cousins in Pasadena, the first commercial airline trip that anyone in our family had ever taken. I remember the postcard she sent of Dinah Shore's house in Bel-Air — "It's quite a life they live out here." And going in to Logan to meet her plane coming home. She walked off with an armload of birds-of-paradise wrapped in foil, specimens from Eden. My uncle had cadged me menus and matchbooks from all the high spots, including the bill of fare from the clubhouse at Santa Anita — with Desi Arnaz's autograph scrawled across the front, for he'd been loaded at the next table.

"The homes!" my grandmother would exclaim, blinking in speechless wonder. These cousins, in the ceramic tile business, had paved acres of terraces straddling the San Andreas Fault. The breakfast oranges came still warm with the morning sun. "They live outside," Nana declared with a flourish of her cigarette, making them all sound like stars. It was the only frontline report I'd ever had of the California good life. None of this was ever connected specifically to Liz or Marilyn or anyone else in the movie firmament, but the West was clearly golden, and I knew I had to see it. Nana promised I would go with her next time.

Sophomore year was banked in a fog of forgettable days. The afternoon tortures continued, soccer and swimming and track, as I parlayed the slightest sniffles into as many medical excuses as possible. We were allowed only six cuts per term, a half-cut for every tardiness, and I hoarded them all for sports. Otherwise we were a group of pitiful regulars at Isham Infirmary Outpatient, we derelict nonathletes who sucked up to Mrs. Furth in her white peaked cap. She knew we were shirking and yet was a pretty soft touch, dispensing three-dose bottles of codeine syrup for our nonexistent colds.

I started Latin that year, the only sophomore in a class of freshmen, and the drill came easy to me. By now I was wholly intimidated by the Apollo and Dionysus juggernaut of my fellow sophomores, who seemed in the intervening summer to have grown into full-blown men, while I still flailed in the shallows of androgyny. Thus did the naked frieze of my midnight longing shift, populated less now with the distant heroes of senior varsity and more with my ripening peers, beside whom I sat with unnerving proximity all day long, from English to Basic Chem to Bible class. I was far less intimidated by the Latin freshmen and so became their unpaid tutor, giving away my Caesar translations to anyone who asked.

In a sort of grotesque footnote, pulling together the queerest strands of life, one of my teachers was Austin Singer's father. This even-tempered man was unimaginably fair, playing no favorites, time for every question. I'd watch him write his four-foot equations across the blackboard and wonder if he knew that his son once licked Vinnie O'Connor's spit. He seemed too nice, with his head slightly fuddled by so many numbers, to believe that boys were capable of torture. Austin himself, I heard, kept getting bumped from school to school, because he couldn't keep up. No chance at all that he'd ever make it to Andover and the safety of his father's ivory tower.

The teacher who most fascinated me for extracurricular reasons was Mr. Nindle in French. A bachelor who drove a Thunderbird, Timothy Nindle was decked from head to toe in the spiffiest tweeds from the Andover Shop. Forty years old, he was master in one of the senior dorms on the main quadrangle, facing the clock tower on Samuel Phillips Hall. He also coached the Romans in soccer, the fiercest of the intramural teams; the Romans always walked away with the victor's cup. At school concerts and Saturday teas at Alumni House, he'd always have on his arm one of the younger teachers from Abbot Academy, our sister school down the street — a tightly smiling woman in an A-line corduroy jumper, with bobbed hair and a Peter Pan collar. Tim Nindle was so eligible he must've made their teeth ache.

But I knew what was really going on, because I'd watch him fawn on his beauties: always a little coterie of Apollos at his table in Commons, as tweedy as he. Or he'd drive a couple of his favorites into town, the top down on the T-Bird, laughing in the wind. His manner with them, even in class, was ripe with flirtatious irony. Nothing overt, very clubby and man-to-man. Was I the only one who noticed the overeagerness, what the shield of his gentleman's wardrobe couldn't hide?

Or was it just weird coincidence that revealed the Nindle subtext of desire? For it happened that the objects of his charm were the very men who haunted me at night — the tennis prince from Lauderdale, the dimpled goalie from JV hockey. If only I could've made them laugh as Nindle did — but flustered lockjaw seized me in their presence. At least I knew the French master's secret, subtle as the twists of an irregular verb. But it left me feeling more impotent than usual, my inability to play either part in the courting dance. Nindle never looked at me. He couldn't stand it when I lingered after class with a grammar question, butting into his private banter with the gods.

Could I have been Apollo myself for a week, I would've seduced him. Not that Nindle appealed to me remotely, but I'd think sometimes what it would be like to have the kind of body and raw power that made him reel. What it would be like to lure him onto the shoals of desire. I wanted to be a mantrap like Liz in *Butterfield 8*. A dark and twisted desire to be sure, and one that was of no use whatever to Nindle or me, since it got neither of us any closer to a night of mad abandon with the goalie. But as long as I couldn't have that, second-best would be to destroy the French master for looking through me as if I didn't exist. And for being a grownup version of me, the overheated voyeur in the locker room.

I don't pretend this baroque tangle of urge and revenge was very conscious — no more than the straight Adonises were conscious of flirting back with a man like Nindle. I only know there were times when I'd be pacing like a trapped thing in the sealed room of the closet, waiting for the slightest rustle at the door, daring someone to knock. So I tuned right in when the sad-eyed man with the wild gray hair came into Nick's one Sunday too often, browsing aimlessly before he bought cigars. He couldn't take his eyes off me, which both disconcerted and thrilled me. From the first I knew the power was mine, for I'd watched it from the sidelines up at school, the fly on Nindle's wall.

As Sunday followed Sunday, we'd chat for a glancing moment while I made change. He was a portrait painter by trade, lifeless full-length studies of women of a certain age, the features slightly cheated, as if by a skilled embalmer. He was called Raf — a fragment of the mouthful of Russian syllables in his name, but sufficient to mark his paintings. Sixty, I suppose, though so battle-worn and unkempt, all I could see was old. Four grown sons, he told me, which meant he lived alone with his wife in the big yellow clapboard house at the bottom of Central Street by the river.

Yes, I knew the house. Yes, I'd like to see his paintings sometime — except I was awfully busy with school. I put him off coyly week after week, amazed at his shameless tenacity, coldly enjoying the power of my casual indifference. Afraid too, but not wanting to give that too much rein, lest I never do anything.

"So when are you coming to see my studio?" asked the Russian. And before I could put up a wall of homework, he added, "You're on vacation, aren't you?"

Spring break, it must have been. I showed up at the appointed hour on the following Saturday, carefully dressed in tie and blazer. I'd had this running fantasy about what I would say if he asked to paint me naked. I decided I'd reluctantly agree if he promised not to touch me. The painting took on an erotic charge more illicit than sex, even if I ran the risk that he'd use it some day to blackmail me. Too many Ava Gardner movies.

He answered the door himself, looking more disheveled than usual and deeply agitated. I held back, thinking I'd interrupted him in the fury of creation, but he ushered me in impatiently and led me right upstairs. Two flights to the attic, passing silent shadowy rooms with heavy armoires. He let me precede him up the attic stairs, and the first sight of the atelier was reassuringly authentic. Several canvases perched on easels, in various stages of completion, done from photographs tacked in the corner of the frame. The smell of art was overpowering, coffee cans jammed with spattered brushes. The atmosphere was bohemian enough to help me overlook the paint-by-number flatness of the work.

I turned to ask a question — and he was on me, fumbling a hand to unbutton my shirt and reaching to paw inside. I recoiled, but didn't run, and now he'd dropped to his knees, fiddling to open my belt. I looked down at his sweaty head, the wild damp strands barely covering his bald spot. He gasped as he released my dick from my pants, then pushed me back into a ragged armchair, hunkered between my legs to take me in his mouth.

I couldn't bear the whimper of his excitement, or the sight of him groveling at my feet. But I got hard anyway and let him continue, too polite, too cowed to put a stop to it. I lolled my head to the side and stared out the attic window. Below, on the back slope, was an arbor black with leafless vines, then the winter-beaten field leading down to the sluggish, swollen river. I remember thinking *So this is it*, with a desolate sense of anticlimax. The naughty excitement of boyish sex with Kite and Richie was long gone. In its place was only grim endurance of the old man's desperate, mauling need.

I came without a sound, gritting my teeth as he gulped me like an elixir. I wouldn't meet his eyes as I stood to pull my pants back on, tucking in my shirttail, relieved at least that he hadn't bared his own geriatric organ. Another minute and I'd be out of there. Then he said, "How much?" I looked at him, confused. "How much do you charge?"

"Nothing," I retorted in a choked whisper, then turned and practically bolted down the stairs. In one of the upstairs bedrooms a shadow moved — the wife? One of the sons? For appearance's sake I let the old man catch up, thanking him volubly for the art tour as we descended to the front door. I gave him a proper handshake, smiling glassily, then escaped.

Hurrying to make it home before dark. Wondering how I had lost the power. Days later, I thought of Liz, counting the curl of bills on the bedside table. What should I have asked for — twenty-five? Would the power have come back if I'd come out on top cash-wise? For months afterwards I berated myself for leaving empty-handed. I never saw Raf again, even at Nick's. He must have found someplace else to buy his cigars.

So *Nothing* was all I had to say — the answer I gave to my mother about Kite, the answer she gave to my brother the day the street toughs called me queer. With a shudder of revulsion I shut the final door, keeping sex between me and my hand, letting no one touch me for the next five years. I was sure I could live without it. Never, never would I become the ravenous creature who did me in the attic.

I grew more invisible every day. I buried myself in books — remember reading *Franny and Zooey* with a physical pang of longing, wishing I had a Zooey to tell it to, an older brother dispensing advice from the bathtub. I sat on a radiator in the library stacks combing through forty years of a magazine called *Theatre Arts*, which printed a new play every month, with pictures of the New York cast. I'd think about becoming a Broadway star, unimpeded by the fact that I'd never acted. I revealed to Francis one day, still my only friend at school, that my stage name would be Landy Monet — the *t* silent in the French manner, Landy a streamline of Landry, my middle name. A crowd of dazzled fans at the stage door. My Tony acceptance speech already written in my head.

On Wednesday and Saturday afternoons I'd always drop in at the Andover Bookstore, in a white-painted barn off Main Street. This oasis of urbanity was owned and run by Jerry Cross, my father's boss at the coal company — started as something of a hobby but quickly growing till it was known all over New England as a book lover's paradise. There was a fireplace with chairs drawn up, coffee and sweets on a table nearby. Ethel Cross oversaw the staff and did the ordering of new books. It's the place where I first understood that books had currency, and Ethel was the first person I ever talked authors with outside school. It was liberating in the same way that having lunch with my grandmother was—nobody watching my moves to see if I was a sissy.

I ended sophomore year by making a brief and very minor splash. The school had a number of obscure prizes in classics—the best essay on a Homeric subject written in Greek, the best lyric poem in Latin, Victorian honors handed down through generations. The classics department was *very* old school, kindly as Mr. Chips but slightly out of it like Mr. Magoo. I don't recall who encouraged me, but I prepared a text to recite in the Latin Declamation Contest. No memory at all of the text itself, a letter I think describing a battle, maybe Caesar himself. But I declaimed it like a house on fire, gesticulating wildly to the assembled dons. And won hands down.

Ten bucks, a real gyp. The Greek essay prize was a cool five hundred. But at least I had finally *done* something, instead of the making do and squeaking through that had so far characterized my worm's progress through the ivied halls. At a place like Andover they encouraged the bejesus out of you, once they've figured out what you can do. So in six months I would find myself starring in the Latin play—five hundred lines of Plautus to memorize, and two hours of leering stage business. Not exactly the matinee idol Landy Monet was shooting for. A buffoon was what the part demanded, half Zero Mostel, half Groucho. My comic timing was generally a mile early or late—but, then, the sleepy audience was composed entirely of Latin students, forced to attend by class assignment, so they just wanted it over with.

I know it's not written down anywhere, even in the shade of the Washington elm, how far you're supposed to have gone at the halfway point of high school. But nowhere is how my halfway point felt. The given of being straight was the only road up the mountain, murderously steep in an all-boys' school. So what if their women were mostly fictitious? The girl at home, with the blue flowered stationery. Or the girl met at a tea dance, trapped in a boarding school of her own, monogrammed notecards from Shreve's. Even the occasional girl from town, encountered by chance in a coffee shop, the class difference oddly compelling, like a duke trying to nail a barmaid.

Necessary fictions, to be sure, since the boys were stuck with each other eight months a year. All *their* real life was compressed into summer romances, sailing in Maine and the Vineyard. But at least they were in it together — blowing off carnal steam on the ballfield, brazenly teasing one another about their masturbatory feats, then comrades in the hunt as the buses dropped them off for the dances at Dana Hall and Miss Porter's. They may not have got much action, this being the last gasp of the Age of Virginity, but the bond of commiseration kept them going forward. The quest for a girl was a team sport.

It wasn't sex I couldn't keep up with, being gay and invisible — it was self. Hiding the truth would require ever more elaborate stratagems: decoy romances and aimless dates. Relations with women would soon take on the hue of the Big Lie. But the hardest part was having no one to bond with, no comrade-in-arms. I was fifteen years old, and nobody knew the half of me. Was I depressed? Shell-shocked rather, dug into a hole, my small and stunted experience of passion indistinguishable from the guilt of being the son who could walk. Betrayal and violation were all I had taken home, so far, from the struggle of love.

Yet what I wish in retrospect is not that I had had a great first love at fifteen. Too much to hope for, given the thickness of the walls I built. Besides, it would take me the better part of growing up to understand that intimacy, more than sex or even sexual orientation, was the universal battleground, and no easier for straight than gay. But I wish I could have shared the state of being loveless with Francis and Gene, instead of that patter of improvised camp so ignorant of its heritage, from Oscar Wilde to Joan Crawford. Camp without a country. I like to think we could have made a first crude sketch of the men we dreamed of loving, because otherwise the dream was as locked up as we were — a closet within the closet. Talking it all out loud, we might have come to see that being different was about something more than just our dicks.

Or as Harry Hay once put it, needling like a gadfly, the only thing that's the same about gay and straight people is what they do in bed. Thus what I wish for the Gay/Straight Alliance at Andover is more than a sex-positive affirmation of self, wherever they make their beds. Let them all come out, of course — bottom line. But after that I wish them the comradeship of differentness, above and beyond the carnal. Or arm in arm with it anyway, as they march down the field butched up in soccer drag and accessorized to the teeth, pearls and boas rampant. Whatever works to keep them from digging a hole. *Go, team!*

For several summers now the Monettes had been taking their last two weeks in July at a rental cottage on Rye Harbor. Along the narrow wedge of New Hampshire seacoast that lies between the Puritan colony of Massachusetts and the untamed wilds of Maine. Mostly I sat on the stone jetty reading Agatha Christie, my swimming in the ice-cube water limited to shrieking thirty-second dunks with my father and uncles. But I loved the rocky coast with its lobster shacks and salt marshes, not yet sucked up by landfill and cluttered with time-share condos. Twice Nana and I took the day-boat from Portsmouth out to the Isles of Shoals, jigsaw crags of weatherbeaten granite carpeted in July with wildflowers. And a swaybacked Edwardian hotel where chowder was served by kerchiefed women as gaunt as Shakers, and island blueberries for dessert.

Rye was the first place I ever thought about telling stories, though I never wrote them down. Shipwreck stories and pirate coves, the curses of one-eyed sailors. My imagination was preadolescent, a boy's garden of tales out of *Treasure Island*, some small midsummer relief from the crazed voyeurism of the locker room. I was thrilled therefore to learn that Jerry Cross had given my father his house at Rye for the whole summer of '61. A big white-shingle cottage right on the water, on a jut of land where the coast road crooked like an elbow. The place had once belonged to Ogden Nash the poet, who to my undiscerning ear was right up there with Robert Frost.

I took the third-floor front room in the gable, the lighthouse view. And decided, on no evidence at all, that this must have been the poet's aerie. Late at night I'd sit on the windowsill and write verse by moonlight, nary a line of which has survived, mercifully. I didn't write much in any case, seized as I was by the dilemma of having to choose whether to be a Broadway star or a deathless poet. When the uncles asked, I still said dentist or lawyer, but that was just a smoke screen now so I could float away and daydream.

Beyond the crook, the beach road swept around a crescent bay lined with the sprawling summer houses of millionaires. Acres of lawn in front were clipped as close as golf greens, not a dandelion to mar the tailored view to the bluff. I'd spend whole afternoons walking up and down the service roads in back, catching a glimpse of the very blond as they crossed in their whites to the tennis court or stalked toward the stables in boots and jodhpurs. I had this drowsy notion, as I peered through the rambling roses and over the fences, that people so rich did only what they liked, no secrets and no shame. I could scarcely have been more wrong about that, but a voyeur is so possessed by what he sees that he doesn't reason. The world is all blinding surfaces.

That summer I started amassing a guilty stash of stroke books. The magazine rack at Nick's was determinedly macho, *Strength and Health* coming about as close as it got to male erotica, assuming steroids turned you on. But recently the distributor had started sending two copies every month of a pocket-size photo mag called *Tomorrow's Man*. Black-and-white pictures of young guys in their twenties, either striking heroic poses on their own or paired with another in a wrestling clench. The studio backdrops were heavy on the satin drapery, with maybe a Greek column to lean against. But what seized the gaze was the state of undress: a pouch of cloth that barely covered the genitals, held in place by an invisible string about the waist, what's called in the trade a "posing strap."

Impossible to describe the hypnotic charge for a fifteen-year-old whose porno diet was heretofore limited to the Parr of Arizona underwear ads in the back pages of *Esquire*. It wasn't just the beauty of the specimens, ripe but not overmuscled, squeaky clean as surfers. It was an attitude of showing off, a sassy wink of something I'd never seen before. When they were shot from the back, they shucked the strap and posed butt-naked, sometimes almost shaking it in your face. I was staring at men who wanted to be admired. And who clearly got down and did it as soon as the shutter stopped clicking.

It was the first clue I ever had that being queer existed out there in the world, with men as real as the shower parade at school. I don't think we ever sold a copy of *Tomorrow's Man* over the counter. One left the store with me, tucked in the pages of *Modern Screen*. The other was surely filched by Alex, Nikos's flaming son, whose feel for the outrageous was so far out as to be beyond ridicule. To call him queer hardly did him justice. He danced through the store with cheerleader pompoms, streaked his hair with Clorox, greeted customers in voices that stretched from Daffy Duck to Mae West. All to the horror of his father, who muttered darkly in Greek and shook his fist at the sky. I thought Alex was a scream. In addition to which, beside him I felt as butch as a first-string fullback.

My brother went into the hospital in October, just shy of his tenth birthday. By then he'd been to Shriner's several times, but this was serious business, bladder surgery at Mass. General. I remember the day of the surgery vividly, a flawless blue and gold Saturday afternoon, with a home game at school against Deerfield. Bobby was under the knife for seven or eight hours, while I stayed home and waited for a call from my parents to say it was over.

Listening to *Judy at Carnegie Hall* the whole afternoon, from the overture through three curtain calls: *I'll sing 'em all and we'll stay all night!* Without any notion that this recent prize acquisition of mine was a gay icon, more telling proof than all the Tomorrow's Men in the world that I was bent. I lip-synced along like a junior Jim Bailey. And at last got the call around dusk that Bobby was out of the woods and in Recovery. So I tramped up to school in time for the victory bonfire, then joined the boisterous crowd for the Saturday movie in George Washington Hall, telling no one my brother had almost died.

Or was just going into the woods. A few days later one of his kidneys stopped functioning. He was running very high fevers, a post-op infection in the urinary tract. Two doctors on the case started butting heads — one of them adamant that the bad kidney had to come out, the other arguing wait-and-see. My parents were treading deep water, not knowing which way to go as they watched their kid sink. The doctor arguing urgency must have prevailed, for Bobby found himself being prepped for surgery, still woozy from the last.

He was on a gurney and waiting at the threshold of the operating theater, when an ambulance came shrieking up to Emergency with somebody even closer to the brink. Bobby's doctors had to yield the theater and reschedule, and in the intervening hours his moribund kidney kicked in again. By now, my parents' nerves were fried. They just wanted him out of there — beginning to have that queasy paranoid feeling that the medical system was more lethal than whatever the body was fighting.

Sorry. Catch-22: hospital policy didn't allow a patient to be released with a fever. So my brother lay there in a kind of prison, days turning into weeks as his temp persisted, unresponsive to a dwindling arsenal of antibiotics. He thinks he must've been in a couple of months, though time starts to lose its borders at a hundred and six degrees. Bedsores bloomed at his hips. I don't know what the last straw was, but a quarter century later my mother still had fire in her eyes recalling the day she stamped her foot.

Enough. They may have been bringing him home to die, but at least it wouldn't be lonely and indifferent. The next part is family legend. My brother home in bed, his fever showed no sign of abating, and the day came when it peaked on our drugstore thermometer at 108. That meant it was off the graph, for 108 was as far as the mercury went. He should've been having convulsions now, but somehow he rode it out. Nothing to do but old-wives' remedies, alcohol baths and icepacks.

And then one day the fever broke and didn't come back. All the red lights stopped flashing. I don't know how easy it was for my parents to unclench their white-knuckle grip on the emergency switch. But we went ahead with Christmas, turkey and mince the same as always, me decorating the top half of the tree, my brother the bottom. Here I'm counting on Bobby's disjointed memory of the crisis and its passing, since on this episode I am more amnesiac than usual. Other than the Deerfield afternoon and the figure 108, I draw an absolute blank. It's stayed suppressed through two courses of therapy and five years of dredging. No further detail yielded up from my brother's duel with the Shadow.

But at least I know why I became unhinged, a quarter century later, as I took Roger's temperature over and over before he crash-landed with AIDS. Ninety-nine point three, day after day, a whisper of something monstrous I had witnessed long before, a single burning match about to conflagrate the world. And the blood-chilling fear of hospitals that I shared with my mother, as well as her bitter fatalism that two medical opinions will always cancel each other out. We are issued our curious armor and toothless weapons by the memories we have blocked, whose traumas seem hardly more real when the details finally do get filled in. Even now this recollection is only the movie of my brother almost dying. The actuality remains the same: a black hole.

No wonder the picture-postcard flow of seasons at school, the yellowing elms and the first snowfall, felt like a different plane of reality than mine. No wonder I was such a loner, processing all the terrors of home. The only connection I could make with the system was aesthetic. In junior year we were allowed a minor elective in art history, a damn sight more nurturing for the soul than the mandatory Bible minor of sophomore year. We were lectured to with a million slides by a teaching fellow from Yale, Mr. Paoletti. He was wonderfully urbane as he roller-coastered us from the pyramids to Picasso, the greatest hits of the West. It was the first time I ever took in the romance of Europe as a place apart, layer upon layer of civilization.

It happened that right on campus we had an amazing resource, the Addison Gallery of American Art. A marble-floored treasure house that was almost always deserted, with one old duffer of a custodian who mostly dozed on his mop. The museum became my private study hall, even more removed from things than Harriet's grave. Especially a faded horse-hair sofa on the second floor that faced *Eight Bells* of Winslow Homer, the collection's most famous painting. But I came to know several others too by a sort of osmosis — Copley, Eakins, Hassam — the silent music of masterpieces surrounding me as I crammed for tests. Downstairs was a whole room of Paul Revere's silver, buffed to a mirror shine. And I remember a special exhibit of modern art, bewilderingly and thrillingly abstract, that I walked through every day it was up. I knew I couldn't be truly sophisticated till I'd figured out why all this stuff was beautiful.

It was there among the moderns that I witnessed a pair of the Dionysus boys horsing around, snickering at the Malevich *White on White* as they made their grudging notes for a paper. Suddenly one of them blocked the other with his shoulder, sending him staggering backward. A flailing arm knocked against a Calder, a swirling knot of black steel rods with teetering mobile wings and fingers. The whole of which fell crashing off its pedestal — setting off no alarm, but the noise brought curator and staff scurrying. The guilty philistines had already vanished.

I watched the staff pick up the sculpture tenderly, cradling it like a big wounded bird, all the while fretting in anguish that it might have sustained some damage. Of course it was fine — that tempered steel could've survived a bomb blast. But I was enthralled by the urgency of their reaction, as if the Calder were a kind of holy object for them. I would be spending a lot of time in museums in the years ahead, consoling myself by means of connoisseurship for the bitter solitude of my life. The lesson of that tenderness, the Calder being restored to its pedestal, stayed with me as I took solace in beautiful things. At least I could feel for art what the laws of desire and my own self-hatred prevented me from feeling for another man.

The temple wasn't inviolate. Some years later, the Aladdin's cave of silver was stolen by overnight thieves, who scarcely had to break a window, security being as lax as the dozing custodian. The museum paid a ransom, recovered the loot and rearranged it in the same creaky glass cases. Two months later it was stolen again, foiling the stubborn New England belief that lightning would never strike twice in the same place. This time all the exquisite objects were melted down for the silver. Insurance is far too high nowadays to permit such masterworks as the Homer to hang unguarded. They are locked in sunless vaults. So I figure I had the last chance to use the Addison as a private gallery, all its glories untarnished. The site where art first came to seem sacred, as fragile and inexplicable as faith.

Not that the watery aesthete was anything like an artist. Already there were two or three guys in my class who were having whole exhibitions of their own, grabbing up the art prizes with wild assemblages and blood-red paintings. We had a fiery actor who dazzled us in *Macbeth*, a commanding bohemian presence clearly destined for Gielgud heights. Then I had a shy acquaintance with a witheringly well-read boy named Terry: burning blue eyes circled by wire-rims, a cascade of blond curls, and a scarf that swept about him like Isadora. He carboned me a copy of his poem, "yes I'm cumming cors I'm late," a stunning pastiche of arcana that I could barely follow, parodies of poets I'd never heard of.

More daunting than anything was the fierce self-confidence, the raw and brazen energy. At sixteen they exulted in being artists, impatient to throw off the bonds of school. Needless to say, I didn't show Terry my own verse, with its wince-making rhymes and Arcadian locutions. I knew I wasn't anywhere near as good as the three or four writers in my class who regularly published in *The Mirror*. But somehow that didn't stop me dabbling.

I decided that if I wasn't a genius in any one art, then I would get to know them all.

Thus I attended every recital the music department sponsored, despite being born with the tinniest of ears. I took parts in plays at the furthest remove from the glamourous pair of main-stage shows, the winter Shakespeare and the spring musical. In my plays, the cast almost always outnumbered the audience, usually a single performance in a drafty rehearsal hall. I signed up for every Sunday museum outing to Boston, once just the teacher and I in the school's blue van, an afternoon of Van Gogh that left me open-mouthed and pounding with excitement. I would've turned the whole world into art if I could, and all the rest of the time my nose was in a book. Anything but reality.

Yet I wasn't a social outcast, even so. My off-off-Broadway career mixed me up with girls from Abbot, rekindling the old courtier skills from seventh grade. I didn't dream of dating them, but they laughed in all the right places. Now it happened that I was friendly that year with a studious boy from Salem, Philip, whose family went back to Columbus. Philip was as nerdy as I, not a trace of Apollo or Dionysus, except he was straight. Because of his lineage he was being heavily tapped to escort girls in the debutante cotillions of the North Shore, though he couldn't have been less of a preppy snob. It turned out that one of the Abbot girls I'd acted with, a girl weighed down with Cabot and Lowell forebears, was making her debut at the winter cotillion in Salem. As she required a pair of escorts, Philip asked if I would come along.

Was that my first tuxedo? I suspect it was, a rented After Six that I didn't quite have the shoes to match, but it fit me all too well. By the time I arrived at the Cabot mansion, I felt as if I were being hummed by Cole Porter. A butler ushered me into the parlor and asked what I was drinking. A dry martini, I told him, straight up. I who had never drunk so much as a swallow of beer before, who'd learned how to drink from reading Ian Fleming. I was drunk on my ass by the time we went in to dinner, seated in the place of honor on Missy Cabot's right. Except for giving a toast that struck me a good deal funnier than it did those thin-lipped Brahmins, I didn't do anything dire. Missy appeared to find me most refreshing.

At the cotillion itself I danced with a lady from England—I mean a *Lady* lady. I charmed the bloomers off the assembled Cabot grandmothers and great-aunts, decked out in their old China trade silks and cameos. A late supper was served after midnight, pheasant and eggs on Rose Medallion. If dining out at Howard Johnson's with Nana made me feel sophisticated, this high-born world in black tie and ball gowns was an earthly paradise indeed. I remember thinking, as I lay in bed at Philip's house, too excited to sleep, how easily one could bring off a life like this if only sex didn't have to come into it.

One night of finery, and already I was trying to figure how to make a dry marriage. What closeted WASPS had been doing ever since they trundled off the Mayflower: a sociable match with a proper lady, passion kept to a minimum, and lots of gin martinis as they pored over their Greek vases, fantasizing about the coachman. If you played your cards right, you could even marry *up*—snare an heiress with banter and cocktail chitchat, as long as you made a good appearance at the club. All you had to give up was your dick.

It would be a while yet before I could spot one of those shuttered unions across a dance floor. The dumpy wife with her gray ponytail, like an old little girl, the smile on her face as strained and pale as the sherry in her glass. The husband a bit too natty in his plaids, his bloodless charm on automatic, and one eye hungering after the barman. Yet even a decade later, foiled at finding a man to love me back, I was still weighing the devil's bargain. Still debating if this woman or that would have me above the waist, and then we could both eat pheasant till it came out of our ears.

The closet is all about compartments. I had grown accustomed now to the nightly parade of Apollo, obsessively narrowed down to a team of six or eight who drove me wild. The ritual jerkoff was my safety valve, a way to put sex behind me. Now that

I had a growing cache of visual aids — a full-color glossy called *Muscleboy*, purchased in terror at North Station while on one of those art field trips — I had everything I needed to keep it to myself. I didn't even feel any longing to incorporate sex into life. The idea was as inconceivable as one of the athlete gods slipping into my bed. I was proud of the little dark corner I came in — nobody's business.

And woe to the faggot who tried to turn the light on. Philip had a roommate from Ohio, rich but nouveau and preppier-than-thou, down to the tassels on his loafers. Charles had a wicked tongue, and he took delight in imitating the various odd-balls in our class. He was tall and rangy, impeccably turned out, and always working double-time to be chummy with the local gods. We laughed at his cruel pantomimes, which often took special contemptuous aim at the "lower" classes — scholarship boys with one-suit wardrobes, the sideshow crew of Commons workers. Yet I never walked away from one of Charles's scathing performances without thinking I would be next to be skewered. He was Dionysus with a mean streak, and enough sweaters to outfit a polar expedition.

Between classes, I spent a lot of time in his and Philip's room, one of the few places among the boarders where I could hang out. It was late afternoon in the spring, the windows wide open. From the lawn below rose the martial sounds of boys play-ing catch and three-man lacrosse. I was studying lines for a Sean O'Casey one-acter, trying to pull off an Irish brogue. Charles had just come in from tennis, all the right white-boy's togs and a racket that cost an arm and a leg. Suddenly he came prancing out of the bedroom, doing a riff on the games mistress at Abott.

Wearing a jock and nothing else. He pounced on me and wrestled me out of the armchair, still in character sort of, the infamous Miss Beale. "Girls, girls, girls," he trumpeted like a sergeant, dragging me onto the floor, then on top of him. "I want you to play fair and play hard. And I want you to run your panties off." He was hard himself and grinding his hips against me.

"No," I whined, then more insistent, scrambling away. In a wounded huff I hissed at him: "That's not who I am." And grabbed my books and beat it out of there, leaving him sprawled on the floor, shot down.

What layer of virginity was I still trying to protect? I don't know if I would have said no so quickly to every boy at school. Temptation by the dimpled goalie would surely have been too much to resist. But Charles was no slouch — attractive and interesting both. Even a brief and glancing affair would have moved me forward, releasing sex from the dark room of my nightly worship. Instead the pattern was set: from now on I would bolt at the slightest come-on, especially from a peer. A full-blown case of homosexual panic, at the mere suggestion of putting together friendship and carnal intimacy. I couldn't stomach the thought that another queer had found me out.

But if that wasn't who I was, I would have to be content with staying no one. All through the following summer I worked nearly every day with flaming Alex, unthreatened by his wall-to-wall camping and vamping. At night we'd go bowling or kick back at his house or mine, putting away whole quarts of Nick's ice cream while we listened to Broadway show tunes. As gay as our hips were wide, but as long as he didn't put the make on me, our friendship pushed no homophobic buttons. Sex would have spoiled everything.

Twice that summer I visited Philip at the Cape, where his grandparents kept an ancient cottage on a private island called Oyster Harbors, with its own bridge over the marshes and a gatehouse. Mellons and Coolidges on every side, for whom sailing was next to religion, glutting their days like the bluefish they ate every night because dammit, the season was so short.

These were the black-tie kids from the cotillions, wearing their summer mufti from L. L. Bean, khaki for days. And here I was inside the compound rather than out, no longer peeking over fences, and the good life looked even better. The Brahmins seemed to worry about nothing and have no secrets, and already appeared peacefully destined to become the lawyers and coupon clippers their fathers were, or their mothers idly arranging flowers and good marriages.

I got it wrong supposing they were happy in a world that left them no wiggle room. But I was right on the money to understand there were places granted by birth, where I could never be more than an overnight guest. My want of name and pedigree would set off the clang of trespass at the gatehouse. I had years of cotillions ahead of me, as well as a spate of white-glove ushering at weddings and being the extra man to fill a table at various brain-dead dinners. Always the invisible radar of the Brahmin aristocrats made me feel like a coal miner's kid who couldn't quite get the grime off. Separate and unequal. Yet in the end it was those very walls, unscalable and glacial, that helped me pack it in and go with being different.

Even for Apollo and Dionysus, senior year at Andover was a forbidding prospect. All of us were required to take American History, the boot-camp course *par excellence*, five classes a week and a grueling twenty hours of homework on top of that. It had its own wing of the library, as well as a monthly exam intended to reduce near-grown men to jelly. We were proudly told no college course would crush our gonads quite so finely — not an exaggeration. College itself being the other prong that goaded us through the year. The clamor of SATs, mass interviews with the Ivy League, the pumping up of résumés. Out of a class of some two hundred and twenty, we would be sending fifty-five to Harvard and forty-three to Yale. Big lifeboats, but you still had to claw for a place.

All of that was secondary, though, when I lucked into Dudley Fitts's English IV. He was the one true Olympian on the faculty. The Sophocles we used in class had been translated by him and Robert Fitzgerald, a feat of erudition that seemed almost Biblical to us. To hear Mr. Fitts talk about Greek theater, how the chorus moved, how it sounded — you were there. The prodigious learning was tempered by a rollicking wit, delivered in an absent-minded drawl, half to himself so you had to crane to listen. Yet more than anything it was the humanness of the questions he asked of a line of poetry, bringing to bear feelings we hadn't dreamed of naming.

The immensity of Antigone's grief for her brother, burying him in defiance of the king. "Why, why does she do this?" Fitts would plead with us. "Doesn't she know she's going to die?" Coaxing from us a halting grasp of the fight between conscience and law, man and the state. Radical stuff — from the Latin *radix*, for root. Then he'd recite it in Greek, from memory, Antigone's dirge, while we followed along in English: *O tomb, O marriage-chamber* . . .

He would have us so rapt, or me anyway, that we all forgot that he never rose from his chair or wrote on the blackboard. Because he was brutally disabled, some kind of degenerative muscular disorder, MS maybe. He'd park his car in the bushes behind Bulfinch Hall, then come in the basement door to his classroom, propelling himself on crutches with arm clamps. Stupid useless legs, just like my brother's. And though nobody ever, ever made fun of Fitts's shaky walk — too much in awe of his mind — it did tend to make people shy and look to the side.

But not me. Ten years living with Bobby had taken all the weirdness away from the specter of disability. Physically challenged, differently abled — the new euphemisms are not just phrases but a recognition of life force, the dispassionate second nature that gets the disabled from room to room. So I'd walk right next to Mr. Fitts, chattering like a bookish magpie, while he made his slow way to his car. And we'd drive over to George Washington so he could pick up his mail in the faculty room, a far better ride than Apollo ever got in Nindle's T-Bird. Because I knew his son and daughter from grammar school, I'd ask about them sometimes — anything to get the great man to talk. I don't doubt I was insufferably fawning, with my small and earnest questions, but Fitts was ever-patient and wry, and encouraged me in my reading.

After that Latin play the year before, I'd sworn never to memorize another line of a dead tongue. But under the spell of Antigone and the fire that breathed through the ancient texts of

Fitts's class, I volunteered again to take the lead. "Tried out" would imply that anyone else wanted it. This time I was stuck with *eight* hundred lines of classical Groucho, another comedy of Plautus called *The Captives*.

I don't remember a moment of it now, a plot so twisted and turned, I could hardly follow it then. The pictures that survive, however, show the scholarly pains taken by Dr. Rohmer, our director as well as my Cicero teacher. Enormous painted backdrops of a Roman town, and our motley troupe in gaudy capes and tunics out of *Spartacus*. One of which gave a side-slit view of my unmuscled body in a skimpy loincloth — necessitating a constant vigilance on my part, so as not to show my slit side to the audience.

What I recall with a flush of pleasure still is that Mr. Fitts reviewed it on the front page of *The Phillipian*, the school weekly. The Latin was as alive to him as the demotic South Boston slang he fell into with such relish. He got all the jokes — practically the only laugh in the house. And when he praised the comic bewilderment of my performance, I felt as if a direct line had been drawn between me and the theater festivals of fifth-century Athens, *Antigone* on opening night.

From this vantage I think it was those Latin plays that got me into Yale. I certainly wasn't any great shakes as a scholar in Classics, given the fact there were boys taking both Latin V and Greek IV, the lofty heights of Ovid and Sappho. But the interviewers from Harvard and Yale were suitably nonplussed by my drama career — "You mean it was all in *Latin*?" And thus I managed to fill some rarefied slot in their calculations, as they rubber-stamped admission to the whole Andover hockey team.

Our triumph with *The Captives* in the provinces was short-lived, however. Mid-winter, Dr. Rohmer suddenly vanished from Cicero class. A younger instructor took over, as Rohmer and his wife and kids were hustled out of the dorm he supervised, a moving van right behind them. The story came to me in unnerving bits and snatches — how Rohmer had taken to giving backrubs to certain of his seniors, and one night went too far. I knew exactly who the victim was, the tennis prince with the flaw-less line of hair bisecting his torso from chest to crotch. He was close to the top of my own pantheon, a gentle-spoken youth who wore his Apollo laurels with appealing modesty.

For his sake the gossip was kept to a Marine-rigid minimum. But the lesson was devastatingly clear, even in the stunned silence that sealed off the scandal. You could throw your whole life away by a single wrong move, a hand that lingered too long on the buttocks. Even marriage was no security. There was one taboo that brooked no violation, a warning to the Nindles of this cloistered hothouse world to back the fuck off.

My father would pick me up late every night behind the chapel, since with all that history to read I never left the library till it closed. We didn't talk about anything much, but nothing felt wanting between us either. I remember the night he told me Nana was rushed to the hospital, a blood clot in her leg. All that week I walked from the library to the chapel, tensing to hear the morbid update. She might lose the leg — they were trying to save the knee — they'd had to cut mid-thigh. By Friday she was amputated, and I still had Saturday classes and a history monthly on Monday. I no more thought of mentioning the tragedy to any-one at school than I had my brother's brush with death. It would have been calling the wrong attention to myself. This, mixed with a curious shame about coming from such a messy family.

One Sunday in the winter, I was taking a break from home-work — leafing through *Muscleboy* with a boner while Judy sang on the stereo, speaking of curious mixes. My mother walked in without knocking, and I managed to slip the magazine under the album cover, but guiltily. The swelling in my pants I covered by hugging my knees. Whatever she'd come in to say was quickly settled, but clearly I was hiding something. Her eyes darted to the album cover, and she inquired with a grisly attempt at empa-thy, "Is there anything you want to tell me?"

Now honestly, what else could I have been hiding except a hard-on and some porn? State secrets? In a flash the two of us were back to being out of our depth, and I was ten instead of seventeen. What is the etiquette, after all, of walking in on your son's jackoff session?

"No," I answered succinctly, but knowing that we'd just picked up the interrogation of seven years before, the question still unanswered: *What were you doing with Kite?*

A moment of prickly standoff, then she said, "You can always talk to us, Paul." *Us*, this time. The beginning of recognition that Dad was the one who ought to be doing the talking. As soon as she left, I stuffed the magazine in the back of a desk drawer, where I kept the omnisexual stash of *Tomorrow's Man* and *Playboy*. I had nothing to say to either of them, but felt dirty all the same at almost being caught red-handed.

And, the next night, walked unthinking from the library to the chapel, having put the whole thing out of my head. I got in the car, Dad and I exchanging the usual laconic pleasantries. Then he said, "There's something we have to talk about. Your mother was cleaning your room this morning . . ."

Hunkered against the car door in the dark, I could see her methodically tearing my room apart, going through everything till she found the evidence. I reeled from the violation as Dad went haltingly on. "There's nothing wrong with those girlie magazines," he declared. "That's perfectly natural, you're almost a man. But the homosexual ones . . . that's not good."

I don't think it went any further than that, no hellfire and damnation. It seems almost decent in retrospect, compared to the ugliness and disownings that have rung down on my brothers and sisters, killing off parent and child for good. I nodded and agreed politely, every nod producing a thousand more miles of distance, from him and from myself. The only thing I would learn from this was to hide the evidence even better. And so with a mutual promise that I could always talk to Dad if I wanted, about anything, we rode home in the dark.

The seniors got the word on college April 15, D-Day in the mailroom. Three letters waited in my box: Harvard, Yale, and Brown. I ran out into the courtyard by the Drama Lab and tore them open one by one—all yes. It still amazes me, the stifling assumption of privilege that advised me to apply nowhere else but these three, with Brown as my "backup." I graduated eightieth in my class, ordinary in every way except for my secrets. Not to say I wasn't insanely glad about winning the triple crown. But ten years later, when Roger told me how it broke his heart to open those rejections from Harvard and Yale — and he smarter than I by a factor of ten — I developed a bad aftertaste for the politics of entitlement.

The politics were obvious enough, even at the time. I was in a delicious quandary, not knowing which way to go. For some reason I never went to have a look at any of the three, though Harvard was only a half-hour away. Still a village boy at heart, for whom the distance between home base and anywhere else was immeasurable. Believe it or not, I was leaning toward Yale over Harvard because they were giving me more of a scholarship — $1600 a year versus $1550. So my future was riding on fifty bucks, when I got a note from the Dean of Students asking me to come in.

This crusty presence had never so much as smiled at me in four years. Meekly I sat down across the desk from him, and he peered at my name on the folder before him as he effused about my three acceptances. And which way was I leaning? Harvard or Yale, I told him politely, but probably Yale. He tutted and scoffed, drawing off his bifocals.

"Paul, I think Brown's where you belong. Harvard and Yale are too . . . too much pressure. Brown's what you want."

Trust me, as they say in Hollywood. The check's in the mail; I won't come in your mouth. I don't think I've ever had such an instant cold-blooded realization that I was being railroaded. He wanted my Yale slot for one of his waiting-list boys, one of those second-string hockey Apollos who hadn't quite made the Ivy team. Deals were being cut. Every purring screw-job I've ever been on the wrong end of, wreathed in Cheshire smiles, always brings me back to that bright May morning when Dean Dunham tried to take Yale away.

"Yessir," I murmured politely, salaaming as I thanked him

for his advice and scuttled out of there. And went right to the library, cutting French, to fill out my Yale acceptance form before Dunham or anyone else could sell me down the river.

Which left only graduation and goodbye. The seniors spent the last few weeks working on their tans and deciding whom to room with the following year. None of the forty-three going to Yale was a friend of mine. Francis was bound for Georgetown, Philip for BU. I told myself I'd be better off starting college without the prep school ties, a chance to have the slate wiped clean. I played no part in the final sentimental burst of camaraderie that charged the green and vivid air of spring. The last teaming of Apollo and Dionysus, hurling their frisbees and pranking the trees with toilet paper streamers. I ended as I began, an outsider—if anything, relieved that I had made it through without being exposed as a queer. No one needed to say goodbye to me, who was hardly there in the first place.

So I was flattered when they asked me to be in the senior class play, a traditional spoof put on for parents and faculty the night before graduation. The boho Macbeth was directing, a sendup of Melville called *Moby Reltney*. I never quite got the joke here, as usual too shy to ask. "Reltney," I think, was a code word for erection. The stage was the deck of the *Pequod*, with a cast of dozens recruited from the ranks of Apollo and Dionysus. Under the guise of satirizing the elaborate symbolism of *Moby Dick*, we were doing a riff on our own sexual randiness. I think.

They gave me the part of a stowaway, a foppish prig called Jonathan Swope von Krohn. The crew of macho sailors takes an instant loathing toward the intruder, teasing his fussy manners and finally prodding him with a harpoon to walk the plank. By then I thought of myself as a serious actor, and thus learned my lines word perfect, working up a portrait of insufferable effeteness. There was only one small problem: John Krohn was the name of a boy in our class. A gangly lad from Texas whose high-pitched breathless voice and slight sashay suggested a sort of Ray Bolger scarecrow without the straw.

The more we rehearsed, the more I understood that they

wanted me to play John Krohn himself, and that the strutting boys in pirate clothes were lynching this homo because he gave them the creeps. I felt horribly uncomfortable now, but trapped as well, too wimpy to raise an objection or walk away. It was bad enough the director kept pushing me to mince more, an act too close to my deepest fear, but the brutal identification with an actual boy was dismaying in the extreme. I kept thinking that John Krohn and his parents would be out there in the audience, too hurt to laugh.

But I went along with it night after night, letting the sailors sneer at me as they sent me over the side to the sharks. The performance was only three or four days away when the year-book came out. Each of us seniors went to pick one up in the mailroom, along with a gold class ring. Here was the record of all the sunny days on Olympus, the sixty-yard runs and the noble profiles, a ruling elite on the brink of manhood. Halfway through was the class poll, a blizzard of categories from "Brain" to "Best Athlete" to "Stubble Trouble," the latter a weird listing of the hairiest among us. Three in each category, nothing too mean, or so everyone would have protested.

The category "Faculty Magnet" was a droll euphemism for brown-nose, the one who kissed the most ass. The three names listed below were these: Monette, Simpson, Monette. I caught my breath when I saw it, stabbed as if by a harpoon. I don't say it wasn't accurate, since I stayed after class with depressing regularity, determined to be liked by the grownups if my classmates had no use for me. But I felt the sting of ridicule in a very deep place, was suddenly ashamed to bring my yearbook home or have it signed by anyone. They really didn't like me, the class of '63. My outsider status had now been cut in stone, to be brought down off the shelf at every reunion, back to which wild horses couldn't drag me.

I walked numbly through the tech rehearsal for the play, then dress rehearsal the night before the performance. The director continued to prod my caricature of John Krohn, embroidering it with broader affectations. The panic and shame reached a peak in me when I spoke that first line. "My name is Jonathan Swope von Krohn," I declared archly, bowing low to Ahab as a sailor behind me made a goosing gesture. Knowing now that they held me in the same low esteem as John Krohn, and that I was a traitor to him, as cruel as any boy who'd voted for me twice.

On the afternoon of the performance we had a graduation run-through, the senior class led to the chapel by a bagpiper in kilts. Then we practiced walking out onto the Great Lawn, where the next day we would make a vast circle two hundred and forty strong, as our diplomas were passed around from hand to hand. My estrangement from the group was total, every face seeming to wear a final smirk at my new nickname, which stuck like a magnet itself.

I had no plan at all to counter my defeat. I showed up on time at the dressing room, wearing my three-piece Krohn suit while the other boys got themselves up in sailors' rags. I held myself apart from their antic laughter, dreading the curtain's rise, powerless to stop the mockery. It wasn't a real decision. It's just that push finally came to shove. I sashayed out on deck between two burly sailors who'd found me under a lifeboat. All around were groans of sneering distaste, as the *Pequod*'s crew took my measure. I bowed as rehearsed to Ahab. But when I said my name, I grabbed for the Irish brogue, mangling every syllable and saving John Krohn by the skin of his teeth.

And that is how I left the place — gay in every respect except my dick, thrown to the sharks by my classmates. But with one tiny victory on my side. For once in my life, pushed to the wall, no matter how much I was no one myself, I'd moved to take the bullet for a brother.

Four

Audieris in quo, Flacce, balneo plausum,
Maronis illic esse mentulam scito.
                                    — *Martial (c. 40–104 A.D.)*

LUX ET VERITAS
You ask at the Baths why all this sudden applause?
It's their habit, Cabot.
Another Yale type has stepped out of his drawers.
                                    — *tr. Dudley Fitts*

ASSUMING THE JUDGE'S THREAT WAS REAL, I was lucky to get
to Yale at all. That final summer before leaving home I worked at
Nick's for the last time. I knew in my bones I was bound for a
one-way trip, that as soon as I hung up my apron in the closet by
the ice-cream maker, I would forfeit the inside track on life in a
small town. That strange amalgam of Norman Rockwell folksi-
ness and the quiet desperation of *Winesburg, Ohio.* Vinnie
O'Connor, having dropped out of Andover High at sixteen, was
already picking up garbage door-to-door in his own truck, his
bully days behind him. And I knew every bachelor and old maid
on sight — the sensible shoes and the rubbers for rain, that wincing sense of apology for their very being. Going no place, the
end of the line.

But if I was about to engineer my flight from same, I was
more overwhelmed than I'd freely admit, especially to myself. I

spent most of my working days with Alex, and after work as well, a ritual stack of records on the turntable, *Oklahoma* to *Candide*. Alex, whose high school C's were making it unlikely that he could take the college route of escape, was already talking cosmetology and hair. But not at the local level, please. His sights were on Madison Avenue and Beverly Hills, centers of style and chic, and not "this Ann Taylor woolen bullshit."

For all his queenly dish, or maybe because of it, Alex had a much more confident feel than I of a world out there to conquer. He had been noisily defying for so long his father's Greek ideal of manhood. "My son is a girl!" Nick would bellow as if accursed, Alex shaking his pompoms in retort. I can't say I actually envied him, but his raw, confrontive style had a certain antic charm about it. He was a drag queen without the dress and makeup, a caricature of a sissy, over the top in a town that had never seen genderfuck at all. Consequently the bullies gave him a sort of theatrical clearance.

In a way I couldn't begin to explain, Alex was defining himself more truly than I with all my school credentials. He said whatever came into his head, nothing to lose, go screw yourself if you didn't like it. Two months later I would have been mortified if any of my Yale friends had seen us laughing together, so desperate was I to pass. But in that summer of finishing life in the provinces I took a curious refuge in the camp of Alex Anestos, who might say absolutely anything and usually did.

"Good morning, sir," he'd greet a bleary customer. "You look like you need a little Ex-Lax, or is it a Kotex?" And they didn't quite hear it, because they couldn't believe it. There was something about these manic sendups, murmured just under his breath, that suggested a marvelous anarchy. Pinning a KICK ME sign on the seat of pompous WASP and shanty Irish alike.

Alex went with me to the mall one day, a half-hour's drive to Peabody. I was meant to buy clothes for school, but I'd been fretting that my summer savings weren't enough to steer me through the uncharted waters of starting college. We wandered around looking for sales, I wistfully passing up sweaters and jackets I couldn't afford. Without any premeditation I can recall,

I found myself at the underwear counter at Kresge's, surreptitiously stuffing a package of Jockey shorts into my shopping bag. I think the idea was to rip off the little stuff so I could buy a sexy sweater. Unless I was simply out to prove that Paul was no longer perfect.

With scant experience at thievery, I was blithely unaware of mall security. In the next store I took my time picking a nice pair of flannel pajamas, then dropped them into my bag. (From that day on I never wore p.j.'s again.) Suddenly a hand grabbed my elbow, and I was dragged unceremoniously to the store's office, matrons gaping at me from every aisle. I broke into a cold sweat, half fainted. The plainclothesman, who reminded me of my father, summoned a cop who formally arrested me. Both stores were pressing charges, and I was to appear the following morning at the Salem courthouse.

All the way home, Alex tried gently to laugh it off as an adventure, but I was profoundly rattled. I told my mother with shamefaced tears. Though she was pained, she hugged me and promised we'd get through it. When Dad got home, he looked like he'd taken a punch in the gut, but as usual he was unbearably decent. The hardest thing was the drive to Salem at seven A.M., just he and I, the feeling I had of his sidelong looks, as if he didn't know what to make of me anymore.

The judge saw us in chambers. After hearing the cop's testimony and a halting plea from Dad, he turned to me and said, "You realize, don't you, if Yale finds out about this, you're out." Now it was my turn to squirm and plead, how I understood the advantages I'd been given and would hereafter be a model citizen—a speech of Ciceronian clarity. He listened with pursed lips, a moment's silence as he toyed with my fate. Then gruffly dismissed the case, with a warning that I was *persona non grata* at the Northshore Mall forever.

We drove back to Andover wilted with relief. And yet I remember being struck by the most perverse thought: *If Yale found out about this, I wouldn't have to go.* Unthinkable really, that I should seek a way to derail my glorious rise to privilege. I buried it rather than face it. But the incident shows how conflicted I was about sailing into the future, as well as an instinct for sabotage. Something in me didn't want more schooling, dreaded the claustrophobia of being one of the guys. Alex's life by contrast was utterly free to happen, changeable as the color of his hair.

But as I say, I buried all that along with my police record. Yale was the next step, period. My mother and Nana dutifully sewed the nametags into my clothes, Nana's dignity much offended by the artificial leg and cane that had lately become her cross. She might have been going to Yale herself, so passionate was the vicarious thrill, for I was the first on the English side to ever get to college. The night before we left for New Haven, my Uncle Dan, with eight kids to feed, tucked ten bucks he couldn't afford into my shirt pocket. "Go buy a round of beers at Mory's," he said with a fond wink, sending the family hero off to claim his knighthood.

The next day, driving down, we stopped at a Hojo's just out of Hartford. ("Is that New York?" my brother asked in an awestruck voice as we swung by Hartford's three tall buildings. "No," we all laughed, though scarcely more worldly than he.) My father and I had a moment alone as he paid the bill, Bobby and Mother off to find the washroom. With an unsettling depth of feeling Dad put his arm around me and said, "Now remember, don't get involved with the wrong kind of girl. Okay?"

I nodded dumbly, seized by a rush of sorrow. Sad that my secrets kept us eternally out of phase, and hopeless of ever changing things.

The homesick blues were intolerable that first fall semester of '63, especially because I denied them. My life in 1068 Bingham Hall was a full-time job, chameleon and ventriloquist, so there wasn't a lot of time left over to feel how lonely I was. A two-bedroom suite, with bunk beds in each. The powers that be had paired me up with a studious lad from Andover, though we had barely been on nodding terms at school. This Russell (never Russ) had already decided on Chinese Studies, arriving at Yale with several thousand vocabulary cards and a placid air that was positively Confucian. He took the upper, I the lower.

Our two California roommates arrived in tandem: Sean and Jake, respectively a rock climber from Marin and a tennis jock from Santa Barbara. Outsize figures from the moment they walked through the door. They'd been buddies at the Trimble School — best of the West, old California gold, where every boy was required to keep a horse because it built character. Jake was third generation Trimble himself, grandson of the founding gentleman cowboy. He and Sean were smart as anybody from Andover, but not so polished, and proud of that. As to the mores and climate of Yale, everything struck them as being so *Eastern*, which only fortified their free-range superiority.

I was smitten by them both inside of twenty minutes. Not sexually, exactly — sexually was the least of it. Though they were strapping good athletes and frontier rugged, they never occupied a slot in the Olympian frieze of my fantasies. I needed them both to be more real than that, or else how would they ever transform my doggy life? For I quickly came to see them as my salvation, the pals I never had among the Apollo and Dionysus ranks of Andover. I'd never been on the inside before, shooting the breeze in a bull session. Never been anyone's confidant about women.

I took to the role with near-demented enthusiasm. To curry the favor of Sean and Jake I underwent a personality change — voluble where I'd been tongue-tied before, flattering them at every turn, adopting their sneering distaste for the East, I who'd never been west of the Hudson. I dressed like they did, took every meal I could with them. *Courtier* is far too pretty a term for my servile hero worship; *sycophant* is closer. Yet it wasn't at all unconscious: I saw my new friends as a last chance to leave behind the nothing I was in high school.

Thus I stopped answering Francis's letters from Georgetown, sealing the tomb on our old playful style, because it felt tainted with faggotry. Till the first snowfall I'd get up with Sean on Sunday mornings and pile in a van with the Mountaineering Club, to spend hair-raising afternoons climbing the sheer faces of northern Connecticut's bony hills. Graceless and panting, biting the tongue of my acrophobia, I clambered up the gorse till my knuckles bled, all for a macho nod from Sean at the summit. Back at the dorm, I laughed myself hoarse at Jake's razor wit, becoming his personal buffoon and comic foil. He wanted to be a writer, and therefore so did I. Prose was his meat and potatoes, and therefore I took poetry.

It amazes me now, that I made life choices for no other reason than to get in Sean and Jake's good graces. Today I haven't a clue where they live or what they've done since Yale. I realize college provides a classic ground for reinvention of self, but self had nothing to do with this. The very opposite: all I wanted to be was the two of them, burying every trace of Paul Monette.

Bury especially the hungry voyeur with the secrets. Jake had what amounted to a knee-jerk loathing of queers, every third remark a withering bash of anybody who seemed the least bit eccentric. He'd pout his lips and affect a nancy lisp and a wobbly wrist, dismissing whatever felt effete or even intellectual. Since there were so many closeted teachers about, Yale was fertile territory for his HUAC-style snipery, every bachelor guilty till proven innocent. And I was the first to go along, frantic to hide my own fellow-traveling. Eagerly I learned how to mock my brothers behind their backs — anything to make Jake laugh.

But more was required to prove one's manhood than just the putting down of queers. In those pre-coed days, Yale men hardly talked of anything except getting laid, unless it was getting drunk. The best of all worlds therefore was scoring in both at once: a dream Saturday night where you'd be shitfaced from the rotgut punch at a mixer and mauling some poor townie girl. Jake and Sean were more than eager to get in on the action, pestering me to set them up with dates since I was the one with the East Coast connections. I could no more admit I'd never dated than I could my heterosexual virginity. So I invented my own modest tales of carnal prowess, cobbling details here and there from other men's boasting.

For Dartmouth weekend I invited a girl I knew from Rosemary Hall, who arrived with a blushing pair of her classmates. I hated attending the football game, having no idea what was going down on the field, but the worst was the mixer that night. Guys throwing up in the bushes outside and a general air of male entitlement, showing off their women and making their moves in the shadows to the tawdry strains of *Louie Louie*. I was engaged in the upstream battle of *not* scoring, avoiding sex at all costs. Here my four-year schizophrenic pattern laid itself out: the requisite girl on my arm, the looking good, the frenzied round of sports and museums and parties, anything to avoid too much time *à deux*, the compulsory makeout.

I wasn't unaware even at the time what a grim sham I was putting the girls through. Oh, I made up for my carnal detachment with frantic charm and witticisms, and for a while at least found dates who seemed relieved not to be mauled. But I would almost never see a girl twice, for fear of the expectations. The girl from Rosemary Hall kept writing till Christmas, and I was too frozen to answer. Every minute of a date felt like a lie, but if you didn't date, you couldn't be one of the guys. My guys anyway, whose opinion I cared about more than my own.

For Harvard weekend I invited Missy Cabot to come down from Middlebury, spending my self-imposed month's allowance just on tickets for The Game. As Missy wasn't due in till six on Friday, I spent the afternoon out at the soccer field, timing the freshman match between Harvard and Yale. I hadn't suddenly developed a fondness for the sport that gave me chilblains all through four rotten autumns at Andover. It was because Sean and Jake were playing for Yale, and I their constant companion could get no closer than sitting on the bench with a stopwatch.

In the middle of the third quarter a campus policeman came up to huddle with the coach. From where I sat, the cop looked like he was crying. When he turned away, the coach walked over to me, who till now was as insignificant to him as a cockroach. "The President's been shot," he said, and at first I thought he meant the president of Yale. "He's still alive. I don't want the players told. We'll finish the game."

I don't think I could have been less political in those days. Because of my endless self-absorption and twenty-four-hour vigilance at the closet door, I never read the papers except for the theater page. The Cuban missile crisis had passed without causing a ripple in my pond. I'd only worn a Kennedy button in '60 because everyone in my family was voting for Nixon. I had no personal investment, in other words, and yet the coach's cavalier priorities offended me for the President's sake. Would he have stopped the game if the news had come in the *first* quarter?

By the time I bleated the horn at the end — a 3–3 tie — Kennedy was dead. Too late to stop Missy from coming. So the weekend proceeded, in New Haven as elsewhere, to the sound of muffled drums. We spent most of our time in front of the one snowy TV in the dorm, the world reduced to black and white. And yet what I remember most is the overriding sense of relief, as Missy cradled her head on my shoulder and cried softly into a handkerchief. Relief that I wouldn't have to make any carnal moves, wouldn't have to prove my hormonal mettle. A chaste goodnight kiss was more in keeping with national tragedy.

A grotesque perspective, to put it mildly. The self-obsession that fears exposure will grab at almost anything to keep the closet door shut. When I bundled Missy off on the bus on Sunday afternoon — just after Ruby shot Oswald — the psychic pain had bonded us, travelers thrown together by a crash. I wouldn't be inviting her again, of course, though I basked for a few days after in Sean and Jake's praise of her winsome beauty and Mayflower cheekbones. I had turned Missy into a "beard" without knowing the term, like the artificial dates those closeted powers of Hollywood take in their limos to all the openings and awards. Except in L. A., the starlets line up around the block for such an honor.

With ever renewed vigor I went on mimicking Sean and Jake, as spellbound and singleminded as Eve Harrington studying Margo Channing. It's a wonder I got any work done at all. Indeed I barely remember those freshman courses — Physics at 8 A.M. with Dr. Dandruff, or the English 25 seminar with sherry in a book-lined study, taught by a loser who used the occasion to get sloshed like a priest on Communion wine. My only intellectual coup was to land in a pair of upper division courses in art history, *Painting and Sculpture in the Twentieth Century* and *Mod-*

ern Architecture. I had to work my butt off to keep up with the seniors, flailing through Kandinsky's theory of the spirit in art, memorizing all the blank walls of the Bauhaus.

But I learned the collection in the Yale Art Gallery cold, forging myself a new sanctuary. What seems in memory a daily pilgrimage to the Van Gogh *Night Café*, the boiling light above the billiards table, the delirium of genius rendering, in Vincent's words, "the passions of humanity in red and green." And to reinforce the spell of art, I had two vivid mentors. Paoletti from Andover, who was finishing up his dissertation at Yale, steered me past the freshman survey and onto the upper floors of the Bauhaus. His comrade in the doctoral trenches, Peter Bunnell, was breaking ground in elevating the discourse on photography as art. I cared about being smart enough to talk to these men in their own argot, despite Jake's dismissal of them both as "fag intellectuals."

They certainly gave me more sensitive counsel than the live-in freshman adviser of Bingham Hall, Entry A, whose roaring binges usually ended with the rolling of empty beer kegs down the stairs. This singular thug, who suited up as an ROTC admiral two days a week, was otherwise distinguished by a bulletin board displaying several pairs of pinned-up panties, trophies of his many conquests. He was also a fourth generation Yalie and pledge chairman of the animal-house fraternity. Not notable for his opinions on Kandinsky.

Over Christmas I worked sidekick on one of Dad's coal delivery trucks, the coldest and dirtiest I've ever been. But the hourly wage was princely, and I needed the money to keep up with the social life at school, the artifice of being straight. So Proulx, the Canuck driver, and I battered our way through a week of blizzards, chuting coal to snowbound customers like Saint Bernards. We filled a coalbin the size of a ballroom in the cellar of Nevins Home, a great crenellated heap of bricks where ghostly Nana Monette was creeping into her nineties. Proulx got a huge charge out of having a Yalie for an assistant, proudly introducing me to all the truckers and jobbers in the diners. "I'm his professor of coal," he'd say.

He also used to tell me how rich I was going to be some-day—with the same grinning pride, as if I would be scoring one for him too. On the afternoon of Christmas Eve we were top-ping the bin at a hilltop estate in North Andover, home to the only daughter of a robber-baron mill owner possessed of Midas wealth. As we were finishing up, the desiccated husband of the heiress came down the cellar stairs to give Proulx his Christmas envelope. He peered at me appraisingly, and Proulx told him who I was.

"Ah, you're the boy at Yale," he said in a reed-thin voice. And as Proulx launched into a shameless brag about me, the guy pulled a roll of bills from his pocket and peeled me a Christmas tip. Two bucks. I mumbled thank you and saw he couldn't take his eyes off me. From local lore I knew he'd been a poor lad who made a brilliant marriage with the heiress, frail of health and mostly confined to her damasked bedroom. Now I saw he was queer. And in that Lawrentian moment in the coal cellar, I real-ized I would be looking to make the same pact one day, with my charm and my Yale degree.

I felt poorer at Yale than I ever had at Andover, partly be-cause the moneyed class was unrestrained by Yankee austerity, the iron rule of prep school. At Yale the well-heeled had cars and wall-to-wall sound systems. They put up their dates at the Taft Hotel and weekended in New York. Those of us on scholarship were something of a servant class. Ten hours a week I worked in the kitchen and dining hall at Jonathan Edwards, the residential college to which the Bingham frosh were assigned and where we would live, come sophomore year. Wearing the white coat of kitchen duty, punching a time clock at six in the morning, clear-ing dishes and scraping garbage — we were menials and knew our place. Our democratic liberal education, free men and equal, didn't extend beyond the classroom. The rich men's sons for whom Yale was built stubbed out cigarettes in their eggs and barked for more coffee, as if we were the help at home.

By midwinter I'd decided to spend the following summer in California, counting on the hospitality of Sean and Jake. I

110

couldn't believe they weren't sick of me already, but I also knew how addictive flattery is, and I doled it out with Machiavellian skill. Instead of going home for spring break, I threw in my lot with Sean and another fellow who'd decided to hitchhike to Florida. I apprised my parents of the adventure by postcard from Virginia, drunk on the romance of being on the road, a well-thumbed copy of Kerouac in my backpack. Not the last time I would trace my life out of a book.

I think I must have been in love with Sean by then. But the musketeer comradeship of the journey ceased when we hopped a flight from West Palm Beach to Nassau. Within hours my two traveling companions had picked up a pair of American blondes on the beach, leaving me high and dry. For the next week they were lost in the throes of spring break mating, while I bummed about on my own. Somehow I hooked up with a young Bahamian girl, a fierce and exotic tomboy who disdained the blond American spring invasion. She took me off on her scooter to show me where the conch fishermen lived. Then into the muggy interior, where we watched the cane workers harvesting and sucked the sweet juice out of raw branches. Midnight before Easter, I went with her to a singing mass in a tin-roofed church, more black than white and more pagan than Christian.

In the end I had as fine a time as my Yale brethren, even if I never got my rocks off. There's a pattern here as well: straying from the traveled path, finding a woman as different as I. In retrospect the Bahamian girl was surely queer, though the matter was all unspoken. I wish I could say I seized with a savoring heart the adventure of going native, but mostly I mooned and pined for Sean, waiting for him to tire of his blonde and hitchhike home again.

As spring advanced, I began to detect a certain resistance in Sean and Jake to my constant tail-wagging attention. Which only sent me into overdrive, doing somersaults of fawning. I remember sitting in the window seat one night, jabbering inanely at Jake, when Russell across the room spun around in his desk chair and flung a box of paper clips in my face. "Can you just shut the fuck up for a while?" he hissed, in a spasm of rage that was most un-Confucian.

There were also the wrestling matches Sean and I somehow fell into, instigated by me, where he'd quickly overpower me and pin me to the floor. Then he'd snap his fingers against my nose, taunting me, till finally I cried uncle through the choke of a nose-bleed. Placidly Jake and Russell would watch these predictable fights, bored as Romans watching gladiators. Did any of us understand I was acting out a crush I couldn't name or handle? I think not. The pointless one-way violence had a rationale all its own, a sort of ritual bloodletting to silence the roommate who wouldn't shut up.

My parents were leery of the California summer idea, especially since I had no job lined up. They were still feeling bruised by my road trip south, but I think they genuinely missed me too, fearing that if I went away in the summers I'd never come home at all. I prevailed by dint of stubbornness, and enlisting Nana Lamb to sing the praises of the Golden State. I knew I'd be on my own, that Sean and Jake had had about enough of my doggy charm, but I had to go and see this other world. Returning to Andover instead, retrieving my apron at Nick's — that would have been backsliding, to the place where I was nobody.

Somehow a deal was struck with an aerospace drone in New Haven who was moving his family to Orange County. We would drive his VW bus across country, and he'd pay the gas and tolls, but he needed the car by June 7. Since our last exam was the third, we would have to drive straight through. There were four of us — Sean and Jake and I and a basketball dimwit from Monterey — driving in four-hour shifts, no stops except to pee and refuel. The radio wailed with the first Beatles hits. By Nebraska we were punchy and seeing mirages, floating onto the gravel shoulder of the interstate and jerking awake. As romantic adventure it was right up there with Kerouac, though we looked more like the Joads by the time we crossed the Golden Gate, disheveled and unshaven.

Jake let Sean and me off in Marin, then headed south to L. A.

Sean's people lived in a big Craftsman bungalow that in memory seems to nestle in a redwood grove, like the house of the Seven Dwarfs. Mrs. Adamson was exquisitely gracious, more so when she picked up the brittle edge of friction in her son, who was kicking himself for bringing home this albatross of a roommate. She even had a job for me, to babysit two kids and three Bouvier hounds in a compound down the road, over-nannied tykes abandoned by their jet-set parents, forlorn and needy as Flora and Miles in *Turn of the Screw*.

But nothing could dampen my drunken wonder at this land of orchids and buff-colored hills, a greenhouse in the desert. Around Sean I moped like a spurned amour, but he mostly ignored me and went his own way, disappearing for days at a time to spider up the sides of cliffs. When he was home, he spent all his time with the girl next door, his beloved Amy, to whom he'd been pinned since junior high. My hero worship of Sean, transformed now into an unrequited crush, produced a jealousy of the two of them that was bizarrely intense. I'd lie awake in the bedroom under the eaves, swooning from the jasmine trellised below, and listen for the sound of the garden gate, Sean tiptoeing home from Amy's.

I reacted with obsessive cunning. By degrees I moved to win over Amy—sunning with her on the back deck while she did watercolors, talking artist to artist, till my courtier presence became indispensable. I wasn't trying to supplant Sean, only to make it impossible for him to shun me. Meanwhile Amy's mother and I got along like a house on fire, sharing a sense of anarchy about suburban pretense and WASP propriety. Sean would come back from climbing rocks and find us all laughing helplessly over barbecue. The subtext being frank defiance on my part: daring him to cut me out.

Even so he barely tolerated me, and I grabbed at the chance to take a break, in the form of a house party over the Fourth in Napa Valley. A classmate of Sean's from Trimble Prep, Skip Bronner, had invited all the Adamsons to "the ranch," but in the end I went alone. Totally unprepared for wealth on such a scale:

thousands of acres of virgin hills, with a ranch house at the summit shaded by ancient live oaks, and a view down the Bay all the way to the Gate bridge. A flock of peacocks strutted past the saltwater pool, with an island sculpture in the middle by Henry Moore. They ate off Picasso plates, were watched over by a wall of Ming horses and jade birds. I was in a state of near hallucination from the moment I set foot there. Rich, where I grew up, meant old polished wood in high-ceilinged houses silent as churches. This was a sybarite's pleasure-dome instead, the California good life raised to the nth degree. A stallion ride before breakfast, oranges right off the trees.

("The homes!" I could hear my grandmother gasp as I entered the dreamscape. "They live outside!")

It wasn't just the layout that turned me into The Man Who Came to Dinner, with a midsummer's lease on the guesthouse. At first sight I fell headlong for Lois Bronner, chatelaine of this whole voluptuous Xanadu. All the women I ever cozied up to before or since, lady or Lady, would be measured against Lois's casual glamour. She had the husky voice and arrogant smolder of Stanwyck in *Double Indemnity*, tempered by a zany streak of self-deprecation, more like *Ball of Fire*. She was about to host a three-day bash for seventy-five, including the whole board of the San Francisco Opera, yet within a half hour of my arrival we were sprawled under a sycamore reading Edna Millay, while Lois shooed off the fretting caterers.

The feeling was clearly mutual, though at the time I couldn't figure what there was in it for her. I only knew I made her happy. In practice, of course, I spent most of my time entertaining the whole family — Skip and his two sisters, the ballerina and the ugly duckling. Also the runny-nosed husband, a zillionaire without a clue despite owning half the natural gas in the civilized world and most of the pipes besides. Even an apolitical sort like me picked up on his wacko Bircher rants, though the rest of the family rigorously ignored him.

I don't suppose Lois and I spent more than a dozen nightcaps under the stars, but it felt like the life I'd been waiting to live forever. She wasn't the first to know I wanted to be a poet, but she was the first who had to know why. I spilled a thousand banalities in answer. Yet she never made me feel ridiculous; she drank in every word as if no one had ever spoken such raptures before. She must have known I was gay, with all her friends in the arts. So was Skip, for that matter, though years would pass before either of us would admit it. For once, gay was the least of it. With nothing to compare it to, I understood I was having this thing with Lois instead of a summer love affair, and that its soul passion was as good as sex, maybe better. Because somebody found me extraordinary just the way I was, and gave me permission besides to be a poet.

Of course it had nowhere to go. I wasn't Dustin Hoffman, and she wasn't Mrs. Robinson. At the end of July the Bronners were off to Hawaii, escaping the blast-furnace heat at the ranch, and I headed out for a two-week hike through the High Sierra. The Adamsons took part in a yearly trek with the Sierra Club, this huge production involving a hundred hikers and a mule train of supplies. I called it The Donner Party for short, making a black joke out of that darkest symbol of westward migration, where the snowbound survivors ate their blood kin. Our own high-country holiday managed to avoid the cannibal, though the antagonism between Sean and me was palpable enough. As one of the trip leaders, Sean rode horseback, but I no longer found him heroic. Fresh from my Cinderella stint with the Bronners, I had nothing but disdain for the Gary Cooper rugged act. All through the long march Sean and I kept our distance, making our beds by separate campfires.

The problem with secret crushes: in the absence of requital the love turns bitter. Amy was meant to go on the mountain trip with us, but a turned ankle had held her back at the last moment. Sean had another two-week group to lead, and I headed back to the Bronner ranch. I don't remember any consciously twisted motive, but I asked the hobbling Amy to come up for a weekend. Did I trash Sean to her, I wonder, or just put on a saintly smile when she apologized for her boyfriend's petulance toward me? I certainly didn't tell her that I was the one who used to beg him to beat me up. Or try to dissuade her when she admitted with a sigh that their storybook relationship wasn't the same anymore.

I don't think they actually broke up, but Sean came down from the mountain convinced I had tried to steal his girl. We hardly spoke again, though we still had to room together for another whole year. No more homoerotic wrestling, though, and no more kissing his ass. I had found my own Golden State by then, the long lambent evenings with Lois as the peacocks chirred in the shadows. Day trips into the city to watch the orchestra rehearse, lunch at the Pacific Union Club and supper at the Blue Fox. The boy who was born to talk in restaurants, the breezy style picked up in coffee shops from his grandmother, had grown into a full-fledged gigolo. Or that's how it felt to me anyway, in my California summer: a gigolo whose dick was not required.

Fantasy being perishable, you can't bring tea and sympathy home. The night before I left the ranch, we went out to see *Night of the Iguana* — shades of Aunt Grace and Sebastian — and the next day, as I got on the plane, Lois and the girls presented me with a cardboard box containing a foot-long live lizard. The joke didn't travel so well, I'm afraid, and the poor freaked creature ended up in a terrarium at Phillips Academy, rooming with an alligator ten times its size. And I went back to Yale, unable to say exactly what the summer meant, but no longer needing Jake and Sean to prove I was real. In 714 Jonathan Edwards they took the bunk-bed room on the left, and I the single on the right. The hero worship was over.

Not that I wasn't as screwed up as ever — still so sexless and secretive, I only came in the dark, wiping it off like a dirty necessity. But at least I decided to throw in my lot with the artsy crowd, even if that meant laying myself open to the rolled eyes of my straight-arrow classmates. On weekends I still bearded myself with dates, enduring the drunken revels of toga parties, even going so far as to try to pledge a fraternity, the last bastion of pig superiority at Yale, white boys only please. Happily I was blackballed, and tried out instead for the Yale Dramat, landing a two-line messenger's part in *Richard III*, otherwise milling about in tights to swell a crowd.

Ten years later a friend informed me dryly that I was the only queer he'd ever met who became an interior decorator *instead of* coming out. I was that kind of actor too. I understood from the first rehearsal that I had found the meeting ground of the queers, a motley troupe whose longest-running performance was being in the closet. With the resources of the mainstage costume shed and makeup drawers, a couple of them camped it up even wilder than Alex Anestos, but I don't think anybody self-identified as gay. In those days camp and *theatah* were a substitute for being out.

As with Alex, I felt a curious butch superiority over the others, reassured by their nelly antics that my own walls of manhood were in place. Besides, as long as I had no sex with them or any other man, I wasn't "like that" at all. My contempt for the brothers I wouldn't embrace was just self-hatred masquerading as narcissism — like people of color buying into the oppressor's code, the higher status of the lighter skinned. But I took it a step further. I developed a backstage friendship with Messenger #1, a burly foulmouthed junior from Kansas City who couldn't stop boasting about his women. More determined even than I to distance himself from the drama fags.

As we waited in the wings together, listening for our cue to run on and tell Richard the war was lost, Doug would fall into an exaggerated sissy act, tittering as he goosed me and wetly smooched my face. And I would reply in kind, just as I had with Jake, hoping to hide my own invert state by flinging a burlesque version in people's faces. As a black man wears blackface, putting on a veritable minstrel show of self-loathing. What was even weirder, the other gay folk in the cast thought we were a riot. At the cast party we did a whole fag parody of Shakespeare, to the appreciative hoots and whistles of the troupe.

For a time after the play, Doug and I were inseparable, even double-dating now and then. When he continued the sissy stuff in private, sweeping me up in a sudden mad waltz or humping my leg like a dog, I tried to laugh it off. But I knew he wanted to push it, was daring me to make the first move that wasn't a joke. Which only repelled me, because even though I found him very sexy, I couldn't figure how we'd ever get out of it once we got in. If I broke my celibate record, I'd be lost.

Last year I had a letter from him, to tell me how sorry he was about my losses in the holocaust. Then a fond and sheepish account of his wife and beaming kids, the lawyerly job in Missouri, still the occasional turn at "little" theater. So I guess he was bi back there at Yale, dipping a toe in the pool of illicit thrills. I've never quite understood the double Janus face of bi — Janus, the Roman god of gates and doors, especially closets. I've met too many who kept the truth from their women and used their men like hookers. Now that I know how to waltz myself, I try not to be gayer-than-thou about bi. Mostly I fail. But I still wish I'd done the wild thing with Doug, even at the risk of being left for a woman.

Instead I did plays, working with semi-pros from the Drama School, just on the cusp of the Brustein years when Yale was where it was happening. I'd long since given up the Tony aspirations of Landy Monet. I wasn't good and knew it, especially when I was onstage with the genuine article. Once I played the Pope in *Galileo*, on a raked disk of a stage, this to show how the scientist had turned the universe upside down. Our Galileo was brilliant, every line a matter of life and death — and I in my popish robes beside him reduced to fifth business. I think I stuck with it because I loved the boho sophistication of the theater crowd, the double-espresso brooding over Brecht's intentions. Also the little cosmos that every production becomes, the bonding fierce as summer camp.

As for poetry, I took the two-semester course in the moderns, Cleanth Brooks in the fall and John Hollander in the spring. These luminous divines could hardly have been more different from one another in approach — Brooks the brilliant exemplar of New Criticism; Hollander a working poet in the flesh, mad eyes and the tongue of a fallen angel when he read.

Though I was never much of a scholar in my studies, I discovered with growing confidence a capacity to walk through the walls of a poem. The hardest stuff made sense to me — the *Voyages* of Hart Crane, the *Pisan Cantos*, *Notes Toward A Supreme Fiction*. I liked being adrift in symbols, beauty for beauty's sake. When Hollander said the subject of the poem was the poem, I was dazzled. Perhaps after all one could live in the temple of art, feeding on air like an orchid.

Yet I came under a much more worldly influence that year, in the way of inspiration. For my scholarship job I'd graduated out of the scullery, and started working in the Master's Office at Jonathan Edwards. The Master himself was a musicologist and bon vivant, impeccably droll, who oversaw a constant round of receptions and soirees for visiting divas and string quartets. His administrative secretary issued more invitations than your average palace, which I rushed around delivering like the White Rabbit. When the RSVP's were low, I cadged last-minute invitations for myself, the proverbial extra man. I'm afraid I went to the concerts more for the deviled eggs and brie that followed, but a little culture no doubt seeped in.

As for the Master's secretary, Jeannette Nichols, she became my vital link to poetry and self. She'd learned how to write on her own, without benefit of academic credentials, and now she was waiting for her first book to come out. A beehive of industry when it came to submitting to magazines, Jan would triumphantly flip open *Saturday Review* or *Tri-Quarterly* to show off her latest appearance in print. She didn't have much patience with the temple-of-art mind-set, or with the filigreed abstractions of Stevens's "invented world." Poetry was lifeblood to her, and her subject more often than not was the blood lust of her sexuality.

Till then, no one had ever managed to show me how a poem could emerge shimmering from the quotidian. Jan took poetry out of the realm of the exalted, making me see that the beautiful didn't have to be pretty, or language high-flown. Every week for the next three years she'd submit to harrowing scrutiny the current crop of verse in the *New Yorker*, demanding why this or that was a poem at all. She kept me relentlessly on my toes, and it wasn't an accident that her mentor was Dudley Fitts, whom she'd met one summer at Bread Loaf. But Jan was *sui generis* all the way, gloriously opinionated, and not afraid to be jealous of work that knocked her out.

She was the one who prevailed on me to nominate Fitts to be a Fellow of Jonathan Edwards. He had a serious Yale connection, after all, as editor of the Yale Younger Poets. Somehow Jan and I railroaded it through the right committee, an Honorary Fellowship that was hardly worth the scroll it wasn't engraved on. But with that in hand, we convinced Fitts to drive down from Andover in his hand-powered VW to give a reading at the college. I busted my buttons with pride the night I introduced him — an impresario's coup, and a chance to tell him over the deviled eggs that I'd started to write some poems myself. Has anyone ever needed so much permission to be an artist?

Awful poems, but let that go. You have to start somewhere, and I started by mimicking everyone I'd read with Brooks and Hollander. A little *Waste Land*, a pinch of Hardy, a sprinkle of Frost. I remember them as fairly excruciating, hadn't reread them in twenty-five years, until just now. They are infinitely more appalling, sub-literate almost. Two pompous, oracular poems in several parts are featured in *The Spider's Web* of March '65, the college's in-house literary rag. Suffice it to say my vision hadn't notably advanced beyond the shepherdesses of my juvenilia. I can only hope I'm the last one who still has a pack-rat copy, even as I consign it to the flames.

Oh well, one verse. This being Part III of *Fragments from the Catacombs*, by Paul Monette '67, though Mr. Monette hadn't the first idea what catacombs were.

> The Rites for the Ceremony of the Burial
> Ring around the rosy
> Do you think that I want my eyes cut out
> Like an Andalusian dog?

But would I marry my mother?
Yes, I must upset the balance
I won't die a traitor
Take the razor Antigone
I don't need a cigarette

The subject of which is Eliot, I guess. (Fear death by imitation.) Plus a recent obsession with Euro-cinema, courtesy of the Orange Theatre, Buñuel and Truffaut double-billed. The incest trope is all my own, alas, and still six years to go before washing ashore at a therapist's.

It wasn't so much the poems anyway. What was necessary was to see myself as an artist, so that my growing sense of isolation and depression at least had the cachet of a Higher Calling. I never stopped thinking about the quandary of wanting men and feeling incapable of acting on it. Fifty yards from the York Street entrance to the college was a cocktail lounge with black-painted windows and a dim blue bulb over the door. *The Blue Note* was New Haven's most infamous fag bar, the gate of damnation and object of countless jokes and hexes by Yalies. I was terrified of even walking by it on the way to the A&A Building, or glancing at the semi-porn in the window of the dirty bookstore beside it. The only outlet I had for the torments of my affliction was poetry, where I could conceal the subject — or thought I could — in the caves of metaphor and monologue. Until I came out nine years later, clear was the last thing I wanted my writing to be. Poetry served as a sort of intellectual wallpaper to brighten up the closet.

If you were looking for a temple of art, the Art & Architecture Building of Paul Rudolph was Yale's most controversial new addition. A primal example of the New Brutalism, defiantly non-Gothic as it faced off against the dreaming towers of the university. It was fashioned of raw poured concrete, grooved like fingermarks in wet clay, with shells and stones embedded in the surface like a cross section of the Pleistocene. In its bowels was the orange-carpeted library where I studied Kandinsky and

Frank Lloyd Wright. In the castle keep of its towering central space, I went to hear Chagall and Louise Nevelson. Somewhere in there, Josef Albers was teaching a master class.

The A&A crowd was even scruffier than the drama crowd, more in-your-face bohemian and fervently iconoclast. Two guys in my class were going for a degree in architecture, and they brawled over lunch and dinner about the arcana of urban planning and solar power. I loved mixing it up with them and watching them build their toothpick and Popsicle models, for they kept the same night-owl hours I did. I'd sit in the corner of Cody's studio, slogging through a Victorian novel while he did elevations. Then we'd head out for coffee at two A.M. in an all-night diner, soulfully trading *aperçus* about Life and Art and being true to your vision.

It was Cody and Burke, my two architects, who took me along to the experimental film series at the A&A. Most of which were about as exciting as watching paint dry, the maddening stasis of Warhol's *Empire* and other home movies of the art elect. But I remember the shock of recognition when Kenneth Anger's *Scorpio Rising* swaggered onto the screen: muscles and jackoff and Attitude to burn, the erotic charge of the Harley outlaw. It rattled my cage profoundly — and even more so afterwards, when Cody and Burke, both so unrelievedly straight, wrestled for hours with the movie's homo kinks. I remained mute, still so starved for images of the male erotic, and all the while fantasizing a walk on the wild side with Cody and Burke.

I could only dimly articulate it then, but I think I believed that Art would give me entry into a no-man's-land where the laws of straight no longer applied. And that once I touched the soul of another artist, a comrade in arms, the bodies would fall into place like the folds of a garment, twining us in a passion of the flesh. Pretty high-falutin', and an awful lot of effort just to get a man to go to bed with you. And seduction by soul-merger didn't even work, I would soon discover, because it was all in my head. But the only other way would've been to ask a man point-blank, and that I could never do.

At least I knew I wanted it, however beyond my reach it seemed. More than anything I dreaded becoming one of the bachelor academics who lived in the college and took their meals with us students. Unfailingly nice and cerebral, passionate about small things like the rules of the Senior Common Room, these professorial live-ins could always be counted on to RSVP yes, ever available as a fourth for bridge. To a man, they were queer but tastefully detached, with highly evolved opinions about Burgundy vintages.

And yet they were very good to me, the bachelors of Jonathan Edwards. The college Dean invited me several times to his country house in Killingworth, long tramps in the woods with his spaniels, and martinis by a roaring fire in his converted mill. No question of sexual advances, ever. He was much more interested in teaching me how to listen to Verdi and how to whip up a Béarnaise. Sometimes there was a young historian there as well, polishing up his dissertation and having his portrait painted by yet another of the Dean's overnight companions. I don't think anyone slept with the Dean, or that the painter slept with the historian. There were lots and lots of guest rooms, and everyone slept alone. At breakfast you'd regroup for more bright chatter, and a little Callas to go with the bowls of dusky French coffee.

As sophomore year ended, Cody Williams and I decided to room together in the fall. I liked the downtown feel of that, the architect and the poet. Already I romanticized him mightily, with his curly red hair and his paint-flecked hands. The whole package seemed very artistic, somehow: the clouds of smoke around Cody's drafting table as he puffed through his nightly pack of Camels, the wine he drank straight from the bottle, and especially his brooding sullenness. In the back of my mind I may have had us moving by slow, inexorable inches toward the bed, but it didn't feel like a crush going in. It felt like a joining of muses.

I'd wanted to go to California again for the summer, but the Bronners were off to Europe, and I needed to make some money. I landed a job at the Mount Pleasant Hotel in northern New

Hampshire — a vast ocean liner of a place, white clapboard, Edwardian grand. I went up with the promise of a waiter's gig, then found out when I arrived that the only job left was "bread boy."

Danish in the morning, rolls at lunch and dinner, carried in a stainless breadbox that hung from a strap around my neck like a mute accordion. I had to be at the bakery by six in the morning and served my last roll at 10:30 P.M. Between meals I ran the coffee shop, which was wedged between the hotel's nightclub — Borscht Belt shtick and ventriloquists — and a small illegal casino, two slots and a green felt table for craps.

Altogether a nineteen-hour day, for the coffee shop stayed open till the last wheeze of the last waltz had sounded in the nightclub. I had no friends among the staff, most of whom were migrant types who worked in the Florida winter-resort circuit and drove up north for the summer. The majority doubled at two or three jobs, as I did, and our brief meals in the workers' basement cafeteria were about as sociable as dining in prison.

My human contact was limited to the small-potatoes gangster who ran the mini-casino. Hearty and self-important, rolling an unlit stogie between his lips, he'd fire off opinions at me about how Harvard and Yale had fucked up the country. The cover for his gambling operation was a cigarette and candy counter. The dice table was fitted on rollers and slid under the counter when state police were on the premises. The slots were quickly stowed in a closet. Every Monday I'd watch the state troopers come in for a Hershey bar, smiling and chewing the small talk as the candyman counted out their cut. Tidy little piles of hush money.

The luridness of the scene was doubtless heightened by the fact that I was reading Flannery O'Connor. My only quiet time was midafternoon in the coffee shop, immersed in the peacock world of O'Connor's grotesques, the flagellants and Bible hucksters. It put a certain sideshow spin on the cast of characters that wandered in: the chubby teens who wanted to cram in one more hot fudge sundae; the "talent" rehearsing next door with the house lights on, polyester clones of Steve and Eydie; the women in rhinestone shades feeding quarters into the slots, rhythmic as a toll booth. Lonely and disconnected, I relished every seedy tableau the hotel threw my way, the pathos and the grift. If nothing else, it was good material.

One Saturday night the headliner was a hypnotist in tails, with a lollipop blonde as assistant. I could watch the show from the doorway of the coffee shop. At one point he had a half-dozen people from the audience up on stage, sagging open-mouthed in their chairs, in full trance. He got them squawking and mooing like barnyard animals, standard stuff, but the audience was eating it up. Suddenly his antic tone changed, and he started heaping abuse on them. Screaming incoherently in their faces — making them writhe, trapped now in a nightmare. Very quickly it stopped being funny. The audience catcalled in protest, and the hypnotist turned, staring in panic, seemingly lost in a trance of his own. Then he bolted offstage and ran out of the club, pursued by the pleading blonde. They lurched by me into the empty coffee shop.

Everyone thought it was part of the act, if an egregious lapse of taste. A moment later Mrs. Gold stalked in, the scrappy little Barnum-and-Bailey owner of this stationary ship of fools — more Leona than Leona, as the French say. She berated The Great Bamboozle and demanded that he cut the crap and go untrance her guests. I suppose she was worried about lawsuits. But the hypnotist was clearly having some kind of breakdown, sobbing now and curling into a fetal crouch in the booth. The hotel's doctor was summoned — a dipso vet whose hands trembled uncontrollably, like Peter Sellers in *The Wrong Box*.

It was fabulous, as if Flannery herself were inventing it. We coaxed and soothed him and fed him chicken soup, while in the club the MC with the game-show pompadour tried to keep the crowd in check, about as amused by now as steerage on the *Titanic*. It took almost an hour to woo the hypnotist out of his "crisis of sensitivity," as the bimbo called it, but only after Mrs. Gold had sweetened him up with a two hundred dollar bonus for the weekend. So I never could be sure if the Jekyll-and-Hyde thing was a fake or not, and I loved not being sure.

Maybe it was that window on the grotesque that finally broke my celibate resolve. I knew one of the waiters couldn't take his eyes off me, and at first it gave me the creeps. Lonnie was too flamboyant by half, smashing plates in the kitchen and shrieking at the cooks if the food was slow. He must've been in his forties, with a Southern delivery my mother would have called "sissified." Wide in the hips, so that he flounced when he led the waiters' parade every Saturday night with the flaming Baked Alaska. Whenever he had to steer me and my rolls to one of his tables, Lonnie would linger a hand on my shoulder or fix my collar, till I thought I'd pass out from the Aramis.

But I let it happen, even though he repulsed me — almost to test myself, though I still don't know if I passed or failed. I started being civil to him, in a low-key sort of way, and he all but wagged his tail in response. We lived down the hall from each other in the tarpaper boardinghouse that lodged the transient workers. In the head in the morning, Lonnie would comb his three hairs again and again, so he could watch me shave at the next sink over. I began to feel this strange detached power over him, all the more thrilling because I had no emotion invested in him, except contempt.

In other words I cockteased him in cold blood, to see what he would do, and then what I would do. *Everything that rises must converge*, as O'Connor had it. On the night of the Fourth we were all on the great verandah that girdled the hotel, staff and guests together as we watched the fireworks burst over the golf course. "Like Mardi Gras," a voice murmured beside me, and I turned and gave Lonnie a taciturn smile. Nervously filling the silence, he began to chatter excitedly about his years in the French Quarter, where he'd had star billing in a drag show.

My skin crawled; at the same time I was fascinated by the lower depths of it all. I kept thinking with dark irony that exactly a year ago I was belle of the ball at the Bronner Ranch. Sure, I told Lonnie with brusque indifference, I'd come over later and look at the pictures.

When he opened the door to his room at two A.M., he was wearing a see-through peignoir and black bikini briefs. More than anything I remember the woodenness of my own movements, sitting stiffly in a chair as he flustered about getting me a beer and pulling down his albums. I could barely grunt in response as he laughingly ran through the pictures: the Scarlett gowns he'd worn to Carnival, the Peggy Lee drag from the Bourbon Street club, his cover-girl appearance in a washed-out magazine called *Female Impersonators.*

He hovered over my shoulder, brushing his crotch against me, and finally he said, "I think you're hard." In fact I was, though I could not have been more removed from my dick, which apparently had a thing of its own for Southern Gothic. Mutely I watched him go down on me, studying his vanishing hair just as I had with Raf the painter six years before. When at last he came up for air, he said, "I think you want to fuck me."

Did I? Frankly, I had no will at all in the matter. I did what I was told. Didn't even get undressed as I hunched beside him in the bed and let him guide me in, smuttily praising my equipment. *This is what they do*, I thought with weird dispassion. The feeling was all in my dick; I was dead otherwise. And no technique or staying power: it was over in less than a minute. "Are you done?" he asked in some confusion, since I'd come without a peep, just the barest grit of my teeth.

I pulled out—I don't think he got off—and wouldn't even look at him as I zipped myself together. "Wham, bam, thank you, ma'am," he drawled in his best Louisiana purr, trying to be light about it, maybe even seeing that I was racked with post-coital guilt. But I wouldn't give him an inch, barking "Leave me alone" as I lurched for the door. "Oh come on, honey," he clucked, bored with the drama already, but now I had slammed the door behind me and stumbled back to my room in damnation.

Leave me alone. I hadn't learned any new dialogue since I scrambled out of Charles's wrestling embrace at Andover. Now, three dry years later, in a paroxysm of self-disgust, I was ready to have those words tattooed on my forehead. I foamed with hate for Lonnie and his kind, feeling violated, molested—though I was the one who'd done all the teasing. I didn't have the first idea that he was the healthy one, not I, he with some hard-won sanity and self-regard from living life bent and proud. It was Lonnie's kind who would start the Stonewall Rebellion four years later, pitching it back in the pigs' faces, while my kind sat in the dark with the door locked.

I never addressed another word to him, staring at the ground if our paths happened to cross. After six weeks on three hours' sleep a night, I'd had it anyway. I called my parents to come and get me. They were spending their summer two weeks with my brother at Lake Winnisquam, about an hour south of Mount Pleasant. I wouldn't admit to myself that the guilt and confusion over the Lonnie incident were forcing me to run away — as if I could escape the darkness in my heart by changing my surroundings. I spent the next two weeks lying on the dock in the sun, as if I were healing. I read eight or ten novels by Hemingway and Fitzgerald, alternated between them, macho and jazz. I'd had enough of the violent sainthood of Flannery's world.

I smiled through my mother's good country suppers, and went out on the lake with my brother in the runabout — a veritable yacht to him, who didn't need legs to fly across the water, the chop thudding against the hull. I may even have been talkative — but inside I felt this terrible silence. How could I want so badly to connect with a man, when the thing itself was always so disgusting and shameful? I didn't know then about self-fulfilling prophecy. All I knew was that in three months I'd be twenty years old, and I'd made love twice since puberty, and love had not come into it at all.

I went back to Yale in September, a ventriloquist's smile on my face, and walked into the propeller of falling in love with Cody Williams. I didn't see it coming and didn't know its name, since my previous hero worship of Jake and Sean had been an amorphous blur of self-abasement. For the first couple of months we proceeded smoothly enough along the lofty ridge of the twin muses. We stayed up half the night arguing aesthetics, taking a thousand breaks from the work at hand — Cody and his toothpick constructions, I and my windy Victorian poems. To match his post-Beat intensity I forced myself to learn how to smoke. By mid-October I could wake up just like Cody did, hacking as I reached for the first Camel before I opened my eyes.

By junior year the pressure to date had taken a further turn of the screw. Men on every side of me were connecting up with steady girls. The girls came down every weekend from Smith and Vassar, with Breck hair and circle pins and Loden coats. They still nominally stayed in the Taft Hotel or the Whitney Motor Inn, for parietal hours were in strict force: no women in the rooms after midnight on weekends. Even so, a lot of them stayed over secretly, smuggled in and out of the bathrooms.

I was the sort who would check if the coast was clear for them, puckish as Juliet's nurse, always glad to assist in the joys of Eros. I charmed the regular girls in the dining hall, everyone's favorite fifth wheel, and they were always trying to fix me up with the shy girl in their dorm. Mostly I managed to sidle away from these good offices, cultivating the role of the solitary poet, too burning with private fires and mysteries to have anything left over for worldly passion. In fact I was the college fool, straining for hilarity and a knockabout enthusiasm, thinking by ingratiation to keep them all so entertained they wouldn't probe too much my bachelor status.

There was one steady girl who resisted my charms completely, barely a thin polite smile for all my manic patter and volley of one-liners. Natalie was from Mount Holyoke, pre-law, with a steel-trap mind and a low tolerance for fools. She was also Cody's girlfriend. They'd dated through four years of high school and two at Yale. A starry-eyed shot of them at the prom, peeking through a rose trellis, perched on Cody's desk. Yet for all her independent spirit and braininess — as if every conversation were a moot court proceeding — Natalie's take on Cody was hero worship, same as mine. And three was very definitely a crowd.

It didn't come to a head that fall, because she and Cody were on the outs. She came down in September and spent the weekend mostly in tears, as Cody snarled and raged at the bourgeois careerism of the architects he studied with. He was thinking of chucking it all and going in for painting, and therefore needed time alone. Natalie couldn't help but take it personally, hearing in his Crisis of Sensitivity a thinly veiled attack on her own careerist dreams. In terms of Cody, she'd always been pre-marriage as much as pre-law. Now she saw she might really lose him; no choice but to give him some latitude.

Her tears only made him harder. I don't think they saw each other at all till after Christmas, just a weekly exchange of tensions on the phone that made the cords stand out in Cody's neck. Did I gloat at the problems they were having? Not consciously, but I also didn't waste a second stepping into the breach. For I would be his muse if Natalie couldn't be, a fount of understanding and encouragement, demanding nothing in return, self-sacrificing and oh so nonbourgeois. I practically held the canvas for him — a human easel.

I deluded myself that this vacation he was taking from Natalie was a window that might admit me in a way that was new for both of us. He certainly liked having me around. As he struggled to free himself from the rigid modernism of the A&A, he began to copy paintings out of books, exacting as an old-school academic. For weeks he worked on a replica of the Vermeer portrait of the girl with the pearl earrings. We talked about the light and color of that damned pearl like monks counting the angels on the head of a pin. We consumed whole cartons of Camels, I sitting blissfully more or less at his feet, reading and writing poems. For me those long autumn nights in the studio were my dream fusion of Art and Soul. I didn't need sex. I needed nothing, if this could go on forever.

Forever? I think I must've been the only person in my class at Yale who didn't hear the tick of reality. It was fall of junior year, time to settle down and plan which way you were going. The pre-med guys were already hip-deep in Biochemistry. The pre-law legions ran practice heats for the law boards a year away. The padding of résumés had begun in earnest. Among other things there was a war out there, and a draft that wasn't kidding. But I took my cue from Cody and spurned the petty politics of careerism. A poet's job was being a poet, and you didn't learn it in graduate school. I made no plans whatever for what would come after Yale. Feeling was what I was majoring in.

I still had to take all the English requirements—courses in Chaucer, the Victorian novel, American Lit. I didn't especially see myself as an English teacher; it was just that literature was the one thing I was good at. So I steered around the disciplines that might have brought me up against reality. No economics, no political science, the barest grunt requirement in psychology. In the latter I lied on every personality questionnaire they gave us—dreams, phobias, sexual habits—even though the questionnaires were strictly anonymous.

My coup that year was landing a place in Harold Bloom's seminar on the Romantic poets, for he only took one out of ten who applied. English was the major major in those days, and certain teachers were accorded superstar status. I can't say I understood very much of what the mythic professor said—about poets misreading one another and forging a vision by mistake, what Bloom called "the anxiety of influence." That all went right over my head. But his day-to-day close readings were breathtaking—the *Ode to Psyche, Frost at Midnight, A Toccata of Galuppi's*. Soundings so deep, you thought he'd never come up for air, and still my favorite poems.

Poetry was better than reality. The imagination was the only country where a man could truly breathe free. Thus the map of my own misreading, believing I could imagine life instead of living it. I got the A's to prove it, a Ranking Scholar on the dean's list all that year. Somehow it ceased to matter that I was having a silent nervous breakdown at the same time. The suffering ennobled me and would teach me how to sing. While everyone else was arguing about the war in Indochina, reading their meat-and-potato texts on the organizational man and abnormal psych, I dreamed my way through the *Idylls of the King*, learning the codes of chivalry and of love that was higher than passion.

The perfect text for me and Cody, longing in our separate ways for a vanished golden age. He'd gone on to copy several Rembrandt drawings and the sibyls from the Sistine Ceiling. Then worked on a series of dark cartoons, *New Yorker* style, yet more like Goya in feeling. The soul bond between us continued to deepen into the winter, till I felt there was no one who had ever understood me half so well. I wouldn't face it that I was doing all the emotional work for both of us, any more than I'd acknowledge how much he was drinking. The picturesque bottles of Chianti had given over now to gin and tonic — lots of gin, a splash of Schweppe's.

But then everyone at Yale seemed to drink too much, almost as a badge of honor. Holding your liquor was the mark of a man, but *not* holding it wasn't such a crime either; it proved a man was still a boy at heart, prone to mischief. I don't know how much I drank myself, a great deal more than I needed, but a small Puritan caution kept me from trying to keep up with Cody, in that at least. Otherwise I was like a mirror of his every word and gesture, increasingly trying to encourage him as his doubts about being an artist made him ever more savagely cynical.

Seething with that bitterness, he would tear canvases in half, then on a sudden impulse invite Natalie down for a midwinter weekend. I froze when I heard him make the phone call, and pretended to be very busy all the week before, so I wouldn't show how devastated I was. When he stayed overnight with her at the Taft, I sat in the dark staring out at the rainy courtyard, feeling as if I would die from the double paralysis of jealousy and envy. So lost was I in the realms of psych, all those lies on all those questionnaires, I couldn't have even said which of them I ached to be: Natalie, so Cody would love me, or Cody, so I could love a woman. I only knew I would never be happy and no one would ever hold me.

I can't recall how many more weekends like that there were — maybe once a month, maybe oftener. But I could see, even with my suffering, how at odds the two of them were — Cody drunk and surly, Natalie red-eyed with crying. But the pain between them made me as envious as their laughter, because it was real and expressible, blood-red with passion, and not the invisible pain of a ghost like me. Sometimes my head filled with a scream that went on for hours but was silenced by the dungeon walls of the closet. My face still wearing its social smile fixed in place as if by a stroke.

Let's go sit with Paul, they all said to their dates in the dinner line. *He's so funny*.

Self-pity becomes your oxygen. But you learn to breathe it without a gasp, so nobody even notices you're hurting. The fool continued to entertain. Every afternoon from four to six he could be found at The Elizabethan Club, an improbable anachronism where tea and sandwiches were laid out daily, to the buzz of literary chitchat. In the club's safe were several rare birds, including various Shakespeare quartos and a snip of Byron's hair in a locket.. A great fat queen of unbelievable pretensions stood guard by the tea tray, his eyes squinched like a nun who has stitched too many tapestries. Every day as I passed him to get my tea, I'd nod at him and pray, *Please don't let me end up like that*.

As for my own résumé, it was turning into an extracurricular nightmare. By the spring of junior year I was editing both the Jonathan Edwards newspaper and literary magazine, the aforementioned *Spider's Web* — jobs nobody wanted, to be sure, but an endless blizzard of paperwork. I had inherited from a mad senior the reins of yet another lit-mag, pointedly called *The Criterion*, as if we were all budding little Eliots. Besides beating the bushes for poems and stories, I had taken over the Yale Arts Festival, a migrainous blur of performances and exhibitions revolving among the twelve residential colleges. My life was a frenzy of getting announcements out, for events that usually drew fewer people than performed in them. All of which felt, even then, like the intellectual equivalent of stringing crepe paper for the school dance.

And it turned out to have certain benefits, being Art Czar by default. As spring advanced, the big push was to see who got tapped for the Senior Societies. This baroque hymn to elitism involved eight "above-ground" clubs, meaning the ones that had actual temples and castles in which the male-bonding mysteries occurred. Skull and Bones was the *ne plus ultra* of them all, rumored to be the site of naked wrestling among its members, and the mere mention of whose name in public meant that a member had to leave the room in a huff. But since each club was limited to only fifteen members, all eight had tremendous cachet. Being tapped for a Senior Society was the supreme example of being picked for the team, and a symbol besides of the influence and power that awaited a Yalie in the cozy world outside. ›

As each Society assembled a list of desirable juniors, they looked to mix a variety of the crème de la crème — heroic jocks, BMOC's, superbrains. And because they all wanted a token artist or two, my role as poet/impresario put me on the short list. I found myself courted by four of the eight Societies, swept up and taken to lunch by the captain of the hockey team and the editor of the *Yale Lit*. For one who had always felt like the last of the last to be chosen, it was a heady time, having my dance card full for once, and wooed by the likes of Apollo and Dionysus.

The only damper on the rush of my excitement came from Cody, who disdained the whole show as "boola-boola," classist nonsense. But even if I had to go against the captain of my soul, and though I muted my enthusiasm in his presence from then on, there was no way I would turn down the chance to be prince for a day. I wanted to belong too much, to be "in" at last. During all those weeks of courtship by the Societies, the wail of loneliness stopped screaming in my head. When pain takes that kind of vacation, you find yourself giddy with possibility.

In the end I went with Elihu, a club whose quarters were an eighteenth-century former tavern on the Green. Elihu had the reputation of being the most diverse and the least preppy of the Societies, politically correct before its time. Where the others reluctantly tapped a token Jew, girding themselves for the country-club fights to come, Elihu chose four Jews to be my brothers, and a Cuban and an African-American to boot. *Quel* melting pot. More to the point, they chose three queers as well, though that would never be spoken aloud, even within the sanctum walls. I give them credit nonetheless for the only real stab at diversity I ever saw at Yale. And I accepted it without question that the main agenda for senior year would be my becoming brothers in blood with the fourteen members of my delegation.

On tap night three men in suits stood silently outside my door, waiting for the stroke of eight to sound in Harkness Tower. When it did, they ran in and tapped my shoulder, and I blurted a breathless yes to the man from Elihu, sending the others darting out into the night to find a backup. I reeled with delight, the phone ringing off the hook with congratulations. I had arrived. And from Cody's room, where he crouched over a pad sketching his gloom in charcoal, came a mutter just loud enough for me to hear: "Welcome to the Mickey Mouse Club, boys and girls."

On the day of the initiation, I was terrified I would have to wrestle naked. But the mumbo-jumbo was minimal, and the alumni dinner following was about as hearty and banal as a law firm's annual picnic. The old Tory Tavern in the basement had a half-circle of chairs around a stone hearth, the same as when Nathan Hale himself sat there and quaffed a tankard of ale, plotting the Revolution. There was a live-in cook and butler who put out breakfast five days a week and dinner on Thursday and Sundays. Thursday would be our tribal night come autumn, when each of us would be required to present an autobiography to our fourteen brothers. We were given to understand that this would be the most naked night of our lives, wrestling or no.

I already knew I would lie when I told my story.

I liked the brethren well enough, fourteen new best friends, and ended the year in a flurry of lunches and dinners, to get to know them all better. I carefully avoided bringing it home to Cody, whose own demons were winning the wrestling match with his soul. Ever quick to rise to the challenge of dysfunction, I only loved him more for the agonizing loss of faith he was feeling over his painting. I've seen a lot of men and women since then who wanted to be artists more than life itself — seen them hit a wall I happen to have slipped through a hole in. I never fail to think of Cody, his fingers numb and palsied-looking as he clutches the chalk that freezes the moment it touches the paper. Dry as a bone and nothing to say. That image of Cody and Yeats's poem, "To a Friend Whose Work Has Come to Nothing."

I had a second stroke of good fortune that spring. I won a summer traveling fellowship from the college, ostensibly to go to England and read the Tennyson letters at Cambridge. Bloom had convinced me to take on the Victorian Laureate for my senior honors thesis, with a special focus on *In Memoriam*, the purple sequence of elegies that had occupied the poet for the seventeen years between 1833 and 1850 as he struggled to quench his grief over the loss of his friend Hallam. In order to get the fellowship you had to come up with a scholarly agenda. I convinced the committee that no one had ever compared the poet's letters with the datable sections of the poem. They nodded sententiously, satisfied as to my Higher Purpose, and cut me a check for a thousand bucks.

Three hundred for the plane ticket left me seven hundred for thirteen weeks in Europe, barely a smidgen over *Europe on $5 a Day*. I remember the last two weeks of school before summer as a time of delicious anticipation, making plans with classmates to hook up for certain legs of the journey, reading everything I could on the Lake District, Paris, Provence, Tuscany. The names of my long bookish life were about to acquire the quick of life, and I was convinced I'd never be the same once I had tasted the dust of the squares and walked in the steps of ancient gods.

Still unrequited as ever over Cody, I mooned in his wake and let him set the bad-ass tone of the garret we shared. I hadn't the strength to admit that his surliness toward me was getting unmanageable, almost as if he were punishing me for loving him. All we needed was the summer off, I told myself. We'd already agreed to room together again next year, the path of least resistance. In the meantime I would be seeing all the treasures of Western Civ, the hundred greatest hits of Art, and come back renewed for both of us. Our muses were surely as bonded as ever, even if we seemed increasingly at odds about everything. I still wanted to believe he was Dylan without the guitar, a rebel with cause, his darkness the stuff of vision.

A year together in 714 had made a most defiant statement, like a kid who paints his room black because the Stones said so. In the middle of our living room was a truck tire full of sand, choked with the butts of ten thousand Camels. In the corner, standing upright, was a plywood coffin, prop from a long-forgotten play, fitted out inside with shelves, as a bar. By year's end, empty gin bottles lined those shelves like a speakeasy. So much did we have invested in boho downtown anti-style. The faux Vermeer hung over the mantel, really rather good, the one thing not torn up in Cody's fits of art destruction. Paperbound outlaws — Plath, Artaud, Genet — were scattered about like amulets.

I promised to write to Cody from every country, and said he could write me back care of American Express, though I knew he wouldn't. A shrug was all he answered lately. It happened that he was leaving for California the same morning my plane left for London, both from Kennedy, so we took a train down from New Haven together the day before, thinking to browse the museums and look up some friends for dinner. We lunched on a six-pack going down, stowed our summer luggage in lockers at Penn Station, then passed a muzzy afternoon at the Frick. Dinner with friends turned out to be cocktails, and then a party uptown afterwards, from which the friends departed without us, forgetting we were supposed to spend the night with them.

After that we closed a bar on Third Avenue — I'd switched to 7-Up hours before — and then just walked the humid streets of midtown. Cody didn't seem to need to sleep, and I was feeling the crush of leaving him for three months, suddenly scared it would never be the same between us after, and no way to say it or that I loved him. Then he announced we must make a pilgrimage to the Seagram's Building, a mock-heroic bow to that totem of utopia. We ran through the East Fifties, whooping and shouting like vandals in a temple.

When we got there, the fountains were silent. Cody opened his arms and addressed the glass tower. "O Mies," he cried, "we are all unworthy of your genius." Then we bent down together and kissed the pavement, rather like drinking out of the tap in Calcutta. From one of his pockets Cody produced a final beer, and we sat on a stone slab above the Four Seasons, feeling very lordly. I took a sip, and Cody guzzled the rest, and then he was sleeping, his head in my lap. The deep sleep of a drunk, so I could stroke his copper hair without freaking him out. Overwhelmed just then with the wish to protect him and save him from the dark inside. And crying, because I could never tell him what I felt.

Change me, I whispered, *change me*.

But it wasn't Cody I prayed to, or God either. As usual, I was quoting somebody, in this case Randall Jarrell, "The Woman at the Washington Zoo." The poem that became my anthem months before, the day I first read it, the woman's caged heart indistinguishable from mine. She walks among the jungle beasts, a bureaucratic spinster nobody ever sees, never touched by wildness. "Oh, bars of my own body," she cries, "open, open!" Cries to the vulture who comes to scavenge the cages, that he should shed his black wings and step to her like a man. "You see what I am: change me, change me!"

All the while rocking Cody deadweight in my lap, closer than we'd ever been and just as far away. Reciting the poem to myself, I think now, trying to rouse the vulture in me to break the cocoon and coma of my secret. These bitter midtown tears were a sort of *bon voyage* as well, a plea that I would find myself in Europe somewhere. As I curled to sleep beside Cody, the first time I ever really held a man, I knew it was all goodbye for us from here on. Time to set forth alone and find out what sort of man I was, instead of being a mirror to somebody else. Swearing a blood oath, even as I clung to this ghost embrace, that I would never hold another man who wouldn't hold me back.

Five

THE DREAMING TOWERS OF CAMBRIDGE were so ancient —
centuries of English rain softening the golden stone like sand
castles — that Yale's cookie-cutter Gothic felt like a cheap sub-
division. I stepped off the train with my duffel bag and walked
straight to Kings Chapel to gape at the fan vaulting, as always
putting the sublime before a place to sleep. I didn't know a soul.
A porter at one of the colleges, eyeing my baggage, allowed as
how he and his wife had a room to let, so I ended up in a thatched
cottage with full English breakfast — full of grease — at five
guineas a week.

Next day, I presented my credentials at the bleak central library and found myself assigned a seat in the reading room,
boxes of Tennyson's letters heaped around me. I was cross-eyed
with boredom within an hour, sitting across from a gloomy nun
in full regalia, her head bent as she scratched a note on her mil-
lionth 3x5 card, looking as if she hadn't moved from her spot
since the Middle Ages. In five long weeks she never smiled or
spoke a word. It wasn't much livelier down in the basement tea-
room, where the scholars dipped and sucked their biscuits like
pacifiers, trading sour opinions of the outside world, anything
Not English being the same as Doesn't Exist — me included.

Itchy and impatient, I speed-read the letters in great gulps, a
language so flowered and courtly it seemed to say nothing at all. *I
was more depressed than Tennyson seems to have been those*

seventeen years of blubbering quatrains over the death of his friend. What irritated me most, I think, was the way the histrionics of grief masked the homoerotic. With all Tennyson's keening about home and hearth, his crushed hope that Hallam would have married the poet's sister and become a brother for real, the whole thing sounded as stupidly unrequited as Cody and I. And the two-line refrain that served as the Hallmark Card of the age —

> 'Tis better to have loved and lost
> Than never to have loved at all

— only made me wonder with a bitter sneer, loved how? *Say* it, goddammit.

But Tennyson didn't have to say it. His brand of soul fusion bypassed the baser passions entirely. Love was the province of spotless knights and maidens pining in towers, all dickless and exalted, perfectly suiting the reign of the widow Victoria. I never felt so much at war with poetry as I did that summer, the prettified sentiment and the long morbid sighs for a lost Arcadian world. For once I wanted poems and life to lead me out of feeling into experience, raw not cooked, and no more perfect phrases.

So I played hooky. I'd planned to spend eight weeks in Cambridge and then push off for the Continent, but every day I revised my departure closer. Meanwhile I hitchhiked all over England — to Stonehenge, Oxford, up to the Lakes for a three-day tramp in Coleridge's boots. But mostly I determined to meet a man and get laid once and for all. Every night I'd wander into the Cambridge pubs, always an alien, too shy to talk and too much a spaz to play darts. In the workingmen's pubs especially I'd get stared at now and then, and I could feel the carnal in it, but just being there was the best I could do. These guys had to break the ice first, and they didn't, because of their own closets. Or else they were the kind you needed to meet in an alley, and I didn't know how to do alleys any better than bars. But I felt supremely ready to be picked up, if only someone would make the move, and that alone was thrilling.

On Saturdays I went down to London to take in a pair of plays in the West End, catching the last train back at midnight. For a couple of dollars I could sit way up in the balcony, close enough to touch the cherubs on the ceiling. Back-to-back one day I saw a matinee of Sybil Thorndike in *Arsenic and Old Lace*, then Noel Coward's *Song at Twilight*, starring the Master himself. I'd seen or read nearly all of Coward's plays and musicals, could hum my way through a good two dozen of his songs. "Heigh-ho if love were all" was my anthem already, and I'd never even kissed a man. I don't think I'd ever put it together how gay the songs were, all those sailor sighs and "Mad About the Boy."

But I got it that night, watching Sir Noel in a wheelchair playing a broken-down writer with the taste of ashes on his tongue. I don't remember much about it anymore, except Irene Worth and Lilli Palmer running in and out with cocktails. And that the point of it all was that he was gay and got married anyway, and his whole life felt like a lie to him now. At the end he sat on the stage alone, reading a letter from a long-ago man he'd loved; then he crumpled the letter and sobbed for what he had thrown away. *I'*d been expecting a comedy, frankly. When I stood to applaud, I felt as if the play had struck like an arrow in my heart, a warning not to lose any more life.

I walked in a daze into Leicester Square, part of me wanting to join the queue at the stage door and try for a moment with Coward himself. Surely he would see the desperate yearning in my eyes. *Change me, change me*. But instead I kept walking the streets, wondering how to find a gay bar, and knowing in my gut that I was letting the last train go to Cambridge without me. I'd either find somebody or walk all night, exorcising the suffocating tameness that had crippled me below the waist as truly as my brother was.

At midnight I was leaning on the balustrade above Trafalgar Square, restlessly surveying the summer throng as it flowed past the fountains and Nelson's Column. Somewhere in there was the man who would change me. Had my hormones finally reached such a pitch that I gave off a palpable musk of desire, a

Yalie in heat? I didn't even notice him standing beside me until he laughed and gestured to the crowd below. "It's all Americans," he drawled with heavy irony, no less so for his own midwestern twang.

He couldn't have been more than thirty, though *older* was all I could think, my pulses beginning to race at the idea of Experience. Rugged-looking and a boyish grin, a streak of unexpected gray like a zigzag of lightning in his crewcut hair. He had my whole story in a matter of minutes, though I hardly knew what I was saying. He seemed to want me to be the preppy sort of Yalie, one of the frat boys, so I played down the wide-eyed poet. He'd been in the Navy himself, stationed with NATO in Scotland somewhere, and never went home when his hitch was up. Good riddance, Illinois.

Abruptly the fountains went off, and the bright lights doused around the Square like a stage going dark. The Underground was about to close; the city was shutting up for the night. Where was I staying, he wanted to know. Uh, nowhere. Well then, why didn't I come and bunk with him — on the sofa, that is. I nodded, as scared as I was excited, but at least nobody from home would ever, ever know.

It was a bed-sitter in Soho, down in the basement. We sat knee to knee on a pair of kitchen chairs, drinking beer and smoking my Camels. I remember him rambling on about Bill Buckley, having once read *God and Man at Yale*. A quarter century later, I blow a kiss to the lovely absurdity of the enemy of my people's being present at my deflowering. I waited for the man to make the first move. (I don't wait anymore, I make the first ten). "Why don't we both sleep in the bed, it's big enough," he said. It was in fact about as narrow as a cot, but I was damned if I'd get hung up on the details.

We stripped to our shorts and folded our clothes on our separate chairs, I too shy to watch him. We lay down side by side, and the moment he grazed my thigh I was on him like a rash. Kissing for the very first time, so hungry I frightened myself. Then he licked his way down my body and gave me head while I gripped his hair and groaned, exorcising a thousand lonely nights of pulling my pud for Cody and his like.

Patiently he maneuvered us into sixty-nine, a position I hadn't even conceptualized before, so stunted was my erotic imagination. He was very big, and he snarled and roared softly when I sucked him, teaching me in an instant what an animal a man could be. When he came in my mouth, it was like a tidal surge in a sea cave, so forceful that the cum streamed out of my nose. When I bucked and shot myself, hearing him greedily drink and swallow, I knew I had tasted life at last — and wouldn't end up sobbing in a wheelchair after all.

I wanted to cry for joy but played it much suaver, not breaking the spell of the Ivy pledge. He fell asleep in my arms, wrapped about his sailor's shoulders, tracing his lats with my fingertips and drinking deep the seawater stink of us. Thinking I wouldn't sleep all night because I wanted to play it over and over in my head. But I must've nodded off, for I woke up in the dark to find him biting at my neck, hungry all over again. Hey, I was game if he was. Now that I'd entered the carnal arena, man to man, sleep was for sissies.

Except he wanted to fuck me. He rolled me on top of him, sitting me up so I straddled his crotch, his horse dick poised in the crack of my ass, the clench of my virgin pucker. I started to balk, bells of panic in my brain, but he found that sexy and gripped my wrists. "I'll go in real easy," he murmured. "Just let go."

Let go? After twenty years of holding it in — swimming my whole life underwater, lungs bursting to breathe. I wanted to run away then, and the only thing that kept me there, gritting my teeth to take it, was a refusal to admit I didn't know what I was doing. From first to last the pain was excruciating, but I was too ashamed to say so. Now I see it would've turned him on to know he was taking my cherry. I was still trying to be suave, a pledge who could take a good hazing. Luckily we were in the dark, suave not being the easiest thing to pull off when you're sitting on a fireplug.

I don't think he got very far in, or that it lasted as long as it felt, about three days if you want to know the truth. Lifting me off, he drew me tight against him, surrounded me with the barrel of his arms, and in a second was asleep. And then the guilt began — that I'd gone too far and split myself in half, the pleasure erased by the violation. Hating myself for acceding to the *woman's* role, when what I had been so desperate for was to prove I was a man. I couldn't have got it more wrong, but didn't have a scintilla of political consciousness to save me. Didn't know about the exchange of power, the wild circle of top and bottom, the challenge two men fucking made to the slave laws of the patriarchy. I was just a scared kid with a throbbing hole.

Is this more than you want to know? as Stevie used to say, listing the weirdo side effects of chemo, the propulsive diarrhea. How was your trip to Greece, his friends would ask. *Oh, fabulous. I shit in my pants in the Parthenon. Pile of fuckin' rocks, if you ask me.* And when I'd talk about this book before he died, balking at the details of my first fuck — even with the man who swam in the sea caves with me, breathing underwater — Stevie would wag his finger at me and say, *Rub their faces in it, Paulie. Nobody told us anything. You tell them.*

He slapped my butt to wake me in the morning — affectionately, no doubt, but it made me cower against the pillow. He was wearing Navy sweats as he poured me coffee, chatting amiably. Asked if I wanted the first shower, hot water being a dicey business Sunday morning. I shook my head, unable to speak. He grinned at me. "You're even better looking in the daylight," he said, then trundled into the bathroom himself. I wanted to cry but had to get out of there first. I waited to hear the water go on. Then scrambled out of bed and yanked on my last night's clothes, checking my wallet to see if he'd stolen money. Frantically looking around in case there was anything he could track me down with.

On the kitchen counter, curled like a megaphone, was the program from *Song at Twilight*. I grabbed it and stuffed it in my jacket just as the water went off with a groan in the bathroom. I ran up the steps to the door, clawing at the deadbolts, all the locks suddenly foreign and my fingers numb as frostbite. I heard him come out of the bathroom. The final lock released. "Where you going?" I heard him call out, bewildered and, yes, wounded.

But by then I was running. Past all the hip and chic of Soho, windows full of glorious kink, groggy couples in leather and feathers shambling home from Saturday's final party. I was afraid to go into the Underground in case he'd follow me there, and I'd be trapped with him in a rocketing tunnel and have to explain myself. I ran halfway across the city to reach St. Pancras's Station, ran onto the Cambridge train without a ticket as it pulled out. Ran very well for a boy crippled below the waist.

My breath didn't stop heaving till we were nearly there. My whole body was clammy with sweat, and I was doubled over with cramps. My mind utterly blank. When I stepped off in Cambridge I looked the same as ever, I dare say, a trifle rumpled perhaps. I walked home to the porter's thatched cottage and prayed that I'd get upstairs without any of them seeing me. But they were all having their full grease breakfast, the two sticky kids in their highchairs, so I had to sit and drink tea with them, nattering on about *Arsenic and Old Lace*, not a word about the Coward.

Until the cramps were so bad, I excused myself and wobbled downstairs to the common loo. I sat on the can, and a great slug of his cum exploded out of me. I stared between my legs at the water, the milky swirl of life. And felt a kind of emptiness and shame deeper than anything I'd ever known. As if I'd aborted the dream of my own manhood, or coughed at the wrong moment and missed the line in the play that would have made everything right. But that's probably more than you want to know.

I fled England about a week later, turning in my library card, never again to sit staring across the table at that nun — which was like looking in a mirror in drag. I got off the ferry in Belgium and hitchhiked up to Amsterdam, with a wired mogul in a Maserati who seemed to be trying to set a world's record in night driving. Three different times he pointed his cigar to the side of the road, showing me where he'd spun out and wrecked his last three cars. And I didn't even flinch, or I found the fear exhilarating. Sure, I was running still from my night with the U.S. Navy, sealing off my sexuality again in its old dark coffin. But the dare and the hunger hadn't died in the process, not this time. Like it or not, I wasn't a virgin, and something deeper even than guilt was clamoring for more Experience.

On paper it looked pretty tame — the student tour of the Top 40, cramming every Rembrandt and Van Gogh I could find. Originally I'd put Amsterdam on the itinerary because of a vague and unsupported notion that it was a capital of homosex. (*Why did you come to Casablanca? For the waters.*) Having had my summer dose of sex — once a year, it was getting to be, up from zero — I averted my eyes from all shadowy doorways and red-lit alleys, steeling myself to walk past sidewalk bins of man-porn.

What was different now was that I would talk to *anybody*. In line at the Rijksmuseum, in student cafeterias, miming my polyglot way like an interpreter at the U.N. And not just with fellow students. I'd hustle over and engage with anyone who looked alone, making him laugh but somehow not feeling the fool anymore. Even men who were cruising me, I'd grin right back at them and ask them what it was like to be Dutch. No one was going to get this little puppy into bed again soon, so there was nothing to worry about from that quarter. What I was doing instead was being a writer, getting to know my material. And letting them all know too that they were in the presence of a Poet.

I hitched to Paris, sitting on my pack at the edges of poppy fields, one thumb out while I lurched through Pynchon's *V* and scrawled notes for a novel. Although the City of Light has become such a totem place for me — all bound up with loving Roger, so riddled with déjà vu that certain streets swarm with previous lives, till I'm the Shirley Maclaine of the Left Bank — I hardly took it in at first sight. I spent two days with the Green Guide, scuttling from museum to museum, but it wasn't the

France I was after. I made my dutiful pilgrimage to the Rue de Fleurus, peering through a gated arch into a dusty courtyard, the very place where Gertrude Stein told Hemingway: *You are all a lost generation.*

Damn right—I couldn't wait to be lost. And for me that meant the immortal South, a jumble in my head of Vincent's burning yellow fields and Scott and Zelda at Juan-les-Pins, knocking martinis back with the Murphys and getting the best revenge. I had a very specific image of myself: baking in the sun while I wrote a novel. Paris would have to wait; I couldn't really see into its heart till I had some writing under my belt.

The first ride, a rattling truck that reminded me of my days in the coalbins, took me as far as Lyon by noon. I still thought I could reach Marseilles by nightfall, even if I made an hour's side trip to check out a Roman ruin in the Savoie. Or perhaps it was a ruined abbey, I was very big on those. In any case I never found it, and the country roads weren't kind to hitchhikers — *autostop*, the French call it. Shorter and shorter rides seemed to take me farther out of the way, till I stopped for dinner in a roadside bar, no village for miles around. The rough-hewn peasants shrugged when I pulled out my map. They didn't live on a map.

Then one grizzled farmer, mustache stiff with burgundy, shuffled over to tell me he was going to Marseilles that very night. He traced the route through Provence with a finger missing the first joint, then beckoned me to follow him out. I dragged my duffel bag after, and we sardined ourselves into his ancient Deux Chevaux, a lawnmower masquerading as a car. But I figured I was in luck and romanticized the journey, perversely enjoying the stink of chickens and pigs that he'd transported to market.

We went about twenty miles into the darkness — south, I assumed, no road signs here. Then he pulled to the side of the road and spoke in a country French I couldn't follow. *"Je ne comprends rien,"* I said politely, whereupon he unbuttoned his pants and pulled out his meat, reaching to drag my head down into his lap. But I was lightning quick and grabbed my bag and jumped out defiantly, not such an easy mark as he thought. Standing alone in the drizzle as he drove away.

I didn't even mind being nowhere, walking an hour in pitch dark and soaking wet, since everything that happened now was in service of Experience. Eventually I came to a village, and slept under a café table shivering like a dog. Nobody in the whole world knew where I was, and that suited me fine. So magic was life on the road, in fact, that it surprised me not at all to wake up bleary to the morning sun and staring at a red Triumph convertible, two women laughing and pointing at me. *"Americain, n'est-ce pas?"* asked the driver, sleek as Claudia Cardinale. Then in quizzical English: "Where do you go from here?"

"Côte d'Azur," I answered brightly, scrambling out from under the table. They laughed as if this was the funniest thing they'd ever heard, then pointed me into the back seat. So I tumbled in behind them and blew dry as we raced down the Alpine hills into full Provence. They shouted questions at me about the Kennedys and Warren Beatty, and I boomed in answer with my schoolboy French, loving the sound of their laughter, their Hermes scarves whipping before me like pennants as we sailed through fields of lavender.

By the time we reached the coast, I felt like I'd walked into *Jules et Jim*, an arrangement in which our every gesture was devastatingly worldly. We pulled into a town called Le Lavandou — no tourists, white powder sand — and had fish-and-garlic soup for lunch with a Provençal rosé. "How come you have no cowboy boots?" Claudia wanted to know, and her friend Monique reassured her, "They're at home with his horse. In Texas." The teasing only made me feel more sexy. After lunch they walked me down the harbor to what looked like a bait shack and turned out to be a drop-dead boutique. They bought me a pearl-buttoned cowboy shirt, the yoke embroidered with lariats, telling me I would need it for the Riviera parties we were going to.

They left me on the beach and said they'd be back at sundown, after they'd made their obligatory visit to a boring friend's château. So I waved them laughing away and walked out onto the beach, stripped to my shorts, and wrote *Chapter 1* on the first page of my notebook. In my head I saw myself spending the next month with Claudia and Monique, perhaps becoming the lover of both — undeterred by the fact of never having gotten hard with a woman before. It was the tossing of my life to the winds that would make such things possible. What I wouldn't admit, of course, was that my one real toss of summer fate had already happened, with the U.S. Navy. And if I'd confessed to my virgin status and he'd gone slower to open me up, I might never have left London at all. Might still be there.

Here in the south of France I was playing a different game. I orchestrated my writer's pose — flung down on the sand with notebook, brooding in a waterfront bar — as if I was creating a character and a camera was always on me. The persona I invented was much more fully fleshed than the pale sticks of characters in Chapter 1. The novel I was writing was really a prop for the novel I was living. An old story, wanting to be a writer more than you want to write, but the pages poured out of me too, so it didn't feel like a pose. I figured I owed it all to the Mediterranean light, that I'd been drawn to an ancient wellspring, like coming home. The truth was more prosaic than even my sunstruck prose: I was furiously reinventing myself as Novelist, to obliterate the memory of being a sex toy. Writing instead of eros would be my passion.

It didn't matter that Claudia and Monique never came back. I found my own way to those parties, bonfires on the beach where the wine was passed in wickered jugs and goatskins, somebody warbling Pete Seeger and Woody Guthrie and mangling all the place names. If I wasn't the only American in that dot of a town, I felt like it. Hair going blond and my skin like cocoa, I was more than a kid on the beach, I was Other, mysterious (oh how I worked on the mystery), like one of those Hemingway types who sport obscure and glamorous scars.

A week later and into Chapter 2, I moved on to Nice. Thinking I could live on three dollars a day instead of five if I stayed in the youth hostel there — a dilapidated villa in the hills, chockablock with cots, like a makeshift hospital. I held myself aloof from the student population there, was the last one in when the gates closed at ten. Though I made several visits to the Musée Matisse, getting lost in the cutouts, my writer's schedule for the next three weeks was inviolable. By nine A.M. I'd be on the beach in front of the Negresco Hotel — where somebody told me Isadora stayed the night before she died, the billow of her scarf caught in the spokes of her gigolo's Bugatti.

And I'd write all day till sundown, though always ready to take a break if anyone stopped to talk. You realize you've been waiting your whole life to answer the question "What are you doing?" with "Writing a novel." Every hour or so, I'd go down to take a swim, though the footing was slippery, stones instead of sand. Afraid to swim out too far, always casting a nervous glance at my stuff on the beach, fearful someone would make off with my precious manuscript.

The novel of course was about nothing, par for a twenty-year-old. *The Beautiful Brick Day*, it was called, because the hero's window looked out on a wall. Took place at a grand hotel in New Hampshire, as if my first task as a writer was to improve the truth of the previous summer. The main characters were a pair of college kids, boy and girl, both eccentric loners, who eventually became lovers of sorts. Though the sexual part was misty enough, under the covers, that they might as well have been playing doctor. I have mercifully forgotten the engine of the plot, though an old dull wince in the back of my mind tells me the girl was determined to build herself a lake. I knew as much about engineering a dam as I did about men and women in bed.

Write what you know, as the first rule has it in Fiction I. But frankly I only knew what I wanted life to be, not what it was. I knew the blank page of life in the closet, and no way would I ever write about that. But I was free to experiment at will, since no one in Nice was looking over my shoulder. In the evenings I attached myself to groups of French kids, café au lait and movie-talk, for they were delighted to have an American to listen to their speculations about the existential Jerry Lewis. They traveled in packs, giving off a general erotic charge that didn't seem to demand — even seemed to avoid — pairing off boy/girl. No one was ever gay that I could tell, but then I wasn't looking any more. Meanwhile I got to feel sexual without having to prove anything.

There were nights when I missed the curfew at the hostel and was forced to spend the night on the beach, huddled between cabanas. With all that caffeine I wasn't sleepy anyway, and let my mind race trying to figure how to pull off this lifestyle as a permanent thing. I flirted with exile, sure I could live on practically nothing. I'd lost about twenty pounds since coming to the Continent, but liked the hungry look of me in the mirror, all my babyfat finally burned away. My tan was beyond cordovan, three layers scorched and peeled till I had that blasted post-nuclear look so favored by Europeans. A shipwreck tan, a philosophical tan, Gauguin in Tahiti.

On Bastille Day I met a trio of American girls who'd been studying French in a convent in Grenoble. I took them on a Pied Piper tour of Nice—the fishing docks and the grittiest onion soup, a vertigo climb to the old Roman road, with cerulean views to Corsica. I described my novel and the Life of Art with boggling pretense, and they ate it up. By the time we got back to the churning holiday crowd in the city, Betsy had staked me out for herself and radared her roommates that it was vamoose time.

I preened appropriately, and somehow didn't feel threatened to be alone with her in the Bastille crush. She had long black hair and a body taut from a life of tennis, standing nearly as tall as I, and fiercely aggressive after a month of irregular verbs. We made out in the middle of the street, all over each other, and I found her aggression exciting, maybe because I didn't have to steer it into a bed. We danced in a conga line that ran for hours on the Promenade des Anglais, then wandered into somebody's open house for dinner, feeling very daring. We watched the fireworks from the park above the harbor and sang the *Marseillaise* till we were hoarse.

We'd long since missed the curfew at the hostel. At three A.M. we sat on the beach in a circle of drunken Frenchmen, kissing and passing the wine. Betsy said she'd always wanted to see Monaco, having been raised to think of Grace Kelly as the pinnacle of Catholic womanhood. Well, why not? We staggered up to the road and hitched a ride in the back of a pickup, sharing the space with a pair of dogs who loved the wind as much as we did.

It was after four when we landed in Monaco, nobody on the streets, and since we couldn't find the casino, we headed up to the palace. The guards in the courtyard couldn't have been more courtly, answering all our gushy questions, though they drew the line at pointing out Her Majesty's bedroom. We carved our initials on the root of a plane tree under the battlements, then wandered the streets till we found a baker opening up. He gave us a half-dozen croissants free, because his town on the German border had been liberated by Yanks in '45.

All day and all night long it had felt like a movie. I *liked* it being a movie, and the way I seemed to watch myself go through the motions of a twenty-four-hour romance. A movie I could take my grandmother to, unlike my night of carnal overload in Soho. The last scene happened just after dawn, Betsy curled asleep in my lap as we sat on a bus bench, flaked with a sift of crumbs. Just then a convoy of French army trucks came rumbling by, each with a dozen men in fatigues sitting knee-to-knee in the back.

As the trucks passed, the soldiers caught sight of us, looking so louche and muzzy with love, and they winked and whistled and waved their rifles. To them — to the whole French army, it felt like — I was their stand-in, a boy with a girl. Betsy never woke up. It was all on me, that final shot, puffing with pride as I stroked her hair, winking back and returning salutes, a man among men. As the last truck passed, a barrel-shaped grunt called out to me: "*Français?*"

"*Bien sûr,*" I retorted, no trace of the schoolboy in my accent. And the men in the final truck cheered, another score for their side. As the convoy disappeared up the High Corniche, I felt near delirious with what I took to be self-esteem. At that moment it seemed the most important thing in the world, to engineer my life so I'd look the right part, a woman on my arm who would garner the cheers of other men. It had nothing to do with Betsy, of course, whom I can't recall saying goodbye to. Once we'd played to the troops, it was cut and print. But afterwards I could summon up the scene whenever I liked, a loop of porn with the sex drained out, always there to tell me the same comforting lie: how it felt to look like a man.

Then I had to move on, having promised a friend from Yale that I'd do Italy with him. Time to go anyway, since my torso was on fire with a toxic rash from sun poisoning. Sixty handwritten pages in my duffel bag, and sure now that I'd found myself a vocation. I hooked up with David in Stuttgart, the most decent straight man I ever befriended at Yale, and we hitchhiked to Venice to Florence to Rome, the Greatest Hits of the Renaissance. The novel stayed in my bag, not necessary just then, though I'd lie awake in the hostels and art-direct my dust jacket, or lullaby myself with rave reviews.

There came a day when the past almost caught me and made me honest. Standing in line at American Express, we met a fellow Yalie who knew my friend Francis from Andover. Francis was finishing up his junior year abroad, and he and the Yalie were on their way south to Pompeii and the Amalfi coast. They had the whole back seat going begging, so David and I decided to tag along. Francis hadn't changed much — still that sacerdotal air from so many years at the organ, but just as wry and flushed with pleasure to see me.

All I could feel in return was distance, bordering on hostility, for he brought back like a bad dream the loser I'd been in prep school. Worse, I feared to be tainted as queer if I laughed at his jokes — though he wasn't any further out than I and passed for straight depressingly well. In a paroxysm of defensiveness I swamped Francis with my writer's airs and boho exploits, laying it on thick about Betsy.

I remember this very specific moment when all those guards came down. We'd taken the ferry to Capri, and after the Blue Grotto tour Francis and I found ourselves swimming naked off a rock below the cliffs of Tiberius's villa. As we paddled back and forth in the cobalt water, I suddenly felt an overwhelming need to tell him the truth. Thought I would die of the pretense if I had to endure it a moment longer. Just to say *How are you handling being queer, because all I seem to do is fuck it up*. It was no secret between us after all, not since the days we'd cracked each other up on the steps of Harriet's tomb. Francis knew I was struggling to speak, and probably knew in his heart what about. I almost, almost said it. But he was as shy to prod it out of me as I was loath to give up being the mascot of heterosex for the French army. We let the moment go, and I went back to living my life as a book instead of a person.

Yet senior year at Yale turned out to be very satisfying, I playing the role of Writer Back from Exile to the hilt. Tennyson had become secondary. My senior thesis on him was supposed to occupy half my time, but mostly what I did was pad the dreary notes I'd made in England. I worked on *Brick Day* instead, revising, ever revising. Though now that I think of it, I worked a lot less than I talked about it — as if I couldn't stop answering *Writing a novel*, even when nobody asked, oh especially then. More than anything it helped me not prepare for the future. I forgot to send to graduate schools for catalogues, tuned out when everyone else was grappling over Harvard Law versus who knows what. I simply didn't care.

Ten years later, finally out, I would say that my senior year was a kind of extended nervous breakdown, but the smiling sort of breakdown that people pretend not to notice. I was still rooming with Cody Williams, yet almost from the first day back we hardly spoke. I felt hardened to him — again that weird disdain for the former object of unrequitedness. Not that I didn't keep up a certain exaggerated courtliness around him, if only to brag about my novel, while he and his own demon continued to stare at blank paper. I certainly paid no attention anymore to which girl he was dating. I even stopped the charade of taking part in the weekend ritual, no more blind dates for appearance's sake. It was the closest I'd come so far to being myself alone, reveling in my writerly intensity, an invisible scarf like Isadora's billowing after me as I capered about.

More by default than not, since everyone else was busy engineering a life after Yale, I was running the whole show art-wise. You couldn't blow your trumpet in public without running it by me first, since I was the cultural gatekeeper. I had at my disposal certain discretionary funds, so I could sponsor a Yale appearance by various troupes on the fringe. I felt like fringe myself, loving the sound of my own opinions, the more outrageous the better.

That fall I invited Pauline Kael to speak in a lecture series officially funded for art history, preferably embalmed. I got to spend three days as her guide, drinking in all that iconoclasm, learning a whole new vocabulary for the decade of movies about to explode. Sat with her one afternoon watching *The Maltese Falcon*, just the two of us, and from her droll running commentary the full heat of *noir* hit me like a blast. All that Hollywood trash I'd grown up on, so irrelevant to the ivied smugness of my education, suddenly had a context. By the time she left, I was ravenous for pop and high kitsch, scorning the good gray syllabus of Eng Lit. Slang was as good as refinement, and if you could somehow put them together—a prose that stretched the limits the way Godard and Dylan did—you could start a fire that burned like a blowtorch.

I spent as much time as I could at Elihu, getting to know my fourteen blood brothers. Most of them seemed as restless as I for a fresh perspective, dissatisfied after three years of the preppy cliques and moldering tweed of Yale. The reason these senior societies sprang up in the first place was the tacit admission that men, left to their own devices, never made friends below the surface, let alone below the belt. The macho gets in the way, the heartiness, the pride in showing no feelings. Or at least that's how the straight boys all complained, as they took to heart the societal oath, in which feeling and bonding were one. If feeling was what they were looking to learn, writer Monette was ready to show them the way.

After each Thursday dinner, the fifteen of us tramped upstairs to the meeting room, its cream-painted paneled walls carved with the names of every member since the founding in 1903. A mace like a caveman's club was placed on the table before the man who was spilling his autobiography that night. I don't really remember the order of events or the incantations, but we took it deadly seriously, for we were about to see into one another's souls. By lot I was chosen to go second—this was about mid-October, just at the cusp of my twenty-first birthday. Tellingly, though my fourteen brothers were to be my collective best friend for the next nine months, the only autobiography I remember is my own.

Because really, it was the first time I'd ever told the tale to anyone. I almost never talked about my brother, till the unsaid had grown to the size of a mountain. And not until that night had I ever shared the miserable isolation of prep school. I began the proceedings by reading "The Woman at the Washington Zoo." All the pieces were there, laid out on the table before them, the scattershot jigsaw of my heart. I held back only the one truth that made it a picture: being gay. The most I could tell them was that I was depressed.

But monumentally so, torn up inside, so bad I'd flirted with suicide. I could see how gravely they took this in, their own sorrows paling for the moment in comparison. For my despair came off as systemic, nothing so banal as losing a game or even a woman. And the unspoken subtext: that maybe I was incurable, a fury of self-destruction in my bones that I would struggle with heroically as long as I could, mapping my soul's condition with blood in my pen, till finally it dragged me under.

Far too much in control of my histrionic rhetoric to let it fall into a whine, which is mostly what it was, I came off like the prince of my own darkness, ever so stylish in black. They didn't know what to say when I finished, my fourteen brothers. They certainly didn't understand how nakedly I was begging them to change me. One of them said, haltingly, he'd never have guessed the turmoil. I always seemed so cocksure and above it all, with my riding-crop wit and my honeyed tongue. Maury, the songwriter from Queens, told me he'd assumed I was raised a landed duke, on account of my arty sophistication. I answered them with a stoical shrug: so much for the deceptiveness of appearances. What they couldn't see was how giddy I was from all the applause, that for me the Thursday autobiography had been a performance piece. Reality was the least of it.

And I got what I wanted. They all decided to cheer me up, make sure I felt like one of the guys, no more the outsider looking in. They also encouraged me mightily in my writer's vocation. Half of them were on the track to law school and med school themselves, and having a poet around was a nice diversion. So I wagged like a puppy when they stroked me, spoke from the windswept hill of Poesy if the mood was right, one-on-one by the fire in the Tap Room. For they tended to draw toward me when they were depressed themselves, now that I was the resident expert on melancholy. And I would do somersaults of empathy, the candle in every brother's darkness.

All of which was so much more satisfying than sending in applications to grad school. My professors in the English department assumed I would go for a Ph.D., and so I took the Graduate Record Exam in case, but grudgingly. Various fellowships for study abroad dotted the bulletin boards along my daily route, and I let my name be nominated here and there, maybe even went after a couple. But the whole scenario gave me a queasy feeling, as if graduate school of any sort — but especially in England — would feel like those five weeks across from the nun at Cambridge, till I gradually turned to stone.

Something would doubtless turn up, I remember thinking, as long as I was true to my writing. I was back to poetry again, in the grip of Sylvia Plath, *Ariel* having just appeared. *What a thrill — /My thumb instead of an onion*, she gasps at the cut of a kitchen knife, mesmerized. To a whole generation of 60's depressives it was a siren call to play chicken on the tracks. The blood lust cries to the father and the husband, flaunting her death, daring anyone to stop her. In fact I didn't read her very carefully, just obsessively, using Sylvia to tap into a rage I couldn't name, where the eros of self-destruction was better than no eros at all.

There was never any real danger that I would turn on the gas myself, having chosen instead a living death, the inchmeal route of the closet. But that's why the poise of the kitchen knife felt so thrilling, even if I was only pretending for the sake of an over-wrought poem. Just look what I can do — *bleed*. There might be no way out of the queer closet, but this courting of insanity and annihilation meant that every other door of feeling blew its hinges. Suffering had a purpose if you could get a good line or two out of it. Besides, when you're working so hard on keeping your wounds raw instead of doing your Stanford application, you can pretty much shrug the future off.

I call it a breakdown, but that's just guesswork. More than any other year since puberty, the details blur. All I can recall is constant motion, running around that Gothic maze of a campus, endlessly performing, working at being everybody's idea of a poet. Somehow I've always blamed Yale for that, but really, what was the college supposed to do? Get me into therapy? Also, I can't think how else I would have ended up a writer without that year of proclaiming it at the top of my lungs. The breakdown's built in.

Yet I still can't look back without pleading for the pain to stop, even from this distance — longing for some bolt of courage or madness to drag me out of the closet before I graduated Yale. Then at least I could say I got something out of those four clois-tered years besides a worthless diploma. For when that longing gets its hooks in me, aching for so much lost time, I think I would have gladly given up being a writer if I could've been queer out loud. Not that it had to be either/or. But another eight years would go by before I understood I could have it both ways: queer *and* a writer.

I remember only a single conversation from Christmas that year in Andover. I suppose my parents had asked me before where I was going after Yale, and I'd probably answered with a certain vague superiority, the whole question beneath my notice. But now they meant to pin me down, especially when I ticked off the schools and careers my friends were getting ready for. "We don't care about them," my father declared, never late for work himself in forty years. "What about you? You must have some idea."

"Of course. I'm going to write."

A pause, in which you could hear the fizz of the lights on the Christmas tree. "But that's not a job," my mother finally sputtered. "It's — it's a hobby. What's all this education been for? You have to *do* something."

Oh I did, did I? The cold defiance must have been naked in my face. My parents probably wanted to beat the bejesus out of the little snot. In retrospect I can hardly blame them. But there are subtler ways, stitched with infinite patience like a crewel sampler. "Paul, don't you understand," my mother intoned with a trace of pity, regaining her footing nicely, "if something happens to us, you'll have to take care of Bobby."

Like the clanking shut of a prison gate. I nodded and mumbled yes, of course I understood that, when in fact I'd never given it a thought. I'd left the world of Stratford Road a million miles behind me, all its certainties, everything taken care of. Not that I wasn't always glad to see my brother when I was home. We made marvelous mischief at the dinner table, trading riffs of rock 'n' roll, talking in circles above the parents' heads. To me Bob seemed completely independent, a kid with his own opinions, unbowed by life in a wheelchair.

He'd finally been sprung from the David Copperfield School, thrown in with the able-bodied masses at Andover Junior High, whose prewar edifice was all vertical, upstairs and down. For Bob every day it was like climbing a mountain hogtied. Forced to take classes on the ground floor, no matter how inappropriate. For one course he had to sit in a janitor's closet, listening in with an ancient ear trumpet that snaked upstairs to the science class on the floor above, like playing telephone with two Dixie cups and a length of string. Education by obstacle course.

And he had his own ache of longing now. Just recently I learned that he used to crawl into my room and rifle through my jerk-off drawer so he could look at the *Playboys*. Now I realize I desexualized him as completely as I had myself — too threatening even to think about. But he was wheeling through those snot-green halls at AJH — where Vinnie O'Connor once made Austin Singer eat a lugie — and gaping at all the nubile girls in the first flush of womanhood, his hormones as wired as any of the other boys'. Except in his case the rattling heat was accompanied by a terrible sinking dread, that none of these laughing girls would ever look at him that way. And it left his heart as paralyzed as his legs.

I bought all the clichés instead: the brave little cripple, the tortoise overtaking the hare. He'd sit in his room playing his guitar for hours on end, singing softly to himself, and I liked the romantic image of that. It seemed Poetic, like me and my pen full of blood. But I hadn't a clue what he felt about anything, and made no effort to find out. If I couldn't face my own demons except in a haze of metaphor, all evasion, there wasn't even an outside chance that I'd confront my brother on his. I mean, what if he asked me to help him become a man? I couldn't be that kind of big brother — couldn't even begin to ventriloquize it.

I suppose it must have made me angry, the prospect of giving up my own life to take care of his. But we weren't very skilled at anger in those days, not where I came from. We were into bearing it silently, like good Episcopalians. (You can always tell how much anger one of them has buried by the crosshatch lines on the upper lip, like a lemon pucker that froze — the opposite of smile lines.) I couldn't cry out the rage, but in January I went back to Yale more committed, not less, to going nowhere. If my brother's well-being depended on my finding a nice safe situation with regular hours and a good health plan, they were putting their money on the wrong horse.

The first half of my Tennyson thesis was due at the end of January. It was still mostly a disarray of 3×5's and fragments spilling off my desk. For the first time I can remember, I played the card of my brother. I went to the college dean and told him Bob had almost died over Christmas, reaching back a half-dozen years to the fevers that broke the thermometer. I had otherwise been so pathologically punctual and perfect in my coursework that the dean was on the phone in a flash, getting me three weeks' grace from the department chairman himself. All through the rest of the year the dean would stop me in the hall to inquire how my brother was doing. A little better, I said, till it finally dawned on me that he might ask Paul and Jackie the same thing at graduation. *All* better, I hastily revised, pulling my brother back from the brink of the grave.

As for the anger I felt toward my parents for saying that writing wasn't a life, the only person I can recall expressing it to was Hilgendorf. By now I was feeling closer to my brothers in Elihu than to anyone else, reading and writing there nearly every evening, always ready to fling my work aside and get into a little soul talk. I tried to give equal time to all fourteen, like a floating delegate at a convention, charming them and interviewing them by turns. But the one who fascinated me most was Bill Hilgendorf, because the realm in which he moved seemed the most unattainable, as far outside Yale as I wanted to be.

Not that he didn't have Yale in the palm of his hand. He was president of our class, respected unto veneration, a jock's jock. In football he was All-Ivy something or other — linebacker I think, but don't quote me — and managed to play a little of everything else, basketball to rugby. He'd lived two floors above me in Jonathan Edwards since sophomore year, unfailingly nice when we passed on the stairs, but I was too awed to engage him much. He looked like the steel engraving of Lancelot in *Idylls of the King*, the subject of the second half of my thesis. Wisconsin-born and rock-solid, Bill had no guile about him at all, and no arrogance either. Nothing to dilute the Eagle Scout mix of authority and decency. Too good to be true, perhaps, but they said the same thing about Lancelot at the Round Table, the envious ones anyway.

Bill and I would walk together to Elihu on Thursday and Sunday nights for meetings, then home again, late, through the Old Campus, I trying to match my stride to his. He admitted to being unnerved by the black hole of despair in my autobiography, never having peered into such deep water himself. But he was convinced, ever the ball carrier, that it would only make me a greater poet, and urged me in his earnest way to charge down the field and run for daylight. So opposite to me, I had no idea what a fellow romantic he was till we got to *his* life story.

Which sounded more or less like the youth of Apollo: cheering crowds in the stadium, his bedroom cheek by jowl with trophies. The middle brother of three, all football heroes, the pride of Whitefish Bay. If Bill had any problems — he groped to find one — it was a struggle with pride, and a certain doubt about being worthy of the pedestal the crowd was always lifting him to. A properly classical flaw, but one you could scarcely lend much credence to in his case, given the seeming total absence of narcissistic self-regard.

I don't know how not to make him sound like a cheap paper saint. He wasn't stiff or holier-than-thou. The aura around him was a sunlit field in a winning season, but he somehow didn't consume the light himself. It always seemed to be shining back on the person he was talking to. Trust me, you would have voted for him in a minute. For that's how it ended up, his autobiography: he was going to be President someday. Understand that most of us around that oval table had a good deal invested in cynicism, especially concerning the powers that be. It was a tribute to Bill's unabashed idealism that we nodded our collective approval, as if we were all extras in a Capra movie, sure that Jimmy Stewart could save the bank if anyone could.

By a curious fluke, lucky for both of us, I never fell in love with him. I *worshiped* him, but it wasn't carnal. And he wasn't afraid of me in the least, or of the wild swings of my feelings. I think he was so self-contained himself, so centered at the core, that he worried a little about being so normal. A restless talker, always stretching, in his way as much of an interviewer as I was. *How do you think poetry helps people?* he'd ask, wanting the whole thing quantified so he could compare it to digging wells in the Peace Corps. He had a missionary streak in him — Christian maybe, but no affiliation, thank you. With him it was more in the nature of a quest, at the end of which he would be a wiser leader.

And, then, he had Star. They had just started seeing each other that year, but the dazzling pair they made seemed more heroic and inevitable than "dating." She was quite the most beautiful girl I'd ever met, maybe because she took to me so fast and wanted to read my poems, *all* of them. She'd grown up in Hawaii, tawny blonde with orchids in her hair, and was surely the most unlikely Wellesley girl around, no circle pin in sight and not a demure bone in her body. Star and Bill were king and queen of a larger prom than Yale, and already I could imagine them campaigning together for a House seat from Wisconsin, White House or bust. They didn't exactly radiate a smoldering sexual heat, both of them still in that astonishment of first love, and therefore somehow innocent. But here it may only be the skewed perspective of the overwrought poet talking, for I thought of her as Guinevere to his Lancelot. Just as I thought of myself as the Laureate of them both, ready to read a triumphal ode at Bill's inaugural.

I'm not quite sure why I felt no jealousy or envy toward them. It's hard to piece it together so far back, since Star is like a sister to me now, the only person I still know from Yale. We've spent so much time since then shaking our heads and wondering: Was anyone ever so young? Trying to get over Bill in our separate ways, what we could've become and how much sooner but for the tease of fate, as Greek as our heroes.

I only know that the two of them seemed to be my biggest fans, and that being a writer became as necessary as breathing when I was in their company. Anne Sexton's *Live or Die* came out that winter, and Star and I read it aloud to each other, loving its smutty vernacular, its snickering at death. She was even taking a course in the Victorians at Wellesley, thus full of questions about poor dreary Tennyson. At Star's urging I actually completed the application to the writing program at Stanford, my one post-college shot, though I can't recall if I applied in fiction or poetry. I certainly brooded long and hard about whether a real writer ought to be going to school to study how. Wouldn't it be better to live on three dollars a day in Nice and write what I wanted? Star responded dryly that what a real writer needed to do was avoid the draft.

I kept forgetting that part. I was still sitting out the war in

'67, totally abstracted from the flood of carnage on the nightly news, paying only the barest lip service to the anti-war. I hadn't anything that passed for a political conviction. It was in the nature of my particular closet that nothing would ever change, so what was the point of trying? I didn't even know I was oppressed.

By March my life was insanely busy, as all the various arts festivals began to take shape in the twelve residential colleges. Where I wasn't actually responsible for mounting an event, my official czar's position demanded that I show up, at every reading and performance — or at least I was too guilty not to, knowing the feeling all too well of outnumbering the audience. The art itself has vanished from memory — the undergraduate angst, the neo-Pop defiance, the spluttering 8-millimeter shorts. But I realized that some of the younger artists, especially the writers, were looking to me for guidance and support. I recognized the neediness and cheered them on, usually coming home with yet another batch of bleeding poems and stories about deflowering. No time at all for my own work now.

As much as I liked playing the mentor, I enjoyed even more the fact that they thought of me as an artist who'd made it, however small the pond. The one-eyed man in the country of the blind. I doled out fragments of my novel to the select few, accompanied by the travelogue of my days in Nice. I was dimly aware that the deadline for turning in my Tennyson thesis was fast approaching, but I kept putting off the revision and polish of my fitful chapters on the *Idylls*. I'd get home too late from the cast parties and be up half the night reading proof for one of my literary rags. As if Western Culture would grind to a halt if I didn't do it all.

So I never pawed through my desk for the *Idylls* file, sixty or seventy pages already typed, if only half thought through, till a week before the thesis was due — and the file wasn't there anymore. Within an hour I knew the pages weren't anywhere in my room or Cody's, with Cody himself more amused than not by my sudden panic, scarcely having sketched the floor plan for his own senior project. But then he didn't have the Paul-is-perfect image to uphold. I began to tremble with fear as I tried to reconstruct when I'd last seen the fateful pages. No luck: I was blank as the wall the hero of my novel woke to every day.

I put notices on bulletin boards, but I knew it was a lost cause. I had to go to the chairman of the department and beg for leniency. Glibly he told me the story of Thomas Carlyle's only copy of his history of the French Revolution being tossed in the fire by a thoughtless maid at the house of John Stuart Mill. And the great man sat right down the next morning and started all over. Except in my case the file included not just my draft but weeks of glazed research across from the tight-lipped nun at Cambridge. I finally struck a bargain: I would expand considerably my not-so-brilliant remarks on *In Memoriam* and let that stand for the whole. More padding of what was already mostly pad, and I knew I had just kissed off my chance of graduating *magna*.[4]

For years afterwards, I couldn't get over the feeling that I'd been about to say something profound about Arthur and Guinevere and Lancelot. But, unlike Carlyle, I never went back. As I lurched around trying to stretch eighty pages to a hundred and twenty, I got my rejection from Stanford, a chill form letter at the end of which someone had stamped Wallace Stegner's name upside down. A dread like a snake in my belly told me I was in deep shit, but during the last ten marathon days with my thesis I couldn't take a break to think about that. The margins felt about three inches wide on either side when I gloomily handed it in.

And was it really the next day — or is memory simply trying to deepen the irony of my comeuppance — that Hilgendorf came down to my room with the *Idylls* file in hand? He'd found it quite by accident in a pile of newspapers on his window seat. I don't know how it got there, left by me or lent to Star, but it's the sort

---

4. But where was the *Xerox* copy, several friends have asked in utter disbelief. Well, the *carbon* copy was stupidly tucked in the file with the original — failure requires effort. The first copy shop didn't open in New Haven till '68, an innovation comparable in magnitude to movable type.

of coincidence that would never fly in a novel—losing the Lancelot study in Lancelot's room. Right up to graduation, those half-done pages mocked me from my desk, twisting the dagger when my thesis came back with a tepid B. The whole incident proving, if nothing else, that the last place I belonged was graduate school.

So I could barely crack a polite smile when my thesis adviser, having pried from me the news of my snuffing at Stanford, tossed me a life preserver in the form of a slot in the graduate program in English. I'd think about it, I grimaced as I backed out of his office. Then ran across the campus through the drizzling green of May to get back to the real work of finishing Yale: the writing of the Class Poem.

It was to be my last star turn in the czarist reign of art for art's sake. An official poem to be read in cap and gown on the day before graduation, to the senior class and their guests assembled on the Old Campus. The Poem would follow the Ivy Ode in Latin and precede the Class Oration, the order of such events having been set in stone when Connecticut was still just a colony. I don't know anymore if I applied for the job or had it bestowed like a bay-leaf crown, but I bent to the task in deadly earnest. Poet Laureate at last.

And found myself quivering with sentimental overkill for the Bright College Years about to end. It suddenly didn't matter how miserable I'd been for the last four years. It was misery on a field of royal blue, shaded by elms that knew no blight, our ties knotted together in a fraternal circle as we passed a silver tankard. In a gush of inspiration I extolled the joys of blood-brotherhood, the hearty embrace and the feelings too deep for words, here at this threshold where boys became men. All the emotional complexity of a greeting card, and serving up the official line of manly comradeship: *for God, for country, and for Yale*.

A poem in five sections, it turned out, each a sort of impressionist sketch of one or another of my futile crushes. The fragment about the painter is Cody, and the steeplejack fragment is Sean. All unconscious, though. You would have had to be a *real* queer to pick up on the homoerotic angle — the breathless pride in being a special friend, the roughhouse games, two loners locking glances. Reality was the last thing in my mind. I let it all be about buddies and the mysteries of friendship, unable to face what I truly wanted from a man, which was nothing so vanilla as friendship.

Meanwhile I went to all the farewell parties, draping arms and singing in the courtyards, the grass awash in spilled beer. I think I was more or less continuously drunk those last few weeks, but was hardly alone in that. Besides, drunk was the best excuse for covering a sloppy embrace, the only time I would ever hold any of these guys close enough to smell them. In my mawkish heart I forgave the cruel indifference of the ones who'd never understood I loved them. This camaraderie of the last days was better than nothing, after all — a taste of Dionysus, dancing for all I was worth, trying to catch the feel of wild abandon before the tribe dispersed.

Two days before graduation, exceedingly hung over, I reported to the main library for a ceremony straight out of E. M. Forster: the planting of the Class Ivy. In a cloistered inner courtyard whose walls and Gothic arches were already choked with vines, the Odist and the Poet were each to plant a little pot beneath a brass plaque that said 1967. Nobody took it seriously, great guffaws all around, but what the hell, tradition was tradition. Here and there behind roots as thick as a man's leg you could see the old tarnished plaques from a hundred years ago, when Tennyson was Laureate.

The Odist planted his ivy first, tossing off some pithy lines in Greek. I remember being surprised that Hilgendorf was there, but as President he probably had to be at every ceremony, however obscure. When it came my turn, I knelt with the trowel where the parched librarian pointed. With the first thrust I struck a rock, the dull clunk of spade against stone reverberating in my tender head. Then Bill was crouched beside me laughing, taking the trowel from my hand and quickly working the rock free. As I bent to lay the ivy in, I suddenly thought I was going to cry, the only one there for whom it had ceased to be a joke. Moved because the two of us were kneeling together, a pair of knights on the brink of the quest, the brotherhood about to disband.

Next day was Class Day, an audience of some three thousand wilting on folding chairs in the sun. I sat beside Bill on the speakers' platform, a canopy rippling above us, suddenly seized with fear that my poem wasn't veiled enough. They would all pick up on the unrequited sigh of it, and I would stand revealed as a deviant. When the Odist took a seat, I stepped to the podium, laying my pages down with shaky hands. Just then a capricious breeze blew up and scattered my poem across the stage. I started after it helplessly, my face burning as people began to laugh. But Bill had already darted forward to snatch the pages up, a save in the fourth quarter. He handed them back to me with a wink, and then I felt strong enough to bellow it out, daring it to expose me.

I needn't have worried. It was plenty veiled enough for that dozing crowd just counting the minutes to the buffet lunch. The rest of the day was a round of receptions, everyone's family in tow, and I was flush with pride as various strangers praised my performance. To me it seemed the perfect rebuke to Paul and Jackie for daring to think that writing wasn't a life — though for their part they mostly just beamed. Perhaps because I finally had a future, for the short term anyway. A fellowship to Oxford had dropped from the sky about a week before. I didn't particularly want it — it seemed like the loneliest year imaginable, all nuns and snobs and greasy breakfasts — but at least I had something to answer when everyone asked what next.

Around midnight I tucked the family in at the Taft and wandered back to the college, grief-stricken that all of it was about to be over and nobody knew me for real. The courtyard rang with raucous singing and drunken laughter, seniors spilling out their windows. Better go find a party quick, I thought, and was trotting across the croquet lawn when I came upon Bill sitting quietly on a bench. Did I say how melancholy he looked sometimes? — though people tended not to see it, since he was the man with everything. I only saw it because of my own. That's how he looked now, grave and still and somehow responsible for all of us, as if he'd just stepped out of the Oval Office into the Rose Garden.

Bottles crashing about us, we agreed there wouldn't be any sleep in the college tonight. Bill had to be up at dawn to begin the muster of the senior class, which he would be leading in to graduation. "I think I'll go sleep at Elihu," he said. Then, like an afterthought: "You want to?"

Sure. And as we walked that way — I still trying to match his stride — I realized I was going to tell him I was queer. At the club we signed our names in the guest book, headed up to the dormitory, stripped to our shorts and climbed into facing beds. Bill had his own trepidations, about to leave for Hong Kong and a two-year stint with Yale-in-China. But he kept lobbing the conversation back to me: Where would *I* be in two years? He was giving me the opening, my last chance to come clean. And I blew it. I talked around and around it — my "problems" with women, how sick I was of being depressed, almost almost saying it — till he finally nodded off.

I never came half so close again to telling anyone, for another five years. Yet even as I watched him sleep, I promised myself I would write Bill a letter in China and tell him that way. He was the only man I'd ever loved without wanting, and I knew I could trust him not to judge me. Thus did I put off the severing reality of graduation, whose trumpets and battlefield logistics all the next day left hardly a chance to say goodbye. There was no last blood-brother moment, with Bill or anyone else. By mid-afternoon the campus was deserted, picked over by cleanup crews.

I don't remember ever being as numb as I was driving home with my parents that night, feeling as if college had never happened. Three days later, the Andover draft board turned down my deferral to go to Oxford, and the fellowship was withdrawn. I thought I was losing my mind, and this time not just in order to write a poem about it. Writhing in shame, I tracked down various deans and professors at their summer places, calling in every last favor. I worked days at the local bookstore, $3.50 an hour, reading everything in print about the war, to catch up on it before I got drafted.

About three weeks later, one of my summering deans came through. I could have a Carnegie Fellowship at Yale for a year, teaching a section of English 15 and taking a couple of courses at the graduate school. I groveled with relief. Then headed down to New Haven for the weekend to sign all the paperwork and get my teaching deferment locked in. The three weeks' panic had kept me from writing my queer declaration to Bill, but in the back of my mind I knew he'd be arriving in Hong Kong in mid-July. Once I got back from New Haven I'd do it, I told myself, beginning to compose the letter in my head. More of an apology than a declaration, but something at least.

I was staying the weekend in a guest suite at Jonathan Edwards. When I wasn't running around getting my fellowship in place, I'd sit in the courtyard brooding, wishing we never had to graduate at all. I couldn't believe 714 was no longer my room. It was as if I wanted them all to come back at the end of summer and rekindle the brotherhood — which was all in my head to begin with. Sunday morning, I took a mug of coffee and the *Times* out to the croquet lawn, trying to feel the place was still mine, even as the shuttered quiet mocked me, the dreaming towers indifferent to boys who wouldn't grow up.

I had to walk past the guard's office to get to the guest suite. The second-string watchman was glued to a baseball game on his portable black-and-white. He'd never have been allowed to goof off like that during term, I remember thinking with a proprietary scowl. Then he jutted his chin at me and said: "When he fell off that mountain, he didn't die. Not for a couple hours."

I thought he was drunk. "What're you talking about? *Who* didn't die?"

"Over there in China. The football player. Hilgendorf."

And I nodded, as if I already knew. Determined — I don't know why — to show no feeling as I made for the stairs. I would spend the rest of Sunday into Monday calling everyone in the class, bearer of bad tidings. Would tell it over and over: his first day in Hong Kong, a hike up to look at the city. Would go to Wisconsin for the funeral, the runt among the pallbearers. But never really cried, even when I finally got hold of Star in Bangkok, who knew too much already about those two hours he struggled not to die.

Eventually it got twisted up with a massive dose of self-dramatization, a version of events in which the wrong man had died—or was it that the Poet had survived to tell Lancelot's story? Theatrics instead of feelings. All I knew was, it became another excuse not to tell my own story. As usual, I missed the point of life outside the closet, that you had to seize it and waste no time, because Now was all there was. Instead, I closed another door. But that day in the empty college, when I learned there was no one to tell after all, that was the day of my real graduation. No more brothers in blood, and no more Idylls to sing.

Six

I CAN'T BELIEVE IT myself sometimes, how fresh the wounds of the deep past sting, how sharp the dry-eyed tears are even at this distance. The very act of remembering begins to resemble a phobic state — feeding on every missed chance, stuck forever in the place without doors. What's crazy about it is, I forget that I ever got out. For an hour or a day the pain wins. It throws a veil of amnesia over my real life, almost twenty years now since I took my first breath of freedom. And I know better than anyone what I wrestled from the darkness of my dead self: three times I've managed to love another man. My white-knuckle grip on happiness, hoarded against the gloating of my enemies, against the genocide by indifference that has buried alive a generation of my brothers.

In those lonely years of wrongheaded crushes, I used to ache for someone to know me all the way through, till the terrified boy in the closet was finally laid to rest. I realize now that I can't entirely shake him. His sorrows and his wasted time still ambush me, the old scars bleeding again, sometimes even when I'm laughing in my lover's arms. Or at least that's how it's felt as I've written these pages. Punchy with rage at how unnecessary it all was, the decade of being dead below the belt. Loathing myself for buying the hatemongers' lies and distortions. Queers can't bond, the shrinks informed us. It's not you, said the Romans, it's the act we despise. And you find somebody to love and prove them all wrong at last, and still the fury boils inside you because the liars made you grow up in a cage.

I understand exactly who I was destined to be, given my frozen state from twelve to twenty-five. Right about now I should be the graying head of an English department in a second-rate boys' school, say, in the Berkshires. The Mr. Chips lessons have long since become automatic, and his classroom patter reeks of ingratiation as he struggles to stay abreast of his post-literate students. Flattering all the Adonises the way Nindle did at Andover. Not that such a career is by definition soul-destroying, but for me the mere fact of the closet would turn it into a job from hell.

Asexual to a fault, too timid even to sweat. Of course I'd be master in one of the senior dorms — forming "special" friendships with the humpy ones, steeling myself to stay away from backrubs. And their parents would thank me at graduation for turning their boys into men, and I would slouch back to my bachelor quarters, always the one left behind. In the deafening summer silence I'd look out over the deserted campus, the green of the hills beyond, and the silent sobs would heave my shoulders. No relief till the pitch of midnight, and then my fumbling hands would guiltily lift the shoebox from the back of the closet. My stash of muscle porn, mail-ordered to a P.O. Box in Great Barrington. I jerk myself to sleep. The cry I make when I'm coming is like an animal caught in a trap, or a vampire's groan at the first light of day.

What steered me from the schoolmaster's fate was coming out. Something I couldn't do on my own: I had to meet Roger before I could take the final step. Yet once I opened the door to him, it felt as if I would never have to look back again. I'd shed the deadweight of Little Paul and his shut-up heart, and now all I had to do was love. Except that love turned out to be not simple at all. Or at least it would get more difficult the deeper it got, asking a kind of honesty that a life of hiding had left me unprepared to negotiate. For it turned out there were closets within the closet, and a lingering self-hatred that even the joy of connection couldn't solve. What love gives you is the courage to face the secrets you've kept from yourself, a reason to open the rest of the doors.

I decided to write this book because so many people told me, after reading *Borrowed Time*, that Roger and I appeared to have a perfect relationship, seamless and undefended, all the bullshit burned away. Especially when the darkness fell, and we had to fight for our dwindling patch of ground, no room to hedge and make excuses. Roger, being Roger, would have squirmed at the thought of being so idealized, even for love. But he knew as well as I did, holding on to the two of us as the tortures of AIDS came raining fire, that somewhere along the way our hearts had fused.

"But we're the same person," he announced with teasing delight one morning, half-blind in his second-last hospital bed. "When did that happen?"

I'm not sure. More remarkable still, how had it happened without either of us feeling smothered or trapped or compromised? And I started to think, if we really got that far and went that deep, then I ought to tell how impossible such happiness looked from the prison of twelve to twenty-five. Convinced I was the most unloved, the most unlovable man who'd ever lived. No window in my cell and no chance of release till I faced the truth that I was queer. That would be my theme, I thought: once I came out, the world was all windows. Suddenly night became day, and I could love like everyone else.

Well, yes and no. It's true I became a new man, with a vengeance, diving into the tribe and crowing my freedom and rhapsodizing my bond with Roger. But the baggage of the past wouldn't go away. I didn't understand how much of a struggle intimacy would be, that when things got tough, I'd shut down. Long after I thought I'd mastered putting *love* and *fuck* in the same sentence, the wild oats I hadn't sowed at twenty came back to mock me. I'd find myself envious of my own lovers, jealous of where they'd been before me, every previous kiss proof I would never catch up. As if I couldn't be happy with what I had now, shut out by my inexperience, my self-esteem too fragile. And I thought if they knew the truth about me — the lonely kid still locked inside, needy and misunderstood — they'd surely run away. When in fact it was I who kept the distance, miles away sometimes without ever leaving the bedroom, and the naked man beside me wondering why the cry I made when I came was so sad.

I'm better at it now, partly because I understand how much baggage everyone else is carrying. In this Puritan sinkhole of a culture, we don't teach children the uses of pleasure, and so they decide we are fools and go their own way, blindly. If we learned to drive as badly as we learn to make love, the roads would be nothing but wrecks. The erotic can be a window into the deepest core of feeling, but more and more doesn't get you there. It's a patch of ground that has to be reclaimed over and over, as much of a struggle for a ten years' marriage as the fumbling grope of a second date. And with all that, you still have to kiss a lot of frogs before you find a prince.

But I also see that it's not for everybody, the exalted dream of romance. To some people I'm just a love junkie. What I experience as being known to the core, appetite and aspiration fused, some queers think of as confinement. Doomed to resemble a bourgeois marriage, straight-identified to boot. I suspect there's a certain defensiveness there, a defiant need to be self-sufficient so nobody else can hurt you. Yet I have friends who don't feel alone being single, and I'm not counting those who've had their fill of kissing frogs. In any case I speak only for myself when it comes to love, careful not to insist that everyone belongs in pairs, or indeed that a couple constitutes the highest reach of earthly passion. The last thing I want to impose is the tyranny of an ideal, the way straight shrinks and the churches do, righteously pushing "traditional marriage."

For my part, I had enough of being solo before I was twenty-five to last me my next three lifetimes. If it's true that you have to love yourself before you can love someone else, then I suppose a certain self-regard must've kept me above water during my decade of drowning alone. But I think that in my case it was the other way — that I learned to love myself because someone else finally loved me. Seeing myself whole in another man's eyes, deeper than any mirror, and neither of us looking away because there's so much lost time to make up for.

If it's romantic mush, so be it. I kept my heart alive in the desert years by turning it into a valentine, holding on to the hope of every romantic cliché like wedding cake under a pillow. If you have to wait as long as I did, you either become an awful sentimentalist or die of disillusion. Somewhere deep inside the closet of lies, I clung to a misty-eyed Hollywood ending: Bette Davis waiting to meet Paul Henreid in *Now Voyager*. Wearing my picture hat with the veil, holding out for the man who would light his cigarette with mine. Happily I would connect one day, with three men who'd waited as long as I, none of them quite believing it would ever come to pass. There was no way we could have known we'd have to do it in combat gear — loving in the middle of all the dying. But not alone anymore, and none of us having to go to our graves thinking we'd missed the brass ring. *Love* and *fuck* in the same breath, even if it's your last.

So when I go back to being twenty-one, to that lost boy who's just buried his college hero, I beat him up in my head for not chucking it all to search for love. For making the worst kind of second choice by going after being a writer instead. Somehow I have to accept it that I couldn't do both, and forgive Little Paul for perfecting his art rather than his life. Going with the intellect instead of with the body. Hell-bent on cutting a romantic figure, I acted out this pop/tragic idea of the Lonely Poet in love with feeling — and not a glimmer of understanding that the pose was mostly a cover for being so conspicuously single.

I rented a cottage out by the beach, about twenty minutes from downtown New Haven, thinking I would teach my three classes a week at Yale and otherwise live in rapt seclusion. I don't know which leaked more, the tarpaper cabin by the Sound or my battered red Triumph. My father, who laid out a grand for the car — my graduation present — had pleaded with me to go with something more practical, by which he meant American. Being a fuel dealer himself, he was even more leery of the squat gas heater in the cottage. I was going to freeze my ass, he told me ruefully when the family came down to inspect my boho digs. My mother, aghast that I was living in a shack—how was this possible, and I with a Yale degree—hauled in a truckload of canned goods, as if I was about to be snowbound.

Who needed heat? All I required was rural quiet and my portable Olympia, for I was ready to work in earnest to finish the great American novel, Wallace Stegner be damned. It took me about two weeks to retype the pages I'd written since Nice. Then, just as the long October drizzle began to glower over Connecticut, I realized I didn't have anything to say. My two characters stubbornly wouldn't fall in love, and without that I had no story. It came to me with sinking dread that I'd made a terrible mistake holing up in a village that closed at dusk.

But I wouldn't admit it, telling myself the lonely silence was necessary if I really meant to be a writer. Knowing in my gut that if I didn't make it work as an artist, I was in *real* trouble, for I didn't like teaching at all. My freshmen in English 15 were mostly overgrown high-school jocks who thought literature was sissy stuff. We lurched from *Heart of Darkness* to *Crime and Punishment* to *Lear*, I identifying like mad with every tortured hero as I strained to make them see how profound it all was. To them it was just depressing and weird, and what did they have to know for the final? Only four years older than they and painfully out of my depth, I felt skewered by their boredom as they rolled their eyes at one another, all of us counting the minutes till the bell rang.

Then I'd drive back to my freezing cottage, never quite sure if the Triumph would make it, a quart of oil a day and great seeping stains wherever I parked. Because I couldn't face the blank page of my novel, stalled on a kiss like its author, I'd stop for a beer in various neighborhood taverns. Straight and sullen places where strangers were not welcome, the local drunks cold-shouldering me while I sat hopelessly waiting. For what? I suppose for someone to pick me up and take me away, though I'd chosen the opposite sort of place. Was I practicing for the night when I'd finally step into a gay bar, or trying to reassure myself that I could still pass for straight? I'm afraid I didn't belong anywhere, and the worst of it was, I accepted it, a fate I had no power to reverse.

I'd still never talked to an openly gay person about what it all meant beyond sex. I still thought of "them" as a dispersed race of exiles, all as scared of their shadows as I was. None of them ever connecting up except for a glancing encounter, hardly worth the attendant guilt or the endless troughs of nothing in between. I couldn't even conceptualize queers being friends, because queer only meant impossible sex. It would be another year before I went alone to an afternoon screening of *Boys in the Band* — one of six people in the theater, the others as furtive as I — before I had my first sight of homosexuals together. Which sent me reeling out in despair, frightened of all that bitter wit and self-flagellation. Today I understand that it told a savage truth about survival, but for me at twenty-two it confirmed my outsider status more corrosively than all the edicts of all the churches. Exiled by my own homophobia, I prefered a life of isolation to being one of "them."

But I also knew, instinctively, that I couldn't change. Unschooled in psychology — stubbornly bearing my pain without illumination because to speak it would have been so much worse — I didn't know any of the theories. Thus in my own crippled way I had no choice but to keep on looking in the wrong places for the thing I'd never even seen: two men in love and laughing. For that was the image in my head, though I'd never read it in any book or seen it in any movie. I'd fashioned it out of bits of dreams and the hurt that went with pining after straight men. Everything told me it couldn't exist, especially the media code of invisibility, where queers were spoken of only in the context of molesting Boy Scouts. Yet the vision of the laughing men dogged me and wouldn't be shaken, more insistent with every lonely month, every encounter that didn't quite happen. The searching became as compulsive as any insatiable need, till I sometimes thought I'd lost my mind — but I also think it kept me alive.

One day at sunset, I was walking on the fetid shore below the cottage, skipping stones. December, I guess, since there was an old couple stringing lights on their front porch facing the Sound. I looked up to see a man in a parka walking his dog in my direction. And as he came abreast of me, he cruised me — the sort of naked look, two parts dare to one part irony, that heretofore had forced my own eyes to the ground. But I gave him as good as he'd given, or thought I did, and looked away only to make sure no one was watching. Just the old folks doddering with the lights. When I looked back, the guy was half-running away, dragged by his panting retriever up the shingle to his car.

I was too shy to call out — standing frozen in my fireman's boots, thumbs hooked in my belt, trying to affect a swagger that would bring him back. As he bundled the dog in the car, he turned and gave me a smiling nod, then slung himself in and took off. By which time I'd dropped my cool and was running, stumbling up to the road and waving at his disappearing taillights, shouting "Wait!" But he was gone, the seniors on the porch staring at me, appalled by such a ruckus.

I came back every day at the same time for I don't know how long. Weeks anyway, till the January blast was so cold off the water, I had to huddle behind a rock. He never returned, and I'm not sure I could've said even then what he looked like. All that mattered was his carnal stare and my readiness to pick up on it. My useless waiting in the freezing cold will stand in nicely for a hundred other blind alleys I spent those next years lurking in. I frankly haven't the stomach to recall the rest; they're all the same anyway. Waiting numbly for a train in a place where there are no tracks.

Then back to that icehouse of a cabin, to heat up a tin for dinner. After which I'd deal out my cache of dirty pictures on the bedspread and give it a wank. Those washed-out shots of barely naked men, never in pairs and their dicks never hard, were state-of-the-art for New Haven. Acquired — with what an agony of stammering shame — from a rat-turd news and candy store out Whalley Avenue, whose Zorba-the-geek proprietor relished every second of my discomfort. I'd grab up *Time* and *Newsweek*, then ask him casually, oh-by-the-way: "Could I see what you've got behind the counter?" And he'd reach down and bring up the stack of manporn, such as it was, nudes without sex. I'd quick-flip through the pile, terrified someone from Yale would walk in. Never buying more than one stroke mag at a time so I wouldn't look too hungry.

Why didn't I go to New York and find me a proper porn shop where the real dirt was, pictures that would've bugged my eyes out? The question has no meaning. Might as well ask why I didn't go out and find myself a laughing man. Shame had so overtaken me that I searched out the least arousing images, not even capable of getting my dirt dirty. Whatever the self-punishing mechanism was, it insured defeat at every turn. When I looked in the mirror, I couldn't quite meet my own eyes, hating my looks the way I did. I spent hours wishing away my big French nose, as if all I wanted was to be even more invisible and anonymous.

My fantasies, even, were stunted. At the pitch of my nightly jerkoff, eyes locked on the centerfold muscleboy, I still hadn't any idea what I wanted to *do* with him. If I started thinking about exploring his body with my tongue, eating the sweat off, I'd block it fast. Judging myself with every stroke — not nice, not right, not healthy — as if each carnal image were being submitted to my personal Legion of Decency, more rabid than the Catholic. And if I started to play with a perv thought — order the kid around, maybe, and get his butt red — the censor in my head would order a total blackout. I'd leave the stash under the bed for a night or two, fearful that sex was getting out of hand. Sometimes, in a spasm of postcoital self-disgust, I'd throw out the whole pile, only to slink into Zorba's shop a few days later and start all over.

What must a self-respecting queer in 1992 make of such a hobbled life? I sound so thwarted and broken, it's a wonder I showed up at all to teach those freshmen, When we got to Kafka's *Metamorphosis* and they couldn't make head or tail of it, I remember thinking that all they had to do was look at me. I was as much of a cockroach as Gregor Samsa, only no one could see it. But that is part of the narcissism of self-hatred, the curious twisted pride that no one's managed to figure you out. Then the contempt for them, who can't see through your charm and your easy patter.

I expect the people whose paths I crossed on campus found me as witty and self-assured as ever, a courtier on automatic pilot. By midwinter I'd begun to avoid going home to the beach house, any excuse to keep me in town — roads too icy, too late to drive back. Several nights a week I'd crash at Elihu, insinuating myself among the new crop of seniors, playing the anarchist poet. I was neither a student nor really a teacher, only a hanger-on, so I had to sing for my supper. Most of the late-night bull sessions were stridently antiwar and anti-LBJ. Though I was still a political virgin, I made up in rhetoric for what I lacked in belief. Railing against the war became a kind of camouflage, a mask of noise that covered the speechless impotence of my stalled life.

Otherwise the 60's counter-culture had barely arrived at Yale, and only then with a few stragglers. In 1968 it still wore its J. Press tweeds, drooling around the silver spoon in its mouth; no long hair and no love beads. If you wanted to play The Doors, you'd better put on earphones. I fought the claustrophobia and the starchiness mostly by smoking dope late at night while the stereo rocked the beach house, but it wasn't the same as finding a comrade, let alone one with a dick. I'd even begun to mouth off about Yale's oppressive whiteness and ridiculous male prerogatives, but mostly as an act of solidarity with the seething ghetto that ringed that ivory tower, and with the mounting cry for co-education. It never crossed my mind that Yale — or the world — was oppressively *straight*, or that discrimination had anything to do with my being nowhere.

I don't recall how I got involved, but I agreed to do some tutoring for one of the campus do-good groups, a program designed to help inner-city kids get into college. All that winter we met in the basement of a church, three black girls and a Cuban boy, the only writing workshop I ever led. They were shy with me and terribly self-critical, but I found their stories and sketches amazingly rich. It may have been an excess of liberal guilt that made me so encouraging, yet these slices of poverty and strangled rage seemed truer to me by a long shot than the phony heterosexual novel lying stillborn in my typewriter.

Especially this one girl Emrald, whom I bit my white tongue not to tell that she was misspelling her name. Of all of them, she was the one who wanted to be a poet. The others were clear enough about why they were there — to get a recommendation on Yale stationery to slip in their college file. They teased me slyly about my overbred diction and fancy grammar. Not Emrald: she thought I hung the moon, and asked if we could keep meeting into the spring for a private tutorial in poetry.

Two afternoons a week, sitting cross-legged on the lawn in front of the library. She had more fire and grit than all my English 15 students put together, and her gaudy extravagant poems were a joy to listen to. I wooed her with my enthusiasm, so carried away I swore to Emrald she had a great future ahead of her. In part I was goading myself as much as her, since I'd started writing poems of my own again — still the perfect form for being vague about my closeted despair. And I needed Emrald's hero-worship, played to it shamelessly: a free spirit drunk on words, assuring her that poetry would save her life.

Till one day she awkwardly announced that she wouldn't be going to UConn next year after all. Not enough of a scholarship, and her mother was sick, three other kids to take care of — so Emrald was going to have to go to work for a while. I understood "for a while" meant forever, and I cringed at how ashamed she seemed, as if she'd let me down. She said she'd keep writing poems, though, "just for myself." And I felt like an ass for so glibly having promised her the moon, all because she'd flattered me. Poetry wasn't going to save Emrald's life at all. She was exactly who Virginia Woolf was talking about in *A Room of One's Own*: Shakespeare's sister, doomed to anonymity and silence. In Emrald's case, because poetry didn't get you out of the projects.

Somewhere in there, Martin Luther King got shot, and my own political education deepened into rage. If Emrald was my insight into the fate of the disenfranchised, she also showed me more than I wanted to know about my own place among the oppressor class, I and my fussy spelling. I took the easy way out: never taught writing again, so I wouldn't have to face giving any more false encouragement.

LOVE IT OR LEAVE IT had already started cropping up on redneck bumpers. When I went home to Andover, I spilled my vitriol about the dead soul of America and threatened to go to Canada if they drafted me into this fucking war. My father and uncles trumpeted at me for being unpatriotic, but my mother wasn't buying the political angle for a minute. Why was I so unhappy, she asked me over and over, infuriating me to apoplexy. *What were you doing with Kite?* was all I could hear in the question, which shows how that ancient guilt still clung to me like a Sphinx's curse. She felt helpless, I realize, was flailing to save her drowning son, but to me it was the razor edge of castration whenever she zeroed in. I'd be fulminating at the dinner table, battering them with images of napalmed children, and Jackie would wait till I stopped to take a breath. Then she'd ask, innocent as a child picking at a scab: What girls was I dating at Yale, and when was she going to meet Star?

My mother's subtext had to do with shaming me back to the straight and narrow by letting me know she had my number. Her dread at having produced a homo son was shaped by her own wounded narcissism: How could I do this to *her*, she always seemed to be saying.

I took defiant refuge in my sexlessness — "I'm not seeing *anyone!*" — flinging it into her face like a glove of honor. Oh, we were equally matched, neurosis-wise. I see now we shared some secret guilt about my brother, vying as to which of us didn't deserve to be walking if he couldn't. Shame was second nature to us both. Somehow we made a deal that avoiding the truth would make it go away. But the lie kept us from loving each other right, and the gulf would only widen, till I would feel my life was my mother's fault. Nothing could even begin to turn it around until I came out. And thus I wonder about so many gay men I've met since, pillars of the community, out to everyone else but Mom, who still refer to their lovers as something between a roommate and a valet. Just who is being protected here, and who thinks queer is wrong?

As for my relationship with Star, it was none of anyone's business, and no one would understand — any more than she and I did. She'd come back from Bangkok for her senior year at Wellesley, only to discover that the last thing a Wellesley senior was allowed to be was a widow. Still in shock from Bill's death, no one to talk to about it, she came down and stayed in the beach house with me, a weekend every month or so. To her I represented some kind of continuity with Bill, the non-jock side of him. For me, she was something else, the unattainable other, whose grief had brought her down into the kind of darkness I could see in.

We constituted no threat to each other, the physical not so much off-bounds as safely out of play. Star's body had shut down; mine had never started. Otherwise there were no restraints, no reason to fear each other's intensity. Before the year was over, we'd read every poem in English worth its salt, anything that put *love* and *death* in the same stanza. Yet it wasn't all gloom either, for that would've been to waste the only time either of us felt real, as opposed to the alienation and misery of the months between our visits. I think we both understood we diverted each other from pain, and that was enough. The gift of being able to ease pain for someone else — it proved to me that I was human, the first glimmer of self-worth I can recall.

We walked on the beach for hours, practically to Rhode Island, talking talking talking. No, I never told her I was gay, but perhaps for the first time in my life I didn't pretend I wasn't. Between us, it didn't resemble a lie, even if I couldn't say the word. And ever after I would measure intimacy against what Star and I achieved that year. And measured what a woman was, for this was the closest I'd come since Lois Bronner. I finally saw the lie in the stereotype which had it that fags hated women. And if one of those sick know-nothing bigotries was wrong, then maybe they all were.

In June I went to her Wellesley graduation, then drove her to New York to catch the plane that would take her to Asia for seven years. The last thing she told me was to keep on writing. Back in New Haven, relinquishing the beach house to the simpler tenants of summer, I told myself that was all I needed to accomplish that year — not to stop writing. The novel was dead in its tracks, but I had a sheaf of poems now, which I would read aloud at the drop of a hat. What I didn't have was a job for the fall, or any prospects either.

How I could have left myself so high and dry again, with my draft board hungering after my butt, I can't even begin to fathom. This boy didn't want a future, clearly, or at least made no attempt anymore to shape it. Hurting as much as I did, perhaps nothing seemed better than anything else. There was still a vague outstanding offer from the graduate English department, that I could sign on for the full embalming of a Ph.D. But the draft board, not into Literature as essential to the war effort, told me to prepare to be called on a week's notice for my induction physical. Curiously I don't remember any fear or drama in the waiting. I simply knew I wouldn't be going. Maybe Canada would be a more congenial place to find me a laughing man.

Meanwhile I'd landed a gig to teach at Andover's summer session — a six-week sleep-away camp for the brainy and over-privileged, but more to the point coed. For me the first time since seventh grade that I'd been thrown in with men and women together. The intern teachers were a hip and shaggy lot, unrelievedly counterculture, the eastern prep division of flower power. Most of them still had a year of college to go themselves, were therefore hardly committed to teaching. They treated this ivy-covered summer as a résumé lark, pairing off for steamy idylls in the staid old dorms once their charges were put to bed. After my lonely winter at the beach, the camaraderie touched me like a thaw of passion and laughter. Overnight I became a compulsive extrovert, manic as a dervish as I ran around becoming everyone's confidant. I cast myself as a cross between a troubadour and a cruise director, keeping the party going at all costs, knowing the induction notice might arrive any day.

Barefoot almost the whole six weeks, cavorting on the very lawns where I'd been so miserable in high school. Having seen *Bonnie and Clyde* four times, I wore a beaten-up slouch hat just like Clyde's and tie-dyed motley and jeans, a clatter of peace buttons across my heart. What I relished most of that summer was strolling downtown to the village, seeing old neighbors and former patrons of Nick's who knew me as the smiling good boy with A's. They looked at me, in my hippie garb, with horror and disgust, the Decline of Western Civilization suddenly plopped in their midst. It was the queerest I'd ever allowed myself to be, all theatrical gesture, my last painted dance before my rendezvous with the Selective Service.

Not that running around dressed like a third-string rock star translated into sexual freedom. The young Turk who ran the Art Studio course came crawling into my bed one night, and I went rigid and feigned sleep till he stopped the stroking and slunk away. A week later, as I closed up the Saturday coffeehouse, the dean of the summer faculty lingered to be my cleanup crew. Married and with five children, he seemed safely outside the changeling world of midsummer, unmoved by my pied-piper enthusiasm. But that night he declared I'd driven him mad and mauled me around the Drama Lab while I laughed him away. A new twist of perversity: I liked the idea of being pursued and felt superior saying no. Driving the dean to distraction was the closest I'd ever come to those Andover jocks who used to torture Nindle with their youth. It felt as good as I always thought it would.

By the time the summer term ended, with still no word from the draft board, I decided on a whim to drive to Chicago for the Democratic Convention. The trouble brewing in Mayor Daley's police state made it sound like just the place to take my hippie theatrics on the road. I made arrangements to stay with a Yalie

I'd met that year, a freshman whose anarchic humor matched my own and who always had a plentiful stash of high-octane smoke. I half-understood that John had a crush on me, and this half had a vague notion that the political heat at the barricades would fling us together like warriors in a foxhole.

We ended up at the wrong demonstration, nothing so bloody or glamorous as the melee in Grant Park. But we burned a dime-store flag and felt like budding revolutionaries, facing a line of Chicago cops who quivered with hate and called us faggots. I remember finding that strange, since most of the demonstrators were just generic students, nobody gay that I could tell. Apparently long hair was enough to make you a faggot in Chicago in '68. But I also felt a surge of something like pride — to have goaded the pigs to spew their poison, to know that I was its target and that they'd kill me as soon as look at me, just for being queer. I can't explain how liberating it was, not to feel battered by the hate but dizzyingly alive. And how it's only a short step from there to what my friend Mark Thompson says: "I eat their hate for breakfast."

For all our revolutionary fervor, John and I didn't quite make it to bed. There always seemed to be a group around us, shouting to be heard above the sound system — especially his friend Julia, a ringer for Louise Brooks and the woman who five years later would finally break the coma of my sexuality. John and I danced around instead, neither of us ready to make the move. A curious paradox here: hand in hand with the political rebellion of the age went a certain omnisexual freedom, but that meant you could sleep with anyone, not that you could be gay. We understood the politics of women and color and war, but gay had no political meaning, to us benighted Yalies anyway. Even with the cops calling us fags. It would take another year of evasions before John and I finally stumbled our way into bed — the day *The White Album* came out, I remember quite distinctly, though he swears it was Joni Mitchell.

I arrived back in Andover from Chicago on a Friday night, and Saturday morning found myself in a school bus bound for the Boston Navy Yard. I had marshaled letters from various doctors detailing my precious allergies to bees and penicillin, but they seemed like such pipsqueak excuses as we were herded in our Jockey shorts from indignity to indignity. A couple of the army doctors actually snickered at the bee letter. I knew and didn't know that push would come to shove in the psychological exam. They sat us down to fill out a Q&A, and there it was, point-blank: "Are you a homosexual?" I looked around guiltily, then checked YES. I remember thinking it had caused me so much pain, I might as well get something out of it for once.

I was called to a cubicle, where a nervous Navy intern shuffled my papers and wouldn't look me in the eye. "Have you tried to change?" he asked irritably, not mentioning the word. The question struck me as incredibly stupid and beside the point, but in case it was some kind of trick I answered sadly, "Yes — but I can't." I thought it made me sound more hopeless. He made a mark at the bottom of my form and waved a dismissive hand, still not looking at me. As I rose to go, I felt like laughing, to think that military policy was so tongue-tied and amateur. I was out of the war because men like this were too scared to talk about dick.

So the future I had no plans for had suddenly been restored to me, official notice of my 4-F status arriving three weeks later. I didn't have two nickels to rub together, having blown my summer savings getting to Chicago. Nevertheless, this was the moment I should've fled, as far as my restless heart could take me. Odd jobs and begging if need be, anything to put some distance between me and too much school. I couldn't have been more lonely, so I had nothing to lose by going alone. All I wanted to be was a poet. I'd never stopped dreaming of California since the day I left the Bronners' ranch. *Go*, I told myself.

And didn't. Instead I moved back into my old bedroom under the eaves on Stratford Road. Taking supper with Paul and Jackie as if I'd never left home, even keeping my mouth shut about the war so as not to bite the hand that was feeding me. I applied to a couple of teacher placement services that specialized in secondary schools, though by now it was September and every job was taken. Not to worry, the placement huckster assured me, someone would surely get sick before long, or a scandal would open a slot.

To pay for my keep, I painted the porches of my father's apartment house, then wallpapered the fetid hallways and lino-leumed a couple of kitchen floors. A handyman who was all thumbs, taking a break every twenty minutes to jot down a line or two of verse. I couldn't stand meeting people in the street, feeling like such a loser, as if they were thinking, at the sight of me in paint-spattered overalls: *But didn't he get all A's and go to Yale?* Self-important despite no self-esteem.

My brother has no memory of this time. He swears I never came back to live at home. But I remember him that autumn, freer than he'd ever been because he'd just copped his driver's license. My mother's '59 Falcon was fitted out with hand con-trols, and the house rang with their shouting matches as she and Bob argued about who'd put on the most mileage and who owed what for gas. My brother says it marked an incalculable change in his life, like going from black-and-white to color: that people's first thought when he drove up was not his disability. After sixteen years of being stared at, he was just somebody sitting in a car.

You couldn't mistake the joy in his face, the aliveness of him behind that wheel, almost as if he was dancing inside. What I didn't know then was that he and Brenda had already con-nected—the two shyest kids at Andover High, two Lauras from *The Glass Menagerie*. Once they had wheels, they probably went to every rickety drive-in in the county, no wheelchair access nec-essary, no compromise to love. I'm sure he wasn't keeping it a secret, not from me. *I* was keeping it secret, maybe because I was afraid to know he'd found himself the laughing friend. Even he who couldn't walk was dancing, while I still couldn't figure out how to put one foot after the other.

Three or four times in late September I was called for inter-views at various private schools, places off the beaten track in the Berkshires and Connecticut. Four brick buildings around a flagpole, barely accredited, ruled with an iron whim by the last of the desiccated spinsters. After a certain age you couldn't tell the schoolmasters from the schoolmistresses, since they both appeared to favor the drag of an army nun. But I begged like a dog for a biscuit, available I assured them on twenty-four hours' notice, silently praying that the bedridden third-form English master would croak so I could have the job.

I remember driving away from one of those schools in Vermont, horrified at the thought of being trapped there all winter. I got lost on the country roads, arched over by the delirious red and gold of October. I stopped beside a lake and walked all the way around it, slogging through marsh and then upland fields. I took off all my clothes and sat on a rock in the chilly sun. Trying to feel free, or daring, or something. And I suddenly threw back my head and screamed: "Somebody find me!"

It echoed across the fields and lost itself in the woods, the cry of an animal dying in a trap. Nobody came, of course, not even a hunter to put a bullet through my misery. I put my clothes back on and drove home in silence, to paint another porch and read in my room with half a heart. When the call came through from the Sutton Hill School, two days before my twenty-third birthday, I said yes before the dean could explain my duties or my salary. I would've mowed the lawns if he'd asked. Of course I would run a dorm of thirty-five boys, and forty-eight hundred a year was more than generous. I was on my way the next afternoon, books and stereo piled in the Triumph, thrilled to have something at all. But nagged by worry too, as I wound my way through the barrens of central Connecticut, wondering how anyone would ever find me here.

It felt more like a reform school than a prep school, and not just because it was run by retired colonels and defrocked monks. The grisly austerity of the place wasn't so much a matter of buildings that looked like barracks or tin-tray meals of prison swill, or even the lockup rules and the petty authoritarian discipline that passed for social graces. Smallness of mind was a given, an aridity of spirit that made schoolwork feel like memorizing a telephone directory. No, what lent the place the aura of a penal colony was the sense it gave you of being every kid's last chance — thrown out of every place else, or fallen through the cracks of a bad divorce, or dyslexic to the point of bed-wetting. A school full of gaping wounds in jacket and tie.

But *tough*. Never a snivel or whine, so thick was the hide of mere survival. Raw and arrogant, trusting no one, and yet underneath pathetically eager to please, squirming like puppies if you gave them a pat. I don't doubt they saw me as a pushover from the start. When I met my classes, they told me proudly how they'd hounded the man I replaced into early retirement. Old and slowed by minor strokes, he'd lose his train of thought in class. Then they'd talk crazy at him, answering questions he hadn't asked and pretending they were in algebra class, till he must have felt vaguely psychotic. In the winter they spread wet newspapers on his windshield, pouring sugar in his gas tank for good measure. "That old homo," they called him — laughing right in his face when he appeared one morning a few days after my arrival, expecting to teach his classes again. I led him out of the room as gently as I could. No one had bothered to tell him he'd been replaced.

A world of Darwinian savagery, like most places overrun by boys. I took on the task of civilizing them with the deepest trepidation, and I'm still not sure why it clicked between us. Perhaps because I was as hungry to be needed as any of them. Or because I couldn't hide how aghast I was at the idiot cruelties and humiliations dispensed by the ruling colonels. The boys came to see me as one of their own, counterculturally speaking, a long-haired older brother who could dance to their kind of music. I was too smart to be kissed off as another old homo. The sons of linoleum millionaires and Ford dealers, these kids had never met a poet before. It made me exotic, a clear outsider — and outside was exactly where they lived. They didn't mind me out-talking them with my torrent of language, because they needed words so urgently themselves, words to lance the boil of their speechless middle-class rage.

I taught about half the eleventh grade, my main task to prep them for their college boards. But I fed them anarchic poetry between every grammar drill, till they got the idea that literature could be as bad as they were. Discussion was unruly, to say the least, sometimes bringing the colonels running with hoses to quell the riot. To them my methods were very bad form, giving aid and comfort to the enemy, which was Lack of Discipline. Happily my department chairman was a man of infinite sweet temper, who gave me my head in scrapping the standard curriculum. So I played "Tommy" and Dylan in class, rocking the walls with relevance, reading comic books for myth, and Native American prayers. Standard late-60's featherhead stuff, but it worked, engaging the truant passion of my lost boys till they roared with feelings. In the process we scrapped *Julius Caesar*, but they never would've read that anyway. *Cliffs Notes* was their only window into the classics, and Cliff hadn't gotten to The Who yet.

Every night would find a gang of them sprawled in my room in the dorm, jostling for my attention and pushing the borders of Lights Out. Too lax a disciplinarian to rein them in and with no life of my own, I relished the street noise of theirs. The Oedipal death-duels with Mom and Dad, the suburban dreck of ranch-house hell in fifteen shades of beige, the parties over vacation that turned into week-long binges, an upper to counter every downer. They were serious druggies, a lot of these kids, whose parents' master bath was a veritable pharmacopoeia, ripe for skimming. They smiled with patronizing amusement when I told them to go easy. I smoked grass almost every night myself, secretly of course, but enough of a buzz that I felt like a hypocrite. I tried to advise them along the Athenian lines of moderation, but I was way out of my depth. Two of my proctors were bodybuilders who traded needles, alternating steroids and heroin. Saturday nights — I didn't learn this till they graduated — there was always some kid being rushed to the infirmary after drinking a bottle of Old Spice or a can of Sterno, usually on a dare.

But, then, they were always climbing too high and jumping off roofs. We had an expulsion nearly every week, one kid caught for what everyone did — a sort of ritual disappearance. This is not to say that Sutton Hill didn't have its share of dweebs and grinds, making their inchmeal way to college. I didn't ignore them either, recalling my own dim cocoon of high school. But the loose-knit gang of bad boys were the ones who fascinated me — cocky and suspicious, spoiled without ever being touched, and therefore having nothing to lose. I guess I thought it was my job to save them, not let them throw the future away. But I see now that mostly I wanted their good opinion. Wanted, if not to be in the gang, to be its coach, with a whistle around my neck, like a horny priest in Boys' Town.

I'd finally kick the last ones out after midnight, the cigarette smoke in my room thick as a Turkish bazaar. By Christmas there were three or four who always stayed till the end. My proctor Harry, with those tracks on his arms I managed not to see, would wander in from his hallway rounds of putting the dorm to bed. Steel, the hockey captain, was usually at the turntable, playing some rabid album he'd brought over, hissing of acid. Over the noise Robbins would read out snatches of Eliot and Rimbaud as he rooted among the books on my shelves. I didn't have a moment's privacy till I fell exhausted into bed, to rise at dawn so I could grade papers and do reports. But I wouldn't have dreamed of shortening those nightly bull sessions, where I never had to think how alone I was. Besides, with all of them so nakedly on the brink of manhood, hormones crackling in the smoky air, it seemed they might carry me over the goal line with them. Swept along in their outlaw wake.

Did they turn me on? I don't think I dared to consider the possibility, or I told myself that I had higher goals. It didn't *feel* sexual, but what did I really know about the displacements and disguises of desire? For once the hero worship was going the other way. They delighted in my intensity, the poet's dare that I could live on nothing but words. I'd ransack all my bookish past for tales to spin, translating every story into street talk they could understand, convinced I was giving them myths to live by. My own performance surfeited me—Merlin among the squires, whipping them up to knighthood. I didn't need the carnal. In those first months the only coming I did was in dreams. Otherwise I stood at the center of their collective male power, eye of the storm, smiling indulgently as they groaned for girls. It felt as if I could live all that vicariously. Better to be a voyeur than nothing, as long as we could keep meeting like this by campfire.

It was Greg who called me Merlin. More of a hanger-on than the others, not so aggressively courting trouble, and no leadership position in the gang. A voyeur himself, I would've said, as well as a bit too obvious in his flattery. Co-captain of the tennis team, but a team that always came in dead last in the league. Not much of a student either, though he talked a good line, especially when he was out to raise the grade on a paper from C to B. Greg got by on his insolent good looks—his insolence in general, I should say, a Holden Caulfield sneer for the boobies who ran Sutton Hill and a rich kid's certainty that he'd never fall very far down. And nobody hated his parents more, which was some kind of feat among so many blood-curdled sons. Greg laughed when the call came in that his mother had cancer; he bragged that he was one step closer to his inheritance.

Did *he* turn me on? Eventually, but not at first. Too self-absorbed, too eager to please, the smile too calculating. The laughing man I was looking for was older than I and working-class, certainly no preppie. So I considered myself immune to Greg's transparent need for attention. Always asking if we could talk in private, and then nothing much to say except he wanted to kill his father. Preppie histrionics. I tried not to give him too much time, sensing an emptiness no counselor could fill. If he wanted to hang out with me, he'd have to take his place among the group, no "special" relationship available. Seeing my coolness toward him, my preference for Harry and the others, with their armor of self-sufficiency and swagger, Greg resorted to melodrama. Unaccustomed to having his insolent charm spurned, he knew exactly how to raise the stakes.

One night I shooed my regulars out early—midterm grades due in the morning and a pile of papers to slash with red. They left pissing and moaning, no other place to have a smoke except out in the rain. I emptied the ashtrays and went around into the bedroom alcove to open a window for air. And there was Greg sprawled on my bed asleep, a book overturned beside him. I hadn't noticed him slip away from the group. It wasn't as if my bedroom was off-limits, since one or another of the gang was always walking through to take a leak in the bathroom. What was out-of-bounds was the hard-on throbbing in Greg's sweatpants.

I shook his shoulder to wake him. He moaned and stretched, arching his torso so as to thrust the bulge in my face. I looked the other way and said, "What're you doing in here?" But it came out bewildered rather than indignant, and anyway I knew in the pit of my gut what the answer was. Groggily he got to his feet, one hand idly scratching at his crotch. "Just fell asleep," he shrugged. "I guess I didn't want to be alone." And, as if there was nothing suggestive in that at all, he scooped up his book and shuffled out.

Leaving me with a pounding heart. More scared that he'd guessed my secret than affronted by his cheek. I don't know how the colonels would've handled it, there being no "it" you could put your finger on. No rule broken yet, just a dare. I suppose I should've confronted him on it, but that would have been to confront myself. I knew we were right in the heart of darkness: teacher molesting student, Dr. Rohmer's infamous backrubs at Andover. But I kept telling myself I hadn't done a thing, and anyway it was all my overactive imagination seeing this as a tease.

My behavior changed toward Greg. I became extra solicitous, including him more and more in the inner group—over the silent disapproval of the toughs. Not to seduce him, no, the opposite: trying to satisfy him with comradeship so he wouldn't resort anymore to the other. A rank delusion on my part, to imagine I could defuse his sexual power over me, or avoid for very long the hunger he had tapped into. I was already in quicksand, panicked that if Greg had my number sexually, then maybe they all did.

After the first volley, a week or two went by. Greg was feeling his oats, knowing he had my full attention, but keeping it neutral and kissing my ass, as if I was still on top. Then one night we were eight or ten around the campfire, *Fresh Cream* blaring from the speakers, and I watched as Greg stood up from the group and sauntered through the tie-dyed curtains into the alcove. Tensely I waited for him to return — five minutes, ten. Abruptly I ordered the other guys out, pleading a headache, terrified they knew what was waiting behind the curtain.

Which was what? A confrontation at last, I thought — no more games, leave me alone. I stepped into the alcove, resolute. Greg was sprawled as before, an arm across his face to hide the sleep he wasn't sleeping. Only this time his other hand stroked the bulge in his baggy shorts, no pretense of innocence now. "Greg, wake up," I ordered him sternly. No move, just the stroking. "You can't fall asleep in here," I stumbled on. "It doesn't look right."

But that wasn't really the issue, appearance's sake. The question was, did I want it? Tell him you don't want it, I prodded myself. Moving to the bed and shaking his shoulder again, bristling with offended propriety, lips pursed like a schoolmarm. "Get up," I said, "you have to leave." And again he raised the dare: pulling down the waist of his shorts so his dick sprang free, pumping it now in plain sight. "Greg, stop it." I tried not to look — tried to stay offended. His eyes were still shut, as if for him it wasn't even happening. I bent down to heave him bodily off the bed, ready to call in the colonels. He gripped the back of my neck, started to pull me down.

Until that second I'd been certain I was resisting, fate and temptation both. But denial is compulsion's middle name. It required no further force to bring me down. I bent and took him in my mouth. I'd come a long way to taste the sweat of this damnation, and knew, the moment I took the dare, that we'd never get out of this alive. He groaned and bucked his hips to drive in deeper. Behind the gritted teeth of the passion I heard the ripple of laughter, so one of us must have been having fun. Must've been Greg, for I was too busy feeding on sin and death to play.

He came in my mouth, but I never touched myself. I stayed crouched between his legs, my face against his pelvis, waiting to hear what we would say. He gave a yawning stretch and rolled away, keeping up the fiction that he'd been asleep the whole time. He shinnied back into his shorts and stood up. "G'night, Merlin," he said, grazing my shoulder with a soft comradely punch as he went away to sleep among the boys, this time for real.

And the pattern was set, once or twice a week for the next year. It was Greg who always chose the time — usually late at night but sometimes right off the tennis court, and once before breakfast, the morning of his history final. I stood ready to drop whatever I was doing to follow him through the flame-print curtains. The pretense of sleep soon fell away, but the encounters passed in wordless silence. Not that I continued to be such a passive player: usually whacking my own meat while I sucked him, even the occasional sixty-nine if Greg was in the mood. We didn't do any fucking, neither of us wanting to take it — a nod to the bullheaded macho of Sutton Hill, where a real man would rather die than submit.

I lived in thrall to Greg's unpredictable needs. This strange underground passion was the only thing of consequence that happened to me in my two years in reform school, and the only thing I think about in retrospect. If I am particular about the fact of being seduced — putting it all on him, the will and the dare and then the control — it doesn't mean I didn't feel the guilt. I racked myself with self-loathing, first to last, a shame that pursued me like the Furies from school to school till I finally bailed out of teaching entirely. For I had become the thing the heteros secretly believe about everyone gay — a predator, a recruiter, an indoctrinator of boys into acts of darkness. Sullying my mission as teacher and guide.

I don't think that now. Twenty years of listening to gay men recount their own adolescent seductions of older guys has put it all in a different light. Indeed, the guilt has abated enough to allow the memory finally to generate some heat. Still, I should've stopped it, if only because it never made me happy and shut me deeper into the closet. I thought I could separate the sex from an unbiased grade when I marked Greg's papers, but that was just another delusion, as foolish as thinking that somehow I'd found love. In fact I felt more dead inside with every month that passed.

No one at Sutton Hill would have guessed, given the manic compensating I did. Never saying no to any kid's need for extra help, doing somersaults in class to preserve my status as favorite teacher. Courtier to the rest of the faculty and their wives, charming the dead-eyed colonels till the bullets of suspicion melted in their guns. Always I could feel the hot breath of discovery at my back. Sometimes Greg would slip out of my room after midnight, disheveled and still half hard in his pants, and come face-to-face with one of the proctors prowling the halls. Naive wasn't part of the program here: there had to be guys who suspected. Especially when I began cutting back on the nightly bull sessions, keeping my space free for Greg.

But nobody ever called me on it, even by way of a third-hand rumor. Perhaps they averted their eyes from the obvious desperation in mine. They had almost as much invested as I in my role of anarchist poet. In any case I resolved every month or so to put an end to the madness, shutting my door to everyone including Greg, on the pretext of being seized by the inspiration to write. But it was like burning the porn at the beach house, a symbolic measure at best, and only leaving me hungrier to start all over. Greg understood better than I that his power increased exponentially after one of my chastity breaks. In the war game of our coupling, a broken will was the best turn-on.

Somewhere in there came the Stonewall riot, when the queers finally drew the line in the dirt and declared they'd had enough. The start of a revolution, only seventy miles from Sutton Hill, but it might as well have been another planet. I don't recall reading a word about it, nothing to do with me anyway. Despite being the school's most vociferous antiwar agitator, running the moratorium for the country towns that circled us, speaking at rallies on village greens, heckled by blue-collar patriots. What had any of that to do with a ragtag bunch of fairies throwing bottles in Greenwich Village? As usual, my leftist politics stopped at the closet door.

I convinced myself that a summer off would put the final period to Greg and me. He told me pointedly that he planned to date a girl back home who'd been writing him all year and was ready at last to put out. Though I was choked with jealousy at the prospect, I also felt relief: I hadn't turned him totally queer. I managed not to think about him much during the summer term at Andover — though he'd call me every week or so, full of that Merlin flattery, keeping his bases covered. And if I was so indifferent, why did I sell the leaky Triumph and go into hock to buy an Opel GT, the lemon of lemons that happened to be Greg's idea of a hot car?

Even so, I worked at being indifferent. Just before school resumed in September, I actually cruised a man in Harvard Square, right off the street. A few years older, more tentative even than I, but I steered us to a motel and wrestled him into bed — over his unconvincing protest that he wasn't really gay. I tried to cadge his phone number, but he balked at that and wouldn't take mine, agreeing only to meet me the next Friday night at Exit 14 off the Mass. Pike, about an hour's drive from Sutton Hill. He was there as promised at midnight, and we shacked up at Hojo's, from which I had to depart at six A.M. to go teach my Saturday classes. An arrangement so cumbersome it hardly seemed worth the brief vanilla sex we had, especially since after he came, he wouldn't talk about anything but his girlfriends. Nevertheless a bird in the hand, and for a month of Fridays he made me feel sufficiently independent that I was able to keep Greg at arm's length.

The only time I ever held the power there, and I could see how it ruffled Greg's feathers, though he affected indifference.

He'd come back from summer vacation more prickly and arrogant than ever, getting in pointless fights and alienating the gang leaders. When his grades started showing up C's and D's, as his dorm master I had to call him in for counseling. He shrilled with bitterness and contempt, how he hated Sutton Hill and everyone in it. All he wanted was to go back to public high school in New Jersey so he could be with Lisa, but his father wouldn't let him. I warned him he was jeopardizing his chances for college, and he shot back that I didn't give a fuck about him either, so stop pretending.

It stung me, the way it was meant to. And then the next Friday my commuter buddy didn't show at Exit 14, and I slept at Hojo's by myself, feeling ridiculous and unloved. Just a few nights later, Greg came in and asked for some time alone, spilling with tears that he and Lisa had been terrified she was pregnant. Finally she'd gotten her period, and now he wanted to beg forgiveness — please, would I help him get his grades up again? Of course I would. I recall the specific relief, that I was no longer included in his blanket contempt of the school, a second chance to prove my doggy faithfulness. So every night I'd give him an hour's tutoring, all across the board, from French to geometry. It only took a couple of weeks before I was sucking his dick again.

This time, it was his frustration at being apart from Lisa, longing to fuck her and have her go down on him. That age-old straight excuse for walking on the wild side: my girl's out of town. He'd stretch out on my bed and curse that he couldn't wait for the weekend. Which was my cue to do him, more wordless than the nights of feigning sleep and no reciprocation at all. Now and then, he'd grip my head and pump hard, groaning Lisa's name, but mostly he remained aloof and uninvolved. Leaving Merlin less and less satisfied, and doubly self-denied for being a stand-in for a girl. A Class-A porno fantasy, I realize — servicing straight men, being their pussy — but not my thing and nowhere close to the laughing man.

But I couldn't put my foot down. Greg's grades crept out of the danger zone, though he still talked incessantly about chucking it all for public school. The fights with his classmates and the sullen attitude continued, till I felt I was the only thing between him and disaster. And that meant keeping him serviced, no matter how debased it left me. Besides, if you hate yourself as I did and think you're a worthless shit, then shit is all you deserve.

It wasn't till Christmas break that I faced my own sense of violation. Specifically New Year's Eve, when I finally walked into the Blue Note in New Haven, having hurried by it in terror for five years now. I stood frozen in a corner, detached from the noisy partying, trying to accept it that this was where I belonged. I ended up with a guy in his fifties loaded on stingers. "You look like you just lost your best friend," he said by way of hello, leering sympathetically. I followed him home through a blizzard at two in the morning, and fucked him because he wanted so bad to ring in the New Year right. "You straight?" he asked me a couple of times while we did it. Which was a turn-on after all, that I could still pass and be as aloof as Greg.

He was out cold within a minute of coming. I put on his robe and walked around his apartment, snooping through his desk and closet to see what a queer's life looked like. I felt the old urge to bolt and disappear, and the sight of his vodka-bloated body sleeping it off didn't help matters. But I also had this tiny impulse of gratitude for his drunken good cheer and friendliness, taking me in off the street for New Year's so neither of us would be alone. And a certain reciprocal loyalty, almost tribal, that he shouldn't have to wake up New Year's Day and find me gone, as if it had all been a mirage. For better or worse this boozy guy was one of my own, and Greg most definitely wasn't.

So when they all came back to school a week later, I was more resolved than ever to keep our relationship strictly student/teacher, four feet on the floor. Hopelessly naive of me, to think I had the power to end it myself. I'd been much more on target the night it began a year before, when I knew we'd never get out of it in one piece. Greg came back from Christmas break in a towering bad temper of his own, so for the first few days we ignored each other. Then I found out from his roommate that he hadn't started his senior project, due at the end of January— shades of me and Tennyson. I confronted Greg and told him there wouldn't be any extensions, so he'd better get to work fast. And no, he couldn't have a weekend pass to go home and see Lisa. He gave me his surliest fuck-you look and turned and walked away.

Shell shock has blurred the sequence of events, but I went down to his room just before dinner, to reason with him and call a truce. He was lying on his bed staring at the ceiling. "Greg, let's talk about this, okay?" But he didn't answer, just shut his eyes and started rubbing his crotch. "Greg, don't do that. It's not going to solve anything." Then he was pulling down his pants, letting his hard dick out. We'd never done it in his room before. No locks on the student doors, and his roommate could've come walking in at any moment. Yet he seemed almost pitiful lying there, begging for it silently and driven back to the pose of sleep.

I sat on the bed beside him, feeling the rhythmic jerk of his body. "Greg, we have to talk," I nearly pleaded. His hand came up and gripped the back of my neck, just as on that first night of damnation. I remember thinking what the hell, one last time, as I leaned down to feed on him. The risk of discovery must've felt like the final dare, all my chips on a single throw. I hadn't even started sucking, just getting settled and feeling the throb of him in my throat—when he cuffed the side of my head and roughly pulled away.

"What the fuck are you doing?" he demanded shrilly. I didn't get it at first, my face going blank with bewilderment. Then he made a motion of spitting at me. "You faggot—get the fuck out of here."

Now it began to dawn on me: he was trying to end it by pretending we'd never played before. That today was the first time I'd ever taken him in my mouth, molesting him as he slept. I couldn't help the bitter mirthless laugh that broke from me. He yelled for me to leave, the door opened, the roommate came in. I stood up from the bed embarrassed, beating a hasty retreat.

I sat in my room with the lights off, frozen, staring at the brick wall we were about to hit. Within the hour Greg ran away without a pass, bound for New Jersey. I learned this at the ten o'clock check-in, from his terrified roommate. It was obvious that Greg had told him about my sex offense. I covered for Greg's being AWOL, writing him a pass after the fact, saying there'd been an emergency at home. But I was only spinning my wheels. I knew I'd just kissed off my teaching career, wondering if the mess about to break would involve the police.

At midnight Greg called from New Jersey. His parents were on vacation somewhere in the Caribbean, and he was sitting in his room with Lisa. I realized he wanted to make some kind of deal, but insisted he come back to school first. "No," he retorted, "I want to talk about what you did. Right now." And then he coldly accused me of trying to queer him while he slept, defying me to say it hadn't happened. In the background I could hear the rustle and click as he fumbled with a tape recorder. So he was going to play hardball, was he?

"Greg, what happened today isn't any different from what we've been doing for the last year. You ready to talk about *that*?"

He hung up. I felt white rage at his manipulation of the truth. Could taste the carnal longing of revenge: if I was going down, I would take him with me, a double drowning. I tore up the pass I'd written and called the dean, told him Greg had run away home. I added gravely that the boy was about to precipitate a scandal, and that I was prepared to take the consequences. I felt as cool then as a man smoking his final cig before a firing squad, a curious relief that there was no place left to hide. The dean was brisk, asking no details, saying only that he would get the head-master on it.

I had to wait two days for the final battle. Good soldier that I was, I went about all my weekend duties and graded the rest of my papers. I could tell the whole school had heard about the incident: so many gazes dropped, so many mumbled hellos as I passed. I figured I'd be out by Monday morning. Though I didn't exactly pack, I imagined myself getting in the car and driving to California. To lose myself in a pseudonym and a job at minimum wage, no forwarding address for the shame and failure I'd be living with forever.

Sunday at dusk, the headmaster called, summoning me to his office. I was putting on a tie for my execution when Harry knocked at my door. Haltingly he informed that all the students were on my side — which meant the gang had decided to cast in its lot with me and would keep the rest of the school in line, whether they liked it or not. I explained that there were no sides here. Greg and I had gotten too close, and the rules of fraternization had so unraveled that someone had to pay. I felt oddly noble saying this, getting deeper into the role of sacrificial victim.

Dr. Richards, the head, sat fatly behind his half-acre desk. We barely knew one another, since he spent most of his time fund-raising and left the daily running of things to the colonels. The younger faculty considered him borderline schizo, given his penchant for sudden rages — hurling boys down the stairs for insubordination, arbitrarily issuing school-wide punishments if no one stepped forward to confess a crime. He had a twitch in one cheek worthy of Captain Bligh and a strange habit of clutching a pair of handkerchiefs in his balled-up fists, to alleviate his sweaty palms. Reminded me of Nixon.

"You understand what he's accusing you of," asked Dr. Richards rhetorically, peering at Greg's file before him. I nodded. "He says you crept into his room while he was asleep and tried to . . . fellatio him." He grimaced at the mere idea. "Is that true?"

I swallowed hard. "No, it's not. We've been having a relationship since last winter — "

But he clearly wasn't listening. He tapped the folder and still wouldn't look at me, awkward as the Navy intern who couldn't say the word. "It was the same thing at his last school," Richards intoned. "He turned on a teacher who tried to help him. That's his pattern."

I was still a full step behind. Turned on the other teacher how? "But this is different," I said. Then realized with a rush that left me faint that there was a ray of daylight here, a crack in my fate. *Shut up*, I told myself.

"I'll take care of it, Paul. Why don't you wait in the dean's office?"

And he steered me out through the back door so I wouldn't have to face Greg and his parents in the outer office. I waited in the dean's anteroom, staring out at the winter dusk, feeling dirtier and more of a coward than I ever had in my life. But no less determined to survive. I heard later how Greg stuck to his story that nothing unnatural had happened before, that he'd had no clue to my deviance till I molested him two days ago. I told myself it was a moral draw: if he was going to lie about how many shots were fired, then let him take the bullet. I'd *tried* to tell the truth, hadn't I?

Well, not very hard. The dean came in to say it was all over—Greg had been expelled. He added with an avuncular hand on my shoulder that "This kind of thing happens to all bachelor teachers." Which kind of thing, I wondered, twisted affair or false accusation? He asked me to wait an hour before going back to the dorm, so Greg could clean out his stuff and be gone. When I returned, Harry and the others told me how Greg had exulted as he packed, bragging that he'd got exactly what he wanted, a ticket back to high school.

I was glad he went with such bravado. It made it easier for me to believe he'd gotten what he deserved. In the weeks that followed, my students bent backwards to convince me nothing had changed: I was still the best, and we were all well rid of the bad apple of Greg. But it was never the same for me at Sutton Hill—I was unable to shake the feeling of being watched, on permanent probation. I punished my dick by refusing to touch it, trying to starve it to death, so revolted was I by the moral chaos it had brought me to. The feeling of being unclean. And, under it all, a vague disappointment that the scandal had resolved itself without setting me loose. As if I had lost by being exonerated, having to stay now and prove myself, no chance to get in that car and drive till nobody knew me.

Somehow I got through the rest of the year. I smiled like a good little eunuch, toed the line and worked my butt off. There was never any question but that I would be leaving in June. I wasn't so self-flagellating as to want to stay and outlive the memory of the scandal, guarding my every move in case a limp wrist or a lingering look betrayed me. I sent out a raft of letters to colleges in Boston, appending a sheaf of my poems and asking if anyone needed a writer-in-residence. I wanted nothing further to do with boys or colonels or country life. Since I had no advanced degree — and no idea at all of the crowd of writers scrambling for slots in the brain hub of the Northeast — I quickly received a pile of form rejections.

But I was accustomed by now to having no future. Anyway I was still choking the water from my lungs after the near-drowning in January. I drifted from day to day, my public self as manic and animated as ever, the rest of the time lying on my bed, hearing that accusation over and over: "You faggot!" My vision of the laughing man died. No chance that love would find me now that I bore the stigma of pederast, invisible though it might be. I would be spending the rest of my life keeping it in my pants so it wouldn't destroy me. How old would I have to be, I wondered, before it hung juiceless between my legs, no more throttling me with the pain of desire? I felt old already, exhausted with life.

In April a group of my seniors placed high in the college sweepstakes — reflecting glory on me, who'd pushed them to go for the top. Their parents sent me champagne and gift certificates, praising me for making the difference and turning their boys into men. This had no effect on the fever of humiliation that held me in its grip. By then I had gotten myself embroiled in an ill-advised backstairs plot by the younger faculty to get rid of the headmaster, whose tyrannical rages had grown increasingly wacko. I let myself be volunteered to present the case to the Board of Trustees. A losing battle before I opened my mouth, since Dr. Richards informed them I was on probation after a sexual incident with a student.

I remember meeting Dr. Richards next day on the quad by

the flagpole. He stuck his jowly Nixon face in mine and hissed: "Your dirty little plot didn't work. And I should've canned your ass when I had the chance. I see now that that boy was telling the truth."

A day or two later, I couldn't get out of bed, short of breath and slightly delirious. By nightfall my fever was 106, and I thought I would die before morning, drowning in phlegm I couldn't cough up. Next morning the dean drove me over to Danbury Hospital, and I was diagnosed with bacterial pneumonia. Dicey, because I was allergic to so many antibiotics. While they played hit-or-miss with medication, I lay there through the whole last week of school, feeling as if I'd finally been expelled. Contagious, I wasn't allowed any visitors, except a brief half-hour when my parents drove down from Boston — required to suit up in masks and gowns and stay ten feet away from me. I had only one call from the school, to tell me my insurance didn't cover hospitalization.

Stuck in that narrow bed, barely breathing so as not to cough, I was a man without any prospects when the call came, out of the blue, from Canton Academy, a prep school just south of Boston. The chairman of their English department had taught with me for two summers at Andover and had been impressed by my fire and enthusiasm. He had no way of knowing the intervening winter had extinguished it. He offered me a job for the fall. Which I accepted without a second thought, just as I had at Sutton Hill. So much for my resolve to eschew the teaching of adolescent boys.

At least the place was coed, I told myself, and anyway I knew what situations to avoid. I explained to the man from Canton that I didn't want to be involved with running a dorm or coaching a sport, the subtext being: keep me away from too much naked boy. No problem: a poet was what they were looking for, not a babysitter or an aging jock. It sounded as if "free spirit" was part of the job description. With the barest regret I let go the fantasy of breaking loose and heading for California. Now I could hold my head up at the Sutton Hill graduation, bragging about my new job, for Canton was as close to the top of the heap as Sutton Hill was to the bottom. That day I was sure I could leave the shame behind, like the seniors flinging their mortarboards into the air, bound for a life free of colonels.

All I had to do was keep my secret — which wasn't just being gay now but the crimes of a practicing deviant. Weak from the bout with my lungs, I couldn't have been more disembodied as I made the pledge to live my new life without the physical. Being a poet would be enough. Besides, I didn't have any more chances. Fearful they would find out about Greg at Canton — or that Greg himself might track me down and expose me — I made no formal goodbyes, left no forwarding address. On a muggy June night I skulked away with all my belongings piled in the car, leaving without a trace the rural green of my two years' prison. Still locked in a schoolmaster's fate, no Merlin powers to change my life, unaware that my rights had been won by the brave queens of Stonewall. All I would have to do was not exist below the waist, and the future was mine.

Seven

THE FIRST YEAR AT CANTON I think all I did was recover from Sutton Hill. The contrast couldn't have been greater: the maximum-security bleakness of the one, the ivy Gothic and pillared neo-classical of the other. The sons and daughters of New England's aristocracy had been polished at Canton for generations, learning the Protestant ropes of austerity and service to others — that is, how to behave modest and just like folks before they came into their trust funds. They had summer homes with names like The Maples and Cliffedge, and grandmothers out of Jane Austen with diamonds as big as their rheumatoid knuckles. Not to confuse it with Exeter or Choate, oh no. Canton was smaller-scaled in every way, with special individual attention to every kid, and none of that vulgar high-poweredness.

There was a boys' side of the street and a girls' side, tensely separate centers of power like contiguous Baltic states. The boys were ruled by the supercilious bow-tied Mr. Phipps, so ingratiating he would shake hands with a coatrack. His opposite number across the street was the parched and flowerless Miss Jameson, last of the iron-gray headmistresses, whose mere presence in a room could lower the temperature till everyone's lips turned blue. To Miss Jameson life was not a cabaret. She and Mr. Phipps oversaw distinctly different faculties, the girls' rigorous teachers tending to see the boys' teachers as overgrown C students with no intellectual backbone. No wonder Miss Jameson had to be dragged kicking and screaming into full coeducation — which had been mixing boys and girls in class only for a couple of years when I arrived, and then only the top two grades. Otherwise the street that separated the sexes was as formidable as the Berlin Wall.

And indeed, the boys' faculty had its share of duds and duffers, men with names like Cabot Adams that sounded more like law firms than people. Gentlemen teachers, they were heavily trust-funded themselves, with summer places in Maine cheek by jowl with the aforementioned Mayflower aristocrats. Canton was very much about keeping things in the family, as tight in its way as a pack of Sicilian mobsters. The older ones had faces mapped with broken blood vessels, tribute to the Martinis they sloshed while grading papers and lab reports, a cocktail hour that stretched from five P.M. to unconsciousness. Meanwhile their wives poured tea at school functions till it came out of their ears.

I taught at Canton for six years, and there were those among the old guard who never once locked eyes with me or addressed me by name, so suspicious were they of "new blood." Yet there were a few marvelous others, crusty eccentrics who'd been there forever and never quite toed the line. Iconoclasts to the bone, who managed to kick the stuffiness out of the place. Archer Smith was their leader, with a deadpan gravel delivery worthy of Bogie, mangling the school's thin-lipped motto — Dare To Be True — by substituting Glue or a baby-talk Twue. Archer would enter a classroom, scowl at his charges and announce with a wagging finger, "Remember, gentlemen — five minutes' pleasure, a lifetime of repentance."

Archer and his raven-haired wife Felicia, who taught Spanish at the girls' school with a wild Flamenco beat, made room for me at their endless dinner table. A vast pot of paella on the stove fed us like the loaves and fishes. Always a spot for Mrs. Washburn, "Chips" to her friends, the dowager duchess of girls' English who suffered fools not at all, her Swiftian wit delivered in a bourbon-dry Virginia drawl. In the salons of Canton, literate meant civilized, and I quickly claimed a place among them because I'd been reading instead of living for years. Besides, I could always be counted on to "square a table," as the Brahmin hostesses went about the delicate business of finding bachelors to partner their widow friends at dinner.

And they all liked having a poet around. A role I took on with a new vengeance, keeping them laughing around the table with horror stories from Sutton Hill, otherwise smoldering with a passion I hoped was Byronic. I sported cowboy boots and various improbable hats, especially a wide-brimmed herder's number. Never a jacket and tie, to the silent chagrin of Mr. Phipps and the old guard. But if my major job was striking a pose as the renegade poet — renegade in a fenced-in yard — at least it got me sitting down to do the work.

It's all I really remember about my first two years among the gentry, writing poems late into the night, usually while puffing on a joint. I lived at the top of Upton House, a big-bosomed mansion with a carriageway and a sweeping drive lined with oaks. The house had been deeded to Canton by a spinster alumnus and broken up into faculty digs. I had the south garret, with dormer windows that looked away to the Blue Hills. There I hammered out my obscure and tortured quatrains, finishing a poem every three or four weeks, then papering my colleagues with copies. Since I didn't have to coach or oversee a dorm, I figured I'd better sing for my supper.

The students were a blessed relief after my scruffy and needy delinquents at Sutton Hill. Mostly they worked with dogged industry, too well-bred to misbehave. It took me a while before their silver-spoon insecurities oppressed me, and the presence of women among them was terrifically bracing. It also happened that I arrived at Canton in the autumn after the school had suffered a general strike. The previous spring a group of radical students and teachers had actually shut down classes for a week. In protest of the war, as I recall, though a lot of mud was slung as well about Canton's world of white privilege, the moat of indifference that separated the school's green suburb from the Dorchester ghetto. Most of the revolutionaries had graduated in

June, but a truculent contingent of seniors remained, sticking it to the authorities wherever they could.

The school writhed in conflicted feelings — dauntless in its defense of free speech, pained at the specter of disrespect and anarchy. Meanwhile the last of the radicals gathered around the school paper, hitherto a gung-ho mix of team standings and satire bland as oatmeal. The new editors meant to change all that, firing up to expose the vast hypocrisies of preppie life. I'd been appointed faculty adviser, so it was left to me to oversee and shape the tantrums. Not that the end product ever seemed very hard-hitting, just a new and more self-righteous form of blandness, but we redesigned it bolder and threw out the old staid masthead. What had been called for eighty years *The Green and Blue* — the school's colors — was now untitled, strictly downtown and underground in tone. The old guard were suitably apoplectic and shunned me even more.

Fine by me. My rad status kept me from having to show up at functions where tea was poured. I played hooky from faculty meetings, and I avoided getting too close to any students — boys anyway. The senior girls were safe, and more open than the boys to the dazzle of poetry and its wells of feeling. It seemed a natural thing for them to have a crush on the bard in residence — the next step after their raptures over horses. Besides, as the savvier ones told me later, they knew I was queer even if I didn't. Queer was part of the romance.

But ever unspoken. In my new life in Boston I assumed my secret was as locked as my determination not to act on it. Poet-not-gay was how I self-advertised, oblivious to the fact that other people didn't bother with the distinction. Because most of them, liberated women especially, didn't have a problem with gay in 1971. They gave me chance after chance to talk about it, but if I didn't want to — well hey, that was my choice. Thus not-gay became my own custom-made suit of emperor's new clothes, the cut fooling no one but myself.

And, having given up the search for the laughing man, convinced I could sublimate my deviance into verse, the sort of relationship that drew me most was the "feeling" sort with women. All Platonic, but no holds barred otherwise. A refinement of the courtier dance I'd been waltzing since junior high, with an existential spin of what's-it-all-about that echoed my long walks on the beach with Star. I was a master of the life sigh, and I knew that women responded to it. Especially those who were waking up to the piggishness of unliberated men, for whom feeling was anathema.

My deepest confidante was Eleanor, wife of my department chairman, the one to whom I poured my soul if not the whole truth. Eleanor and Hugh were my downstairs neighbors in the drafty mansion — to my mind the effortlessly perfect couple, reeking sophistication like French coffee. Or was I so lavish in praising them because they took me in all the time? Underneath the mantle of the poet I was a stray dog with quivering tail, always out for scraps. I spent *hours* every day with Eleanor, perched on a stool in her kitchen while she cooked, picking up her kids' toys, anything to keep talking and not be alone. Eleanor was doing a major avoidance number of her own, not finishing her dissertation. I don't recall what we talked about, except she was so encouraging about my destiny as a writer. I was very big on destiny at the time, a latter-day "Beast in the Jungle." Mostly I was grateful not to be asked about the disparity between my swooning passion for Art and my curious celibacy.

Two afternoons a week I raced up Route 128 to Chestnut Hill, where I had a part-time gig at a women's junior college. This one was in a vast stone house built by a robber baron whose wife had left him sonless. I swear, there's a sermon in every mansion in New England, the vainglory and the failed dream — all that's left of the second-hand castles of men. I met my creative writing classes in the grooms' mahogany parlor above the stables. I remember the young women of Chestnut Hill as achingly lovely, liquid as models when they moved, and shiny-haired, thoroughbreds themselves. They'd come to this marginal finishing school because the only A they'd ever received was for being pretty. To them writing was a decorative hobby like making silk flowers, as they dotted their *i*'s with circles and groped for Hall-mark sentiments. Meanwhile they all had serious boyfriends and no time for crushes on poets, treating me as a sort of exotic pet. I rather liked being petted by them, though feeling more than usual like a eunuch in a harem.

And after those classes in the stable, I'd drive up the street to Myra Golden's house. Myra was the mother of one of the gang-leaders at Sutton Hill, who'd had me down for spring vacation in Florida after the Greg affair exploded. We'd hit it off in her cabana at the Surf Club in Lauderdale, where I became the per-fect escort when her husband was on the road. Ash-blond and Vogue stunning, Myra at forty-five had just woken up to an empty nest, her three kids off to college. With the husband al-ways away on business — a traveling girlfriend in tow, it turned out — Myra had no one to share a Chivas with at sundown. Ex-cept me, on Tuesdays and Thursdays. She'd bitch about being trapped in a gilded cage in Chestnut Hill, a twenty-eight-room house where no lights burned except in the den and her bed-room. And the scotch would blur with the Valium, till Myra was weeping for her beauty about to crumble, and that was my cue to reassure her that she was still a knockout. Then the maid would serve me dinner on a TV table while Myra went up to take a Seconal, and a half-hour later I'd be summoned up, to hold her while she fell asleep.

I don't know what the stages were that brought us to such a place — a sort of neurotic intimacy, a torrid affair without the sex. But I felt unbearably worldly, slipping between those Porthault sheets and taking Myra in my arms. She'd purr and whimper against me, telling me I was the only man who — what? Under-stood her? Made her feel safe? I can't remember the exact terms of our delusion, as Myra slurred into unconsciousness. This was what it must feel like for straight people, I thought, falling asleep in their vast suburban beds. Thus did I try on the role of husband and protector, another new suit for the emperor.

Eleanor and Myra constituted the poles of my intensities with women. They weren't all so bizarrely co-dependent as

Myra, but I clearly had a thing for married ones. Call it an instinct for empathy, which would be my main qualification for my upcoming career change. It was a trait I shared most notably with César, the man who became my first real friend — no, more than that, my blood brother for the next fifteen years. César taught languages at a school about an hour south of Canton, in a sleepy harbor lined with shingle-style palazzos, another enclave of summer millionaires. César had landed there after a dozen years of voyaging — born in Uruguay, lived in France, traveled everywhere. He was fluent in four tongues, and when we started laughing together in the fall of '70 he'd just returned from a four-month trek overland, Paris to China. Sleeping with lepers in railroad stations, outrunning bandits, bribing his way into various Holies of Holies from the Vale of Kashmir to Singapore.

And then, all through the winter, he dined out on the stories, riveting the tables of the richly divorced and widowed around the harbor — just as I did at Canton, acting the poet. In fact we made a terrific tag-team match when I'd visit overnight, a pair of raconteurs who played off each other wonderfully. César was the single most social animal I ever met, with a Proustian appreciation of the chess moves of a party. In conversation he could keep a dozen balls in the air, his juggling punctuated by irrepressible laughter and gasps of fascination. He made the dreariest people feel sparkling and witty within the magic circle of his charm, and was smooth as a gigolo when it came to drawing out the coquette in an older woman. But somehow never glib or fatuous, too much of an anarchist for that, his noisy opinions too hard-won. He managed to pontificate — especially about the foibles of Americans — without sounding judgmental. He was a travelogue in 3-D, circumnavigating the civilized world, and if you happened to engage his florid attention, then you became a pin on the map of his itinerary. And considered yourself blessed to be part of so momentous an expedition.

He was smothered with invitations, as students and townspeople jockeyed to be in his company. He used to say he'd have to eat dinner in shifts, three times a night, to accommodate all the demands. Yet he always made time for me alone, dropping all else when I came down to visit. And though we often squared a table together, providing anchor for *two* widows, César and I never laughed our way into bed. I knew he was queer and could see he knew the same about me, who usually ran at the first suspicion on either side. Yet I wouldn't let us talk about it — my choice definitely, not his, just as it was my decision not to let our friendship flower into love. César would've gone that way in a minute, but staunchly kept his feelings to himself, permitting me to define how far we would go. Not far enough, not soon enough. But at least I had a gay friend now, even if it dared not speak its name out loud.

Late at night after the parties, after we dished the guests, we'd sit by the fire in his fisherman's shack and trade our pasts. We'd both been the loneliest kids on the block growing up, practically mute from not fitting in, though no one would have known it now to see our extravagant public selves. He told me his deepest secret, that he'd been raped by the gardener when he was six. By the time he lurched into puberty, he weighed more than three hundred pounds, his only moving part the hand that stuffed his face. He never had anything close to a friend, only children who laughed at him. When he was eighteen, he decided he had to go to Europe, and lost a hundred and fifty pounds so they wouldn't laugh at him there. *The other César*, he called the lost weight, a demon exorcised. He still had the rolls of deflated skin around his torso to prove it, which made him proud rather than embarrassed.

He also had the largest, most expressive mouth I ever saw, a wind cave of languages. In one eye there was a flaw, a black dot by the iris, which made his gaze more penetrating but also unbearably poignant, like a visible bruise on the soul. And I could do no wrong in those eyes. I felt helpless to give him back the love he needed — deserved — even as I drank in his constant delight and appreciation of me. He settled for the intimacy without the sex, a bargain I would be making all too often in the next few years, as I strung along those who wanted to love me. They could have everything else, but not my body. A fanatical purity that had no higher purpose than fear: if I did it with someone I cared about, I might have to give up the shame and self-hatred, which was the only place I could hide. Besides, how would I ever get out of such an arrangement, once I got in?

To experience love as claustrophobia. In such a twisted paradigm lies the sick legacy of a lifetime in the closet. I couldn't see myself honestly enough to understand it was the closet making me clutch for air, struggling to breathe, not César's laughing embraces. So I toyed with his great heart, feeling guilty and paralyzed as I stiffly crossed my legs and kept my buttons buttoned. Not that he ever upbraided me for it or held the slightest grudge. Having survived the Benno Blimpie torments of his youth, César had no more time for resentment of his chosen life than he did for self-pity. If I wouldn't be his great love, then he'd just make do with a great friend. It was he who made all the compromises, smoothing the fur of my fear so I wouldn't run away, and teaching me in the process what it meant to love without boundaries.

And how successful was my commitment to a life without the pleasures of the flesh? For those first two years in Boston the eclipse was nearly total. Sometimes after midnight, wired from writing dickless verse, I'd drive the twenty-five minutes into downtown and browse the one dirty bookstore I knew. Its queer pornucopia didn't represent much of an advance erotically from the under-the-counter stuff I used to buy in New Haven. But now at least I'd half-cruise the other skulking patrons, older men in trenchcoats from the suburbs, who seemed as lost as I.

Once, though, a burly grinning fellow about my own age found the guilty furtiveness of the place downright silly. He winked and nudged me, pointing to various gaudy members as he flipped the smudgy pages. It was the snicker that drew me more than anything, and before I knew it he'd proposed to follow me home. Where of course my major concern was not to appear inexperienced — a dread that I might not get an A, the self-doubt grading my every performance for years. But he merrily took the lead and soon had me laughing as smutty as he, pouring honey on my dick for lubrication. Leaving me with the messiest sheets since infancy, and making me want to hang them out the window like a banner. He even gave me his number as he lurched off into the night. But my dour and hopeless morning brain couldn't cope, and I let the number lie there on my desk till the fuck-buddy statute of limitations had passed.

Over New Year's I was in Puerto Rico visiting a family I knew from Sutton Hill — the fifth wheel at every gathering, mournful in the tropics, and not a clue where men went to meet in San Juan. At midnight on the thirty-first, wandering out of a party and standing alone on a terrace above the lights of the old city, I resolved not to run away the next time somebody wanted me. Then, in the crush of flying home the following day, I was bumped to first class, where the man with the cordovan tan beside me set about getting me drunk on champagne. A college administrator at Tufts, Armenian and opulent, with rings on four fingers, he didn't so much as drop a stitch as he bragged about the men he'd done in the islands. No hedging at all: he assumed I was queer the moment I sat down. Which for once didn't send me into twitches of paranoia, my New Year's resolution being so fresh.

Of course I couldn't keep up with his tally of tricks, but tried to maintain a certain cool unshockability as he reeled off the gritty details. Somewhere over the Carolinas he nodded toward the bathroom beyond the galley: "You ever done it in one of those?" I shook my head, speechless at last, as he spilled the gaudy story. I'd never really heard a gay man strut his satyr's stuff before. I don't recall if he proposed that we do the bathroom thing ourselves, since by then I was woozy and nodding off. Waking up to find he'd put a blanket over both our laps and pulled my dick out of my pants. I was too nonplused to protest as he guided my hand to his own throbbing love muscle. I stared around the cabin with a thrill of terror, sure we would be arrested but too turned on to stop.

His telephone number I kept, and a few times went to his high-rise in Charles River Park for a wank. I liked his gaudiness and his dirty mouth, but didn't at all appreciate his grilling me about my closeted life. No matter how evasive I was, or how fast I disappeared after I came, he wouldn't let it rest. Who were my gay friends? What bars did I go to? Who knew? Things were turning problematic anyway, since he wanted to fuck me and I stubbornly refused. I think he assumed The Lady Doth Protest Too Much, which was probably true enough, but I only grew more defiant the more he pushed. *I'm not that gay*, I remember thinking self-righteously, still all mixed up about compromising my manhood if I took it up the bum. The last stand of I'm-just-dabbling-at-this: the sphincter clenched like a rosebud.

The final time I saw him was in the spring, arriving late on a Saturday night, lured by a shipment of dirty pictures he'd just received. I walked in on the coffee end of a dinner party he hadn't bothered to mention, seven or eight men in their thirties who gave me the laser once-over when I pulled up a chair. They couldn't have been more civilized and welcoming, but I squirmed at the proprietary hovering of my Armenian buddy, who puffed with pride as he showed me off. A couple of his guests rolled their eyes gleefully, as if to congratulate him on his latest conquest. I went icy cold inside, dismissing them all as Boys in the Band, nothing to do with me.

And when they all left, we had our final go-round — no kissing, no fucking, yeah I guess you can suck it. Perhaps he got off on my playing so hard to get, so accustomed himself to having what he wanted. I never went back, and hung up when he called: I didn't want an older gay brother, however well-intentioned, leading me out of the closeted dark. He continued to send me Christmas cards for years afterwards, big religious jobs with flocking and glitter on the Three Kings' robes. And a scrawl of a note inside about his latest cruise of the islands, always ending with some variation of *I hope you're happy*. Meaning out.

Was I happy? Busy at least, surrounded by friends who gave me strokes for being a poet. The squirming shame of Greg began to fade. In 1971 I didn't think of myself as dead inside; I thought of myself as reasonably happy and successful, now that I was writing poetry for real. When the pain and loneliness in my life surfaced, I made contorted images of it, every poem a closet of words. But I have to face honestly the disparity between my experience then and my memory now, because from August '71 on, there's evidence in my own hand — a journal.

A journal so numbly unconscious, it takes my breath away to reread it today. Not to mention the prose style, which favors sunsets over self-analysis, banal as the silky bouquets of my girls in Chestnut Hill. How fast the Paul of '71 would've run from a man like me, who's a hundred times more insistent about everyone coming out than the Armenian ever was. No, I cannot blame "the other Paul" for keeping his distance, staying out of my reach emotionally, given how harshly I feel toward him now when I read his white-bread pleasantries and chameleon accommodations.

But before I start challenging the Chronicle, one other memory intrudes from that first year at Canton — a clap of recognition that left me in shudders. School was already out, and the faculty hanging around to do the slopwork of final reports and meetings. The June weather steamed like a sauna, especially under the eaves of Upton House. I was lying naked in a bath of sweat, trying to nap, when suddenly I smelled smoke. I jumped up sniffing, tracking it to the connecting door between my apartment and the north garret, which was occupied by a ghostly bachelor in his sixties. A liver-spotted classicist who'd been there forever, lips so pursed you figured he had to be fed by IV, and so appalled by the school's new blood that he stared at the ground whenever we crossed paths.

"Allston," I called, rapping the door between our places. No answer. Terrified of fire, I didn't think, just pushed the door open and stumbled in. The smoke was thicker. I darted about the suite of rooms, then realized the smoke was coming in through an open window, from a barbecue on the ground floor. False alarm. But as I turned to go, I looked at the wall above Allston's bed, and it was covered with photographs in dime-store frames. Allston and his special boys, grinning shoulder to shoulder in tennis whites, some of the pictures cracked and yellow and reaching back to the 40's. So long ago that Allston was my age. On the bedside table, a triple frame with three pictures of the same boy, from puberty to college. Cringing, I realized with a shock that I was naked and ran back into my own place, shutting the door on that sad museum. But the feeling wouldn't go away that I had seen the very face of death-in-life, a melancholy eros that had no expression except the mute longing of self-denial.

That summer I taught at Andover again, having inherited the theater course. With a troupe of twenty students we put on a high-toned repertory of plays, Lorca to Kopit, the intellectual headiness designed to hide the amateur theatrics. Glad of the break from grading papers, I relished wearing an impresario's cloak. Such a mercurial role let me swing from brooding intensity to high camp without fear of being labeled queer. And the bounded world of summer school itself was not unlike the theater — the sudden family, the backstage politics, the frantic busyness, the in-jokes. I let myself play the free spirit in a near frenzy of acting out, a true character, madly hyper and keeping everyone dancing.

In that heightened atmosphere every friendship had the quality of a shipboard romance. I spent most of my time in groups, playing the jester, and made no move to single anyone out. But found myself more and more in the company of a brainy young woman just out of Smith, the teaching assistant in the painting course, whose studios happened to abut on the main stage. Alida was a dusky redhead from an old Mississippi plantation family, the latter long gone with the wind. She had the ripe curves of a Rubens Diana and floated when she walked, a curious paradox of earthy laughter and a fragility like spun glass. As passionate about painting as I was about poetry, and struggling as much as I to stop getting A's and do something new.

Alida seemed to understand the rules — that I wasn't available for serious boy/girl stuff, that I'd staked a ground above all that. Thus we would keep it in the realm of loftier feelings and claim our intensity there, poet and painter equally matched.

I was the only one who bought this bullshit, and didn't notice Alida's growing infatuation. Besides, she seemed so self-possessed and self-sufficient — but that was a screen too, thrown up so I wouldn't run away.

Not that the psychodynamics were clear to us at the time. Mostly we laughed the summer away, grasshoppers rather than ants, no threat to each other and wildly productive. When Alida heard that I stole a couple of hours every day to sit under a chestnut tree and write, she asked if she could bring her easel and join me — then asked if she could paint me. Or maybe I was the one who asked, since my narcissism was operating at full volume that summer. In a *folie à deux* it's always hard to reconstruct how the maze gets built. Before you stop to think, you've taken so many turns through so many hedges that everywhere you look is green, and anyway there's no going back.

So Alida painted my portrait under the tree while I scribbled lines on a pad beside me. We couldn't stop talking either — how to live a life that worked and still be an artist, how not to compromise. Alida was going to Princeton in the fall, to start the slog through a Ph.D. in art history, somehow trapped by all her A's into having no other choice. Now she realized how angry she was at the spinster academics at Smith, how they'd pushed her out of the studio and into the library. You can paint on the side, they told her patronizingly, wincing at her work because it was so . . . figurative. Color-field maybe they would've allowed, even Pop, but the human figure just wouldn't do.

This touched a chord in me that hadn't stopped echoing since the day I stumbled into Allston's room and stared at his wall of boys. "I have to get out of teaching," I blurted out, "or I'll asphyxiate."

How did we get from there to starting a business together? It seemed more idle than anything, playing out our fantasies of where we wanted to be instead, like tracing faces in the summer clouds. Alida said she'd always wanted to be an interior decorator: to spend other people's money on beautiful things, plundering the antiquaries of Europe, putting it all together like a stage set and then walking away. The walking away was very important; that was the whole point of the life of the high Bohemian, dabbling in bourgeois pleasures without getting caught. Taking the fat commissions and buying that idyllic farm in Provence with a barn for a studio, thus beating the swords of the rich into ploughshares.

There was a flaw in this logic a mile wide, the assumption that one could keep one's hands from getting dirty in the process. If you help to construct the suburban hell, you may forfeit the road map out. But at the time all I wanted to do was encourage Alida, praising her for her taste and sophistication, sure she could make a go of it. My own participation seemed hardly more than a playful afterthought. "I love old houses," I said, "and old things. Maybe I could do consulting work for you. Like for restorations — you know, the structural stuff."

The butch stuff, I guess I meant. It makes no more sense now than it did then, the balmiest decision of my life based on nothing. I had not in fact ever pulled apart an old house or restored a blessed thing. I couldn't have told you the difference between Greek Revival and Regency — still can't. But Alida jumped at my offer, envisioning us as a company of the highest class, bringing old beauty out of the ruins, working with ancient craftsmen. Reality played no part in our speculations. We awarded ourselves the White House contract, the Williamsburg account. No job too grand.

In other words, the sort of pipe-dreaming that dies with the summer light as the days grow shorter. It was too late for Alida to pull out of Princeton, the first semester already paid in advance, and I had my double teaching job to go back to in September. Even so, we left it that we were open for business if anything dropped in our laps, and I started telling friends I was a part-time designer now. It was a company without so much as a pencil to its name, but why get hung up on the details? Though various jaws dropped when I made the announcement, my friends all hastened to support me. In retrospect, I think that so many of them were waiting for me to get it over with and come out, they hoped this new persona would help me blow the hinges on the closet door.

It had everything to do with the closet, that much is clear. Somewhere inside me I was clutching at the thought of finding a place where gay was acceptable, where it didn't have to hide itself in lies and vicarious longing. To leave the world of furtiveness and go where the laughing men were, and maybe find one of my own at last. The only thing I knew about decorating was that it was populated with queers. In the end my self-hatred foiled me even there, for once I got into the party, I clutched. I felt smothered by the effeteness and the naked cruising looks, which only made me stick closer to Alida. Putting out the vibe that we were a couple so the queers would leave me alone.

But all that self-sabotage came later. At the end of August, when the journal begins, I'm on my way to Paris for a two-week soak in art. A trip that turned out to ravage me with loneliness, as I trekked from museum to museum, jotting my earnest *bon mots*. I couldn't understand why I was so depressed. Getting back to Paris had been my fondest dream for years, to see it at last through a grownup's eyes. But everyone seemed to be in pairs, filling ashtrays in the cafés and leaning over the balustrades above the Seine, wrapped about each other. As for me, I hadn't any better idea in Paris than I did in Boston where the men of my kind gathered. All I knew how to do was museums and monuments, eating by myself in bleak self-service dives to save money, squirreling images of the glamorous world that passed by, figuring it would make a lovely poem anyway. A poet's depression, I finally decided, which somehow made it nobler.

Now I see my Paris sorrow was trying to tell me something about the self I couldn't run from anymore, whose lies and evasions made every relationship false and desperate. But I wrote a poem instead of confronting the truth, and came barreling back to the new school year in a state of breathless manic cheer. Seven classes to teach between Canton and Chestnut Hill, two or three hours every night writing poems, and endless cups of coffee with my team of feeling women. Most of whom were thrilled to hear that I was contemplating a change of career, since they knew how stultifying I found the life of a schoolmaster. I basked in their approval, hearing it as permission to be gay.

And yet I know they all thought I was having an affair with Alida, whom I mentioned in every second breath. Two or three times a month I seemed to be driving down to Princeton to visit — that is, if Alida wasn't coming up to Boston. We slept on one another's sofas, virginal as a monk and a nun, but nobody knew that or would've believed it. For we were a dazzling team at a party, two hyper types who knew how to charm and could talk about anything. Not so different from César and me — and my denial was just as acute, my refusal to think about what Alida really wanted.

We studied antiques and visited every old house we could find, memorizing styles with a fervid determination to get an A. We had business cards made, our two names linked, with an office in Canton and another in Houston. The latter was a total cheat, being Alida's mother's address, but we thought two offices made us sound more legitimate and cosmopolitan. *Interiors and Restorations.* I'd still never held a swatch of fabric in my hand or ordered a stick of furniture. Had no credit *anywhere.* It was still only part-time after all, no irrevocable decisions.

Then around Thanksgiving Alida decided to drop out of Princeton after the first semester, so she could move to Boston and get going on this enterprise of ours in earnest. I remember being thrown by her suddenness, but my deepest anxiety had to do with her expectations of me sexually. I had it out with her one night, stumbling and red-faced, explaining that I was sexually confused and couldn't perform. "Are you gay?" she asked me gently, but I couldn't bear such honesty. Not exactly, I said evasively, just terribly ambiguous and fucked up. I made it sound like one of those obscure war wounds in Hemingway. When Alida swore she had no expectations at all, that she was just glad of what we had, a friendship unlike any other, I was so wilted with relief that I would've opened a used-car lot with her. Unhappily she wasn't being honest herself, still believing deep inside that she could change me if she was patient and loving enough. We were caught in a double bind of hoping for the best and not wanting to hurt each other.

I flew to Houston over Christmas. A strange week with Alida's family, during which I couldn't shake the feeling that I was being "looked over" as husband material. And I did nothing to counter that perception — on the contrary, did somersaults to win their approval. Alida and I were a couple, because it was far too complicated to explain what we were instead. Besides, right away we found ourselves too busy to linger over the proper pose to strike. We suddenly had a client — a plastic surgeon and his wife who lived in a bloated tract-house Tara in River Oaks, Houston's whitest precinct. Though they had already uglied up most of the house in a sort of barbecue-baroque, they wanted a music room so their squeaky little girls could give recitals.

Not my style. I couldn't wait to get out of there, glad to turn it over to Alida. Meanwhile back in Boston, another job fell in our laps — a woman who wanted to build a room around a bunch of deadly Early American portraits. None of this was what I'd had in mind, especially not the fawning or the winging it. But checks were actually coming in, so I just had to *do* it. I picked an upholsterer blind from the Yellow Pages; sold forty yards of fabric wrong side up. I remember one bewildered evening: Alida and I sprawled on the floor with my brother on Stratford Road, trying to learn how to keep books and do sales tax.

To Bob this whole designing enterprise had seemed from the first a crazy aberration, but then so was being a poet. I kept saying how happy I was to be changing careers, and he took me at my word. He sparked to Alida immediately, and thought we might as well give it a go if we were having as much fun as the laughter we gave off. He didn't know a hysterical laugh when he heard it. He also thought that Alida and I were a couple. Even recalls asking me point-blank if she and I were sleeping together, and my squirming retort that it wasn't really possible because my dick didn't work. However vague and tragic I tried to make it sound — gored by a bull in Pamplona — he understood it as an admission that I was gay. While I thought I was still protecting my secret.

Now I read the frenetic itinerary of that winter, how I ping-ponged between my two teaching jobs and raced into Boston during free periods to order ten yards of damask. Out with Alida three or four nights a week, dinner with every marginal rich person we knew, drowning in banalities as we tried to drum up business. And I pick up the casual reference here and there to what was really going on outside the distracting circus of my life. "Scott dropped by," it says between bites of paella and lists of errands. Back and forth to Alida's new apartment in Brookline as she and I addressed our official announcement to everyone we'd ever met—"and Scott came along for the ride."

One of the senior editors on the school paper, Scott was an exhaustingly bright kid who never stopped interviewing the world at large. So cocky, he'd known for years that he'd have his pick of the Ivy League. Not my type at all, scrawny and kind of an ugly duckling. But that was how I fooled myself as the whirlwind gathered through the winter: since I didn't want him sexually, I had no fear of repeating the obsessive pattern with Greg. Besides, Scott was after something else entirely: he wanted to be a writer. Worse—a poet, just like me.

I started out flattered and charmed, answering his thousand questions and parsing his little verses for him. I told myself I could actually do something altruistic before I phased out of teaching, helping Scott write his own way and not like a parrot. My special tutorial with Scott was just the sort of one-on-one Canton took such pride in. Nothing to hide, unlike the dark business with Greg. It was all on the run anyway, since I had to be in three different places at once on any given day. I didn't even hear the warning when I wrote it down myself. Sunday, January 30:

> I had library duty this afternoon, saw S briefly and found out he has a tryst tonight and might be late coming over here to work on lines. This disappoints me, I hope for

innocent reasons. I hope I'm not jealous of the tryst. That is an ache I would beg off right now.

Words to walk into a propeller by. By mid-March the poet-talk with Scott has clearly become the center of my day, and I will rearrange and juggle everything else in order to leave us an hour free. Though I hadn't the analytic skills to know it then, I'd already begun the process of "de-selfing" — my own word for the craziness that's turned my life into a minefield, this wanting to be somebody else instead of me. Such projection may be every bit as sexual as desiring someone's body, but it felt bodiless and annihilating. For months I romanticized Scott and me as a relationship of near Athenian purity, the ephebe and the master. But I got to like Scott's life better than mine — especially his easy heterosexuality, and the puppydog eagerness with which he faced a future uncompromised by secrets.

During my two-weeks' spring vacation Alida and I returned to Houston, where I began the slow dissolving into breakdown. All of our leads on new clients evaporated, horrible cups of coffee with Stepford Wives whose style was confined to the tuna surprise in *Family Circle*. We still had a major presentation to do for Dr. Plastic and his wife, but I just wandered through while Alida did the sketches and bids. I spent most of my time in bed, ostensibly fighting a neurasthenic flu, but in fact I was writing a poem to Scott. A set of rules, mock-didactic, on how to become a poet.

The tension and uncertainty were palpable now between Alida and me, as we wondered if we were really suited to the decorating trade. Neither of us liked the clients we'd met so far, nor the endless coddling required. And as I read her the stanzas of Scott's poem fresh from my overheated brain, she must've understood better than anyone that I was writing a love letter. But there was no turning back. Alida had burned the bridge of Princeton, and I'd given notice to both my schools. We had to make the business work — if only because we'd *told* everybody. Bailing out now would've been like canceling a wedding. A metaphor chillingly close to the bone, since Alida had finally begun to see that my heart knew what it wanted even if I refused to listen to it. And that she definitely wasn't the one.

One morning she came in to wake me in the guest room, to tell me she and her mother had been bothered all night by a crank caller. A surly drunk who identified himself as Greg from Sutton Hill, demanding to talk to me. I was in bed, Alida told him, I had the flu. She was clearly rattled and frightened, editing out the obscenities he must've spewed in my direction. I wept and told her what I could about the curse that seemed determined to pursue me, the shame that wouldn't heal. I don't know how Greg tracked me down in Houston, and it never happened again, but at the moment I thought he wouldn't stop until he destroyed me. Alida held me close and swore I would leave all that behind once I got out of teaching, at the same time reaffirming her commitment to our glorious enterprise. Neither of us mentioned Scott.

So I returned to Boston and careened through the final term on a manic-depressive rollercoaster. For my senior spring elective I offered a seminar on the poems of Wallace Stevens — an exercise in counting angels on pinheads which drew a group of Canton's brightest. Stevens was the ideal mandarin text for my perorations about the primacy of Art, the palm tree at the end of the mind from which you could pluck the truth like coconuts. I was practically speaking in tongues by then, so focused was I on the private hours I spent with Scott, often after the seminar broke. To the group I preached with a kind of desperation, exhorting them to seek the poem more perfect than life. It was all displacement of course, trying to build a temple of Art around my relationship with Scott so I wouldn't have to call it by its name. An obsession that kept digging deeper the hole in myself.

But the students ate it up. Stevens under their arm, they walked about the campus and waxed pretentious, a last fling at being high-school literati. Four or five of them trailed after me like ducklings, hoping for scraps of wisdom, in the process providing a certain cover for my hypnotic fixation on Scott. He'd finally decided on Yale over Harvard, which choked me with joy to think he would have the happy time there that had eluded me. I swore to myself I'd be content to send him off to a life of triumph from which my secret barred me. He could write about anything, after all, while I had to couch everything in code. So in the end it was Scott who would make it as a writer, and I would be lucky to occupy the footnote of having been his mentor. This was what it meant to be selfless, I thought, as I nailed myself to a wall more melancholy than Allston's.

Somehow I kept all the balls in the air. I took on a new project in Cambridge to redo the conference rooms in a hotel. The prospect filled me with hopeless dread as I felt more and more trapped in a business that made no sense. Another horror was the finish of school in June, when Scott would graduate and the long Platonic sessions of poetry end. By now I was under a bell jar of suffocating despair, hearing the mocking echo of all my chatter and laughter, ventriloquizing like mad so no one would guess I was coming apart. Only when I sat to write my poems did the madness vent — in twisted paranoid images, swarms of ravenous bees, a gunman blowing away the locks and lunging in at me. These fever charts of misery were the closest I could come to a cry for help, and yet the pain sits prettily in neat, fussy, decorative stanzas. When each poem was finished, I made my dutiful copies and passed them around as usual, hearing the technique praised and what a marvelous wordsmith I was. No one asked me if I was going crazy for real.

To most people I seemed a little more excited than usual, with a slight consumptive flush to my cheeks that was entirely appropriate to a poet mining his battered heart. When I was by myself, I was blank, staring into the middle distance. All I could do was try to save my energy — clutching my wounds like an animal losing blood — and make my appearance at every graduation function. Swinging into overdrive, talking so fast I thought I would burst, but still enough social skills to keep everyone laughing.

I don't blame Scott for keeping some distance at the end. He was valedictorian, after all, and had copped the literary prize to boot, the latter awarded by me. Flush with his own successes, he did what he could to keep open a daily slot of private time with me. Upbeat and breezy, always some new poet to ask about. But he'd also started the process of separation from Canton, ready to put it away with childish things. I felt abandoned but not betrayed, since the disintegration of Paul Monette was all my own fault. Meanwhile the obsession throbbed like a brain fever, as I wondered minute by minute what Scott was doing.

Thursday, June 15. I don't know what this journal is for anymore. I can't even accurately write down the crippled times, what it's like to just stare at the clock.

He stayed on for a week after graduation, bunking with friends in Cambridge, so the final smashup kept getting put off. We'd meet in Harvard Square for coffee, or walk by the river reading Lowell and Berryman. In those brief hours I would act as if nothing was wrong, like Garbo laughing to hide the cough at the end of *Camille*. The rest of the time I stumbled around like a zombie, knowing I needed help but paralyzed to find it. I remember dropping Scott off at the airport, the most casual of goodbyes, then heading up to Andover, knuckles white as I gripped the steering wheel. I'd promised my parents I'd stay with Bob while they took off for a week's vacation.

And that's where I hit bottom — in the very room I'd grown up in, or *stopped* growing up in. The room where I hid my first porno and jerked to the nightly frieze of my jock classmates at Andover. All that week I bumped around the house on Stratford Road, reading *Between the Acts*, wondering who would self-destruct first, Mrs. Woolf or I. My brother only recalls that I was subdued — odd for one usually so voluble, but nothing more remarkable than that. He was pissed at our parents for bringing me home to babysit, since he could damn well take care of himself. At twenty he'd finally taken charge of his own life, having just completed a year of junior college and about to start a four-year business course in the fall. A long way from the factory job that had seemed his only option after high school, two dead-end years of putting widgets together till his brain was nearly as atrophied as his legs. Now he was so happy, he had to pinch himself to believe it, out with Brenda every evening in the Falcon, beginning to plan a life together for real, marriage and all.

I remember thinking that I mustn't cloud his joy with my pathetic problems. There was nothing he could do anyway, nothing anyone could do. Yet I tried to stay in contact with people, especially my feeling women, pleading for direction, finally letting them broach the subject of therapy. "You can't go on like this," they told me. "Nobody has to live in this kind of pain." I took down the names of their shrinks and promised I'd call, then froze at the telephone. Wrestling with the terror of turning myself in, thinking I would rather die than tell my shameful story. Finally a girl I knew—a social worker who said I was starting to "look like a suicide"—called a friend and begged him to see me, because she didn't want my blood on her hands.

His name was Cantwell. Mid-twenties, a preppie jock with a brush mustache, relentlessly straight in demeanor and groomed to the teeth. I think I was one of his first private clients—twenty dollars a session, as I remember. I sat there rigid with terror, responding in monosyllables. "I gather you've been depressed," he said.

"I'm a homosexual. Why wouldn't I be depressed?"

"You sound bitter. Tell me about that."

And it poured out in a torrent—Greg and Scott, the search for the laughing man who didn't exist, the polar swings from celibacy to obsession. I couldn't stand it anymore, fitting in nowhere, always feeling less than. But wait—did I think there was something *wrong* with being gay? I squirmed, guardedly admitting it seemed to work for other people. But I'd never met one like me, or one who wanted me back. I was a misfit among misfits. And I didn't especially want to learn how to function better at something that made me feel so wretched.

"What *do* you want?" he asked. I blinked, and he repeated it.

It seemed to be some kind of trap. He persisted. "What would you *like* your life to be?"

I snorted with contempt. "That's easy—I'd like to be straight. So what?"

He nodded. "So let's work on that." He didn't seem to notice my look of stupefaction. Very businesslike, he proposed we see each other once a week for the next six months. I remember feeling offended, that he made it sound so easy. Did he really think he could undo in six months the lies and desires of twenty-six years? In my deepest heart I resisted the deal I was being asked to sign—a first stirring of pride perhaps, or just a stubborn anchor in reality. How would I ever teach myself not to eroticize men? It was as deeply rooted in me as the fact of gender itself.

Yet under that flutter of indignation was a hunger to believe him. My being queer was inextricable from the depression that was destroying me. But maybe my certainty that I couldn't change was only the sickness talking. Besides, Cantwell's startling challenge had a seductive appeal to my intellect: that we could take this bundle of neuroses and understand it to death. It was like enrolling in a graduate course in self—with a reading list and deadlines, as well as a chance to recite and show off in class to an approving teacher. Another shot at another A.

I walked out of that first session convinced I was a new man already, intoxicated with the will to change. I didn't even feel so oppressed by the continuing obsession with Scott, since that represented in a nutshell the self-destruction of my disease. So taken was I with the thrill of change that I handled without panic Alida's decision, a few days later, to drop out of the business. She'd had enough of my falling apart, was sick of hiding her own feelings and playing the saintly nurturer. Very well, I would make the business succeed without her. I was broke and had no certain income, but liked the feel of being free to make my own mistakes. Meanwhile my department chairman at Canton offered me a part-time job for the fall—only two courses, I'd be out of there by noon. I knew I could live on the half-salary—five grand—as long as I found a cheap place to live in the city.

Then I fell into the perfect situation. A Harvard professor and his wife, whose daughter I'd taught at Andover, were on their way to China, Nixon just having opened the door. They had a beautiful place on Winthrop Street in Cambridge, a stone's throw from Harvard Square, surrounded on three sides by the red-brick bastions of Harvard's residential houses. By contrast, the professor's house was a nineteenth-century throwback, a farmhouse really, with a split-rail fence around the yard and an apple tree that made a shady courtyard by the kitchen door. They asked if I'd like to housesit for them till Christmas, sharing the place with their oldest daughter, a nurse who kept a hatchet by her bed because of the constant stream of burglars.

It was like moving into a ready-made bohemian life, glamorously funky, burglars and all. The daughters' friends were always hanging out on Winthrop Street — a ragtag bunch of dancers and rock musicians and body-painters, people who didn't go anywhere without a tambourine and a couple chips of hash wrapped in tinfoil. They were glad to have a poet around. And I had the exhilarated feeling of starting over every day, the post-hippie street life of the Square being the perfect surroundings for making everything new. I remember walking barefoot to Ninni's Corner to buy the morning paper, checking the kiosks for poetry readings, dozing on the riverbank as I read my way through Forster. If I still thought of myself as paralyzed with depression, I must've had to work at it.

In fact I was working hard on my therapy. From the day I started with Cantwell I couldn't stop talking about it, practically collaring strangers on the street to announce that I was coming back from a nervous breakdown. For someone whose every feeling had been masked since puberty, I was compensating in spades, conducting a public airing of dirty laundry in all the cafés of Cambridge. I poured out the truth to any friend who'd listen. I'd been the perfect ear for so many women for so long, they owed me one. Besides, it was part of the urban chic of the times, in Cambridge anyway, to talk about the progress of one's therapy. We were presumably sitting on the same mythic café chairs where Sexton and Plath traded razor scars and overdoses.

But my agenda wasn't madness now, it was going straight. In Cantwell's office I went after the usual suspects, raging at my parents for the body shame that entered the house when my brother was born, the feeling that our seed was cursed and that maybe we deserved it. I might be afraid of sex with women, but that didn't mean I didn't want it. Once I was able to grasp that in theory, I was wild with impatience to test it out, to play it through with an actual woman — and the obvious choice was Emma.

She'd graduated from Canton in June, in Scott's class, and though never a student of mine, had always hovered at the edges of the literary crowd, smiling enigmatically at my noisy opinions. Emma lived in the Blue Hills south of Canton, at the end of a dirt road through rolling fields, by a black pond at the foot of a meadow — the perfect place for a changeling to live. She had a long elegant face and the saddest eyes, being unaware of her own considerable sensuality, and liable to start like a deer at any sudden move. I don't know what drew us together, but I suspect it was a shared sense of being out of step. Her father had died of cancer, pointlessly and abruptly, a couple of years past, and the wound at the center of things was still raw. We fell into spending time together while I was still packing up to leave the garret in Upton House. We had no expectations going in, either of us, just a willingness to give one another permission to be sad.

But as soon as I understood I might be a closet heterosexual, every encounter with Emma became freighted with the possibility of romance. I was tentative as a twelve-year-old, terrified and thrilled to get as far as a dry-lipped kiss. We went camping in Maine with her older brother, Emma and I holding hands between our two sleeping bags, shyly skinny-dipping in the iceberg waters off Winter Harbor. She felt like my first girlfriend. It was for me a reaching backward to reclaim an innocence my tortured youth had never tasted. Emma was infinitely patient and undemanding, fascinated by the twists and turns of my psyche as I got shrunk. Her own blue-nosed New England upbringing had ranked the expression of feelings somewhere below dancing on Sundays, a thing that was Simply Not Done. She had repressions of her own to peel away, and to her I was a veritable circus of acting out and getting in touch.

Of course I'd still see men on the streets of Cambridge whose beauty would stop my heart, throwing the whole matter of my sex change into question. Dutifully I would tell myself I wanted to *be* that guy, not have him. That was what I should try to visualize, said Cantwell: not fucking the men I lusted after but becoming one of their own. I'm putting this idea in Cantwell's mouth, but I'm not sure. For if there was any theme that recurred with dismaying frequency in our sessions, it was my ravenous need for approval. So extreme, that I would say anything to be liked, take on any persona if I thought it would ingratiate me. I think he was trying to tell me that I'd decided to be straight because that's what I figured everyone wanted of me, Cantwell especially. By then, of course, I was checking out every woman I knew as a possible relationship. Have I got it right yet, doctor? How about this one?

Yet it was Scott's approval that mattered most. I'd call him once a week, he at a phone booth outside a drugstore in Jerkwater, Michigan, where his family spent their summers. I'd narrate the breathless tale of my struggle to overcome my sexual dysfunction, while he steered the conversation to books and poets. By now it was only a reflex of good manners keeping him in touch with me. He was cool and distracted, counting the seconds till he could hang up. I didn't care. Wait till I showed him I was as straight as he was.

Emma and I never made it to bed, but we did the best we could with a chaste romance, delicate and courtly as figures in a tapestry. We managed to end the summer tenderly disposed, neither of us bruised, as if we had prepped one another for a greater love waiting just around the bend. I'd gotten what I needed from the experience — a chance to be vulnerable, a taste of intimacy without the fear of being asked to perform. Not that all this attenuated eroticism served to blunt my baser needs. Though repeating my mantra to be and not possess the humpy numbers who crossed my path, every now and then I'd let one follow me barefoot home for a quick blow job. And berate myself as I watched them disappear down Winthrop Street — as if it had all been a lab experiment to prove the virtue of my higher goal. And of course a chance to rack myself with guilt in Cantwell's office for having fallen off the wagon.

September, and Emma was off to Sarah Lawrence. Scott came through Boston on his way to Yale, stopping long enough for a couple of rhapsodic walks along the river. The words that passed between us were so carefully composed, we might have been speaking in blank verse. I experienced again the Platonic heights of the previous spring, convinced that we could bond like Wordsworth and Coleridge — or was it Byron and Shelley? — now that I was on the road to sexual normalcy. Around this time, Cantwell broke his therapist's silence to call me on my delusion that I wasn't turned on carnally by Scott. Bluntly he warned me to beware of the self-destruction here, not to dress it up in lofty sentiments.

Oh, all right. Deep down I knew I could show Cantwell that I could have it both ways, the princely soul-passion of poets and the earthly physicality of a man and a woman. Which was where Julia came in. I suppose it must have been my friend John at Yale who put us back in touch — he of the *White Album* suckfest — having first introduced us four years before in Chicago. Julia had settled in Washington, working "Style" for the *Post* — sassy and gorgeous, quick to be bored, and utterly certain she'd win on her own terms, no matter how much of a men's club journalism was. John sent her some poems of mine, but more to the point he passed on to Julia the eye-rolling gossip that Paul had decided to go straight.

She called me in Cambridge and said she had to come up to Boston for a story. Which may have been an excuse, but she couldn't have been less coy about her motives. "I never really thought you were gay," she informed me, "because gay men don't turn me on, and you always did." The perfect mix of dare and flattery. Sure, we could see each other while she was in Boston. Whatever trepidation I had was mitigated by knowing she lived five hundred miles away. I expected her on Friday; she showed up two days early. Knocked on the door of Winthrop Street, her bags beside her on the stoop, the friend she'd vaguely been planning to stay with having fallen through.

For the next four days, we were up half the night talking, me spilling every detail of Greg and Scott and whatever else I could think of, because Julia couldn't get enough. We slept in the same bed, curled together, Julia insisting that we not move too fast with the sex. Fine with me, whatever she said. I let her take my hand to explore her body, seeing how it turned her on that I was a virgin in these matters. She told me I had a beautiful dick, which got a blip of a rise from it. We made out for hours on end, read poems aloud in the bathtub, and she'd waltz naked around the bedroom singing Carole King songs.

I was mesmerized by her, and not even scared when she warned me, before taking off on Sunday, that she was falling in love with me. All I knew was, I'd just spent four days not thinking every other minute about Scott. And the calls poured in all week from friends who'd seen us together, whom Julia had dazzled as much as she'd dazzled me. It was the most heterosexual I'd ever felt — the luxurious pride of having a fox on my arm, as smart as she was beautiful and doting on me shamelessly. "We look good together, don't we?" she'd ask whenever we passed a mirror. And checking myself out in mirrors was crucial to this heterosexual process, Narcissus needing to see what he looked like arm in arm with a woman.

I begged her to come back the next weekend. A few nights later I was walking in the Square and saw one of my half-hour tricks riding toward me on a bicycle. I tried to look away, but he stopped anyway. To inform me he had VD, and I'd better go get checked. With a cheery smile he was on his way, and I stood there hardly breathing, racked with shame and hating the pull of men. I thought Julia would refuse to see me anymore, but she couldn't have been more supportive. "That's all in the past," she assured me, insisting on coming with me when I went to be poked and swabbed at the clinic. Of course we couldn't have *real* sex now for a couple of weeks, but Julia didn't mind. It would do us good, she said, to let the anticipation build.

When she left on Sunday night, I declared in my journal that I loved her — a feeling I'd never experienced before without pain, and for once there wasn't any pain. Yet four days later, I'm grappling with it like Jekyll and Hyde, still trying to balance love and obsession:

> We are the lucky, Julia says. And this is what it's like to be happy. But I'm so much in the middle, fearing that in loving them both I am playing both ends against the middle, that it's surely not possible to complete the possibility of Julia with the way I feel about Scott.

Saying the truth, however, didn't make me face it. When Julia arrived for the third weekend in a row, I told her that though I loved her, my manhood felt trumped up, artificial. I feared I was using her to compete with Scott, trying to mimic Scott's libido because I had none of my own. She shook her head fondly. Didn't I understand yet that she loved me not in spite of my confusion but because of it? "I even love the faggot in you," she said. "I don't think he's anything to be ashamed of. I just think he's becoming superfluous."

Sounded good to me. And of course I had all kinds of backup to reinforce me now. I was servicing four or five clients in the suburbs, women who couldn't wait for the next installment of the Monette soap opera. The business had shifted since Alida left, away from draperies and the acquisition of things. Now I was installing lurid supergraphics, turning previously white rooms into "color environments." These migraine-making experiments in hot pink and four-foot polka dots were all the rage for a while — my signature. I don't know how anyone ever slept in one of those color-field bedrooms, but it seemed to make the bankers and their wives feel very Pop/Op hip. Especially because I did all the painting myself, a sort of latter-day Renaissance fresco maker. Tossing off lines of poetry as I worked, while my client ladies held the ladder and brought me coffee. Then I'd regale them with every grisly detail of my dick that didn't work, and they'd root for me and Julia.

Twice I went down to Washington to see her, enjoying the feel of reciprocation as Julia showed me off to all her friends. More confident now, I was boyishly eager to get to the fucking part, but still Julia cautioned that we shouldn't go too fast. When I champed at the bit, she sighed and clucked that I was beginning to act like every other man. She also didn't seem to want to spend as much time naked, preferring that we go out carousing with her friends in the bars. I began to think she kissed me more when we were out in public than when we were by ourselves. But I tried not to push — afraid that it was all so fragile, and that I'd lose my grip on straightness if I lost her.

Then I'd stop off in New Haven for a couple of hours on the way back to Boston, to goose the Platonic delusion with Scott. Of course I wanted his body, even as I bragged about my new life as a het. I'd arrive back in Boston confused and schizophrenic, and Cantwell would hammer at me that I couldn't have it two ways, or at least not the way *I* was doing it. If I wanted to be bisexual, fine, but the male half needed to be workable and satisfying, not tortured and self-denying the way I was with Scott. Anyway, when was I going to stop thinking so much about my dick and more about relationships? He seemed to feel I was losing something in this heterosexualizing marathon. Did he mean the same thing Julia did, that I was turning into "every other man"? But that was the point of it all, wasn't it? Cantwell wouldn't commit himself, except to say that I needed to stop living my life like a novel.

I resisted this notion mightily. I was finally living my life, and the drama helped me feel the tang of it. I had no idea how to turn the volume down. On October 19, I drove to New Haven — three days after I turned twenty-seven — ostensibly to consult with John on some graphic design, but of course it was only an excuse to see Scott. I called him and proposed we go see a play at the Long Wharf Theater. Driving out the turnpike, we were just going to make the curtain, and I was in my usual manic state with

Scott, shaking the palm at the end of the mind. We stopped at a red light near the theater, an eighteen-wheeler in the lane to my left. I was talking so intensely I didn't notice the light go green — or the truck start turning right across our path.

The driver never saw us. I looked out my window into the underbelly of the semi and realized that the huge rear wheels were about to crush us. I tried to wrench the Opel over the curb, but wasn't fast enough. The big tire flattened my side of the car, exploding the window and spraying me with glass. I screamed and pushed away from the door, so that my hand caught the full force of the wheel's battering progress. Then it was over. I knew I'd broken some bones, but dismissed the pain with an airy wave of the injured hand, more concerned just then with how annoyed and embarrassed Scott appeared to be.

How loud does fate have to shriek in your face before you pay attention? Still not loud enough for me. At the emergency room they told me I'd broken two bones in my left wrist, my writing hand. Fine, fine — no problem. It must've been shock, but I acted as if nothing at all had happened. Apologizing profusely, I made Scott leave and go back to the college. John collected me and next day took the bus to Boston with me, Julia meeting us at the station with blood-red roses and a shower of kisses. And as I remember, even that night I wanted another lesson in heterosex, so driven was I not to lose any more time, or think about how self-destruction worked.

For the next month the journal is mercifully silent, because I couldn't even hold a pen. Except for two loose-leaf pages tucked in at the back, covered with one-finger typing, run-on without any caps. The first page is a flat account of the accident and the days that followed, Julia smothering me with tenderness. If I'd thought she was cooling off to me, my broken wing changed all that. Now she just wanted us cocooning together, everyone else be damned. If in fact there are no accidents, maybe that's really what I was after — pay more attention to me and my terrible need to go straight.

The second typed page is back at fever pitch, recounting the first weekend in November. A friend from Canton had given us the keys to his house on Cape Cod, and Julia and I spent three days there, she putting me through my midterm exam in love-making. Working at it in deadly earnest, outwitting my unco-operative member by waking up in the middle of the night, going at it before I had time to be scared. I was doing the wild thing at last — the *normal* thing. I strutted around all day in a swoon of self-satisfaction. Didn't even balk when Julia announced that she might move up to Boston. Was I ready for that? Well, sure — could we fuck again now?

The memory of those days in the house on the salt marsh is a strange blur of ecstasy and pain. My throbbing wrist in its clumsy cast lying frozen on the pillow as we gasped with passion, swimming in tandem at last. If Cantwell had asked his question then — "What would you *like* your life to be?" — the answer couldn't have been more self-evident. This right here, islanded with the woman I loved, the torments of the past behind me. A real man at last, with the notches on my gun to prove it. Let's stay like this forever.

When the journal starts up again, on November 17, you can see the handwriting's shaky and distorted, as if I'm starting from scratch. By then I'm sleeping with another woman, though it has to remain a secret because she's practically engaged to a friend of mine. Julia and I have not quite broken up, but it's just a matter of one of us getting the gumption up to say it. Scott is staying over at the house on Winthrop Street, telling me he's decided he's more of a novelist than a poet. Something we must discuss to death for another month while I try not to stare at his pants.

And how am I? Oh I'm fine, couldn't be better. Happier than I've ever been. And the crippled hand that writes all this is completely unaware of how it will look nearly twenty years later, the jagged crooked letters a Rorschach of denial. A young man — well, not so young, just not grown up — living his life like a novel with too much plot. Running as fast as he can to stay in one place where everyone can see him, applauding their approval. Not quite like other men, but getting there.

Eight

I HAVE TO KEEP MY LATER SELF on a short leash as I negotiate those hurricanes of feeling that propelled my time with women. From the vantage of life outside the closet it's too easy to scathe and ridicule. I see the manic posturing and the agonized self-doubt as I tried to cram myself into a straight man's suit of armor. Every move I made seems driven by that engine of approval-seeking. Therefore I'm as tough and cynical as any of the Boys in the Band as I fling aside the journal of my sex change: *Girl, when are you gonna get real and find yourself some dick?* I have to force myself to remember that it wasn't just more wasted time, loving those women. That they were the ones who finally broke the ice skin that sealed me among the living dead. That I couldn't have ever opened myself to Roger or any other man if the women of '72 and '73 hadn't been there first. Unjudging and tender, taking their own risks in the open country of the heart, no kiss ever a waste of time.

I don't know how things would've gone differently for Julia and me if we hadn't had to contend with those five hundred miles. I grew impatient with the weeks that separated our visits. The long commute, cadging rides like students on a road trip because neither of us could afford the shuttle, was taking its toll in nerves. We continued to *look* terrific together, never missing a literary party, and for me at least our lovemaking grew wilder and more anchoring. But Monday to Friday would leave me prey to emptiness and doubt, as if we were doing it all with mirrors.

Somehow I couldn't fall back on the old Platonic talking relationships with women — that seemed bogus now and neutered, a repression of my new-found maleness. I'd had enough of talking — I wanted action. Even at the risk of preening like a satyr, of putting sex before everything else. I wanted my due at last in male entitlement.

The summer I moved to Cambridge, an old friend from Yale had split with his wife in Vermont and taken a place in Back Bay. Justin was a radical architect determined to put the world under a dome and power it with solar panels. His work had so far been confined to ski houses that looked like crashed spaceships, as beautiful as they were strange, stubbornly avoiding all bourgeois compromise. His bathrooms were as pared down as outhouses. Justin was noisy and pushy in his opinions, growling and pulling his mad Tchaikovsky hair if anyone said anything stupid. He drank heavily, was built like a bear, and lived on practically nothing a month to defy the egregious riches of his parents. Relentlessly, raucously straight — or so I'd always thought. Because we courted different muses, we constituted no threat to each other as artists, and so hung out together, trashing pretense and easy art.

Sometimes I'd spend the evening hunkered in Justin's window seat looking out on the somber façades of Marlborough Street, working over a poem as Justin tinkered at his models and elevations. But more often than not I'd be waiting to have a laugh with Sally, who breezed in around eleven to spend the night with Justin. The most electric woman I'd ever encountered, with a smutty mouth that loved to shock, seeing *everything* in sexual terms. Sally had everyone's number, but most of her jokes were self-directed — a formerly fat girl who'd learned to bury the hurt by being one of the guys. Her brazenness was all the more startling because she looked so demure and vulnerable, with the peaches-and-cream skin and honey-soft hair of the Breck girl. To me she seemed the most sensuous of creatures, her fingers grazing the hair on my arm as she talked, her voice a low thrill perfect for secrets. And so urban-hip and self-assured, a cross between Holly Golightly and her namesake, Sally Bowles. I was weak-kneed with envy of Justin.

"Monette, you're not getting laid enough," clucked Sally when she heard about my weekend arrangement with Julia. She promised to find me something steadier and closer to home among her own girlfriends. To that end she set up a couple of exploratory lunches with one and another, but it was Sally I couldn't stop looking at, and she knew it. I'd also begun to bristle at the hardball toughness that passed for banter between her and Justin. Digs and sneering and jokes that left invisible scars, all on the pretext of a certain liberated openness. From where I stood, Sally had signed on to be treated like shit by a petulant artist — where being an artist excused cavalier self-importance, not to mention the flight from commitment.

I don't know who seduced whom. But when Sally told me fretfully that Justin was now demanding a couple of evenings a week for "independent development," meaning so he could go out and get laid, I leaped at the chance to be gallant and protect her. Within a few days we'd begun our own independent development, Sally and I, and it was weeks before I even caught my breath. She ate up the challenge of my newly minted heterosex identity, turning me on in ways that nobody ever had. And I made up for the caring too many men had withheld from Sally. Two wounds healing, that's how I thought of us.

She knew how to conduct an affair at true soap-opera pitch — appearing suddenly at one of my classes at Canton, dragging me off to make love in the woods. She left me notes on the apple tree on Winthrop Street, or raced over from work for a quickie at lunch, or woke me with a spray of pebbles at my window, wanting in for a night in my arms. Sally was the first secret I ever had that made me happy instead of ashamed. A secret she kept much better, probably, than I, who spilled it to my client ladies as the next installment of my cliff-hanger life. I even told Julia — or at least she figured it out, since I couldn't stop recounting Sally's bawdy lines. Oh, and we were terribly grown-up about it, Julia and I, convinced it was just what I needed to tide me over. Sportsex, with no entangling alliances. Besides, I announced proudly, having a weekday paramour left me no time to think about men.

The four of us actually had dinner when Julia was next in Boston. A bizarre evening of *Rashomon* dimensions, nobody quite knowing who knew what, but all of us acting devastatingly worldly. "I'm not jealous of her," observed Julia as we drove home, following up with a few quick razor slashes on the subject of Sally's looks. "But you do know that Justin's gay, don't you?"

I didn't. But if that was the drift of Justin's evenings out — leaving Sally for other men — then I was only more determined to be the "good" lover. I was doing the opposite, rejecting the self-defeating hunger for men in order to be with these women, no backsliding and no regrets. I certainly thought I could keep things going with Julia — indeed, was convinced that having my sexual education doubled would only make our relationship deeper. Besides, Julia seemed to quicken to the challenge of not being jealous, more playful in bed as she teased about whether her moves were as deft as Sally the hooker's.

I like to think they were both too smart to be used. Or at least I've always taken comfort in knowing that neither of *them* has any regrets, that they remember the whirlwind days in Cambridge only with fondness and laughter. That I managed to be, for both of them, some kind of anchor in painful times. But I was barely conscious at the time, running so fast between bedrooms that my life began to feel like a French farce. I guess I counted on the scale of my emotions to get us all through, the running monologue of my fear and uncertainty, my eagerness to talk all night if it made me learn to love a little better. And, with that, a compulsion to know everything *they* were feeling, as if all our lives depended on nothing remaining unsaid.

Over Thanksgiving I went to Washington, four nights at Julia's place. We seemed to be happier than ever, and once more tossed around the notion of Julia's moving to Boston. We argued only once, when she accused me of not taking her writing seriously. I was stung, having read the chapters of her novel over and over, thrilled by their passion, bragging about them to friends. It was something else, less tangible, a clash of writerly egos, a certain self-satisfaction I couldn't hide about the higher calling of poetry. I never meant to use it as a wedge between us, but it must have felt isolating when I walled myself in my notebook for an hour's fixation on a line or two.

I certainly didn't think we were anywhere near to breaking up. I returned to Boston, and Sally and I resumed our surreptitious romance, spending her two nights off from Justin at her apartment on Concord Avenue. The Harvard prof and his wife had arrived back from China, and I took another house-sitting job, this time just for a month. But I was hardly ever there except to feed the cat, my boxes never unpacked. When she finally reached me, Julia said she'd been calling for days without an answer—this was before answering machines, when all you had to do not to be caught in the wrong conversation was not be there. Effusively I apologized, swearing I hadn't been trying to avoid her—

"It's all right, Paul. It's just over, that's all." She couldn't have sounded less upset. I tried to pump up the volume, genuinely shocked. "We're too strong for each other," Julia declared. "We both want the same things, so one of us would have to win." I understood none of this. Julia seemed so far advanced in deconstructing the psychology of it all. I was already scrambling to think how I could see more of Sally to fill the void. "Breaking up is usually the part that sucks, believe me," Julia said. "Someday you'll see how lucky we were, because we knew when to say goodbye."

Sure felt painless to me. I didn't take a minute to be angry or sad; I was out of there in a flash, trotting through the snowy alleys to Sally's place, snuggling in under her covers so I wouldn't have to be alone. I may even have been so dimwitted as to announce that I could be with her full-time now. Never having truly gauged how deep her need for Justin was, or how complicated the game she'd been playing to hurt him for running out on her. The next morning, I saw the trapped look in Sally's eyes, so I bent over backwards to let her know how glad I was to be free to play the field. I had to convince her I wasn't needy, because otherwise she wouldn't let me love her.

So I dated with abandon, living on capuccino and cigarettes at the Blue Parrot and Café Pamplona. I would read my poems aloud to an audience of one, then segue into the tale of my brave quest to go straight. As a line of seduction it had a certain uniqueness, pleading rather than aggressive, and promising miles of foreplay. I wasn't afraid anymore, knowing the naked intimacy would satisfy the two of us even if my peter wasn't stiff as a tuning fork. Meanwhile I couldn't wait for Emma to come home for Christmas vacation, so we could finally consummate our summer of tender feelings. Making love began to seem the simplest thing in the world. At the back of my mind I even played with the shadowy notion that when Star returned at last from Asia, I'd be ready to be her lover.

Such a liberating idea, to transform by passion relationships that had heretofore been ambiguous and problematic. Or so I must have presented the case to Alida, who'd been having a lonely time of it in the dating department, admitting at last that she'd never stopped being in love with me. Great, I said enthusiastically, then why didn't we have an affair? All through the playful negotiation that followed, Alida was the one who kept wondering aloud how we would ever get out of it once we got in. An argument I dismissed out of hand; that was precisely the sort of logic that had kept my heart in chains so long. We'd worry about goodbye when we got there, I assured her.

So we went for it, swearing we wouldn't become too involved. Thus did I juggle affairs, proudly sharing it all with Sally, for she was now my mentor and love adviser as well as my main squeeze. As for Scott, he detoured through Cambridge at either end of his Christmas vacation, spending the night on Sally's sofa while she and I shared the bedroom. I strutted with pride at being able to show off to Scott a woman of my own, and Sally in turn showered him with affection, giving him pointers on how to get laid at Yale.

I thought I had everything now, running from tryst to tryst. I tried not to notice Emma's sadness as she took off for college after New Year's, clearly not as certain as I that it had done us both good to devirginalize our relationship. Or did she pick up, in me, an impatience to have it over with, an arrogant calculation in my New Man's equation that a few rolls in the hay over Christmas was all we were worth anyway? I shrank even more from the restless sorrow in Alida's eyes when I'd leave in the morning, not free to see her again till the end of the week. I didn't think of myself as controlling, had always assumed my outsize presence was enough, since I prided myself on having learned to live completely in the moment. For the space of an evening, a couple of hours' loving, we enacted a kind of poem. Who needed a day-to-day commitment when we were blessed instead with the spirit of High Romance?

Cantwell heard me out on all these florid theories, the litany of my galloping, rampant manhood. I assured him I barely felt the homo side at all anymore. Cantwell cut to the chase: my approval mechanism sprang from my desire to recover the relationship I'd lost with my mother the day she found me with Kite. I see now how tenaciously he was questioning my whole commitment to straighthood, what an evasion it was of confronting the unreason of my shame at being queer. I nodded agreeably but ducked the analysis. Since starting therapy, I'd become more and more distant from my parents, finally breaking the pattern of weekly visits to Andover, laundry in hand. I'd told them, with some defiance, to leave me alone to work out my life. So who needed approval?

Besides, Sally had just invited me to share the apartment on Concord Avenue. She must've been fairly convinced I was making a life for myself by then, or perhaps she had some thought that we could reconfigure our relationship and just be roommates. I know she'd finally told a couple of girlfriends about our affair, and they weren't amused at all. They told her she'd end up losing Justin. I don't know quite how I envisioned our living together, but I remember thinking that if things went well, we could end up married. I moved in mid-January, taking the tiny second bedroom, a mattress on the floor amid vertiginous piles of my books. But I slept in Sally's bed, alone if she was spending the night with Justin, otherwise wrapped about her. As far as I was concerned, I'd achieved a level of heterosex completion beyond my wildest imaginings.

Two weeks later, early one Saturday morning, Sally came back from Justin's. I woke up to find her packing a bag so they could go off to Vermont for the night. She climbed into bed to kiss me, let it grow more and more passionate, then pulled away shaking her head. It had to stop between us, she said, because she couldn't handle the cheating anymore. Justin had promised to be more committed — something he did periodically, usually when he found he had the clap, the reason Sally eventually gave him the nickname "disease du jour." I bit my tongue to keep from protesting *I love you better than he does.*

But I cried. I bawled. A wail of grief that went on and on, shrugging off the comfort of Sally's embrace. Mostly it was a tantrum of self-pity, but the loss and the hurt and the dread came down to a single immutable certainty: *I would never be straight.* The whole elaborate drama of my interlocking affairs seemed to fall in a heap at my feet. *You're gay, you're gay,* throbbed a voice in my head, *you'll never get out of it now.* Sally wanted to call Cantwell, but I said no, I needed to feel this pain all the way through.

It was a crossroads in my heart, though you never would've known it to see us later in the apartment on Concord Avenue. For Sally's resolve lasted about three days, and then we were back to doing it whenever we had a night free. It was different though, because I understood she wouldn't be leaving Justin for me. I even understood that she needed him to punish herself, and that she had to come out of it on her own. Which was more than I understood about myself, as I raced around trying to fill the gaps in my dance card. Within two weeks I'd found another pair of players, and this time one was a man.

But first came Edie, a blazingly colorful presence in the Square, feathers in her hair and her eyes made up in Day-Glo and sequins. She was a part-time cook in the café of the moment, classically trained in voice and ballet but preferring instead the spontaneous song-and-dance that erupted in the coffeehouses of Cambridge. She was also a Mayflower blue blood, a fact of pedigree that cracked her up. Edie seemed to live as fast as I did, juggling as many amours. We found ourselves bored at the same parties and finally split from one of them together, ducking into Barney's for coffee. There she was a sort of resident diva, popping into the kitchen to fix me eggs, embracing all her regulars at the bar. She collected artists, she told me point-blank.

Okay, I thought, so collect me. Edie seemed to love having me around, though she had intimacy problems in bed. Sometimes scared like a little girl, sometimes terribly melancholy, crying into my neck. So I went slow and treated her as gently as I could, moved as always by anyone else's sexual fears and traumas. The only thing I found odd about Edie was that she never ate in my presence — though she was always cooking for me, merrily waltzing naked around her kitchen as she boiled up pasta or baked a pie. She was neither thin nor fat, and never talked about dieting. She just preferred to eat by herself.

I liked her eccentricities — the bizarre late hours, the glitter clothes, the singing in the streets. She also didn't judge me for having met Pip. Of *course* I was bisexual, Edie declared cheerfully, prodding me to have it both ways. Well, as long as somebody gave me permission. I'd met Pip at a party at Justin's, where he was sipping Jack Daniels out of the bottle and plunking jazz on a flat piano. He was an architect too, though mostly unemployed. A strapping boy from Minnesota, Swedish and big-boned, with always three days' growth of beard to give a rough edge to his cherub's dimples. What César used to call an *ange tombé*.

I'd taken him home to bed that very evening, knowing I was playing with fire — the first man I'd slept with in months, the first ever who wasn't more or less anonymous. After we came, we sat up half the night talking about what "bi" meant. We both decided that our overriding instinct was for the normal thing with women. Having it on with men was a minor variation, a chance to reexperience adolescent comradeship, but mostly just for play.

Two men could never reach the depth of feeling available to a man and a woman, because a woman led the way when it came to feelings. As usual I went along with all these half-baked stereotypes, not wanting to come across less of a man than Pip. And careful not to show that I was ready to fall in love with him, the last thing he was looking for.

So for a couple of weeks I had the experience of loving both Sally and Pip, but not telling either one for fear I'd lose them. They in turn seemed to think the main event in my life was Edie, whom I did see every day, but with the increasing sense that we made a better couple at Barney's than by ourselves. Cantwell warned me that Pip appeared to have more guilt over his gay side than even I, and if I really wanted a man, I had to find one who took joy in it. He was equally uncertain what I was still doing with Sally, who'd told me I would never be first. I countered stubbornly that I liked the free-floating arrangement. What better way to find out how bi I was than to have one of each?

On the last weekend in February, Edie and I drove through a blizzard to my friend's place at the Cape, picking up groceries on the way for a house party that was meant to be eight of us. But nobody showed up on account of the storm, and by nightfall we were snowbound. The idea of being stranded appealed mightily to my romantic nature, but Edie promptly cracked at the seams.

While I was making a snowman, she locked herself in the bathroom and plucked out first her eyebrows, then all her eyelashes, then her pubic hair. She emerged, frantic with anxiety, admitting she had a food problem and warning me to fasten my seatbelt. Then she proceeded to cook and eat six bags of groceries — a ten-pound roast, a turkey, two pounds of bacon, on and on, all night long. Every half hour or so she'd go in the bathroom and throw it all up. She was curiously polite about all this, apologizing, even making jokes about it. But I swear she would've come after me with a butcher knife if I'd tried to get between her and any of that food.

The plow didn't come to dig us out till noon the next day, and we drove home in stunned silence, stopping every ten miles so Edie could eat in a coffee shop. When I left her off at her place in Cambridge, she said with rueful understatement, "I don't think I'm quite ready for a relationship."

The terrors and dysfunctions, the self-battering and self-hatred. The more I experienced the struggles of intimacy, the more troubled and lonely I found almost everyone. Of course it may have had something to do with the people I chose, drawn like a magnet to hearts as damaged as mine — but I don't think so. At twenty-seven I thought I was uniquely fucked-up for having choked so long in the closet. But my belated journey through the minefields of the bedroom gave me abundant proof that the fear of connection and openness crossed all borders — men and women, gay and straight. And just getting into bed with somebody wasn't the magic solution, because people could hide their terrors in pure technique — depersonalizing so completely the body embraced that they felt nothing at all.

Yet it was all still so new to me that I kept believing passion would save everyone in the end. I even would've continued seeing Edie, since she'd tapped into something protective in me. Anyway, after so many years of being a chameleon, I was nothing if not accommodating. Other people's pain never made me run the other way. But Edie had revealed too much, and couldn't look me in the eye anymore when I'd drop in at Barney's. So I redoubled my one-way commitments to Sally and Pip, who for all their problems of self-esteem seemed positively sane after Edie in the blizzard.

For a little while we kept a precarious balance, acting as if the incestuous relations among us were the height of bohemian freedom. One long Sunday, Sally and Pip and I lay sprawled on her bed in our underwear, passing a bowl of out-of-season cherries as we laughed our way through the papers. We'd take baths together, the three of us lined up in the claw-footed tub washing each other's hair. But the camaraderie couldn't mask the fact that when Pip and I finally crawled into bed on my narrow mattress, he wanted it over quick and without any love talk. Mostly just *frottage*, and almost a phobia about kissing. Once the sex was done, he'd happily laugh and talk all night, and I'd pretend the half-measure of passion hadn't left me hungry.

And Sally didn't really like having a queer relationship in the next room. It reminded her too much of what she was struggling against with Justin. "Are you in love with Pip?" she asked me abruptly one morning at breakfast. No, I demurred. Then, two mornings later, as if she'd been thinking about it ever since: "If you're not in love with him, why are you acting this way?"

What way? Lovesick, I guess. Putting up too much of a breezy front when Pip and I were together, then moping when he didn't call. Sally fixed him up a couple of times with girlfriends of hers, which I found pretty hostile but didn't express it aloud. Somewhere in there, Justin was over at Concord Avenue for the night, and he and Sally invited me to share their bed. Justin's idea, not Sally's, and not much fun either. I made love to Sally while she sucked Justin off. The mechanics worked okay, but there was a desperate undercurrent as Sally worked frantically to keep Justin and me from touching each other. She needn't have feared: Justin was the last person I wanted to touch.

But the moping got worse, as I felt increasingly estranged from Sally and angry at her debasement at Justin's hands. To complete the circle of deceit, Justin had started secretly seeing Alida, who'd been smart enough to end the blurred affair with me but whose sense of being left out overrode her better judgment. It was beginning to feel like a hothouse, clammy and claustrophobic, being Alida's confidant about Justin and having to keep Sally in the dark. For me the only positive thing to come out of this round-robin of musical beds was Scott's thin-lipped disapproval of me and Pip. At last I was able to shed the lingering tentacles of that obsession, deciding he could go sit on it if he didn't like it. One less approval sought.

I was seeing Pip maybe twice a week, and one of those times he'd usually be drunk on his ass. He reminded me then of Cody, my roommate at Yale—the same unfinished projects on his drafting table, the same chaos of dirty laundry and unopened mail. If I visited him over at his place, a commune in Brookline that Sally called the Addams Family, he'd sit in the drafty solarium two-fingering the upright piano. Please don't go, he'd tell me. But please don't make him talk either. So I curled up in a ratty overstuffed chair and worked on a poem while Pip made lonely music.

I thought we needed to get away, so we drove to Provincetown for an overnight. But all he wanted to do was drift from bar to bar, drinking boilermakers, and it ended with us sleeping in the attic of a guesthouse, rain beating down on the roof a foot from my head. I watched him sleep and thought, *This isn't the one.* Not that I had the strength to say so and pull out of it, but I knew I was angrier now than anything else. Tired of his pontificating about building a real life with a woman, sick of coming up short because Pip was straighter than I.

Then I met Ellen. It was a dinner reunion for several of us who'd taught together at Andover, but I don't remember anyone else who was there. Ellen was the roommate of the hostess, not really there for the party, passing through to get herself a cup of tea. We locked eyes and smiled, and right away all other bets were off. Her thick chestnut hair was down, tumbling nearly to her waist and rustling when she walked. Her beauty had nothing to do with pretty; mysterious was the main thing. A wide brow that hooded her probing eyes, the smolder of her dark skin, a haunted smile. Otherworldly, and something about her that beckoned you there.

We talked on the stairs for an hour, halfway between the party I no longer cared about and the sanctuary of her bedroom, where she repaired to recover herself after a week in the trenches. She worked at City Hall in Boston, writing the script for the city's two-hundredth birthday, two years away and already a nightmare of logistics. But none of that mattered to Ellen, now that spring was coming on. She couldn't bear the hibernation of New England winters, and bloomed in the sun more than anyone I ever met. Three mornings a week, she went to the Zen center in Cambridge to chant. She had a mystical passion for things Native American, and was always reading the speeches and prayers of some holy chief, when she wasn't devouring Joseph Campbell.

Depths upon depths she suggested, and I was ready to dive before the evening was done, hating to let her go upstairs alone. In my journal I cautioned myself not to be so precipitous, to try to figure out first what I wanted. But I think all I wanted was life to happen without any figuring from me. I'd been honest with Ellen, spilling the tale of my tightrope walk between gay and straight, especially my upheaval over Pip. She was at the lingering end of a wrong-headed relationship herself, the long good-bye, so she didn't seem so ready to jump herself. I let ten days go by before I called her, an eternity for me.

Pip was delighted to hear I'd met a woman; that gave him license to talk about Barbara, his on-again-off-again girlfriend who sounded, if possible, more co-dependent than I. Pip said he drank less when he was with me, so he must've been nearly comatose with her. But I never said no when he called and asked to come over, even if it felt more and more like walking on eggs. We didn't have sex unless he proposed it, because I was afraid of scaring him off. We'd lie in bed with a sort of invisible sword between us, Pip bemoaning the confusion of his life, berating himself for being afraid of making a commitment to Barbara. Not a word about him and me. Then he'd turn the light off, and I'd wait to see if he moved to touch me.

Cantwell suggested bluntly that I not see Pip anymore. He thought I needed to face being alone and let the despair of that wash over me, and then we would see what I really wanted. But I waffled all through April, waiting for someone else to make an irrevocable move. Sally and I fought over stupid little roommate things, and more than once she snapped that Pip and I were "counter-productive." Then I'd spend the weekend at Ellen's, hoping the bi confusion would go away. I loved her exotic intensity and her willingness to talk for hours about emotions. I wasn't exactly afraid to make love to her, or even especially impotent, but I couldn't shake the feeling that I was faking it.

Notes from a session with Cantwell, first of May:

No goals, Monette, no purpose, therefore no commitment, no self-command, no self-respect. Started from getting no direction or goals from parents. And the relationship with Pip is therefore directionless.

A note from Ellen, May third:

My friend, what I fear from you is the response from my soul to greet you, aching and surging and loving the moorings below where life is in one sense complete, even then rising up to laugh in the joy we meet again and again. Never before has such communion in energy been unmirrored and respectfully separate . . . I need you, yet I am in flashing tremors panicked by the space between us that I feel powerless to enlighten. You do not know why I do not force myself upon you? Then I shall say it again. Because I am afraid I will grow to love you more than I love myself and because I fear you believe you don't know what commitment is. You do know, you are given, but your mind etches splendid diagrams of warning, distrust and invalidation, so that while conscious you are still not responsible. The understanding I have for you, windswept and alone as I am in a dark core, is recognition of and sorrowing with you over your own spaces, the intellectualized emotions baited for withdrawal. And yet these are darkening my own, even as you fill me with life.

Writing in my journal at the Casablanca, May eighth:

Very depressed, very bad. Called Pip 20 minutes ago and told him I couldn't handle it. He sd he wasn't trying to avoid me but he is, and he sd "it" was sexual but couldn't talk about it . . . What *do* I want? What do *I* want? I don't know. Cantwell has been saying all along that it's a bad relationship with Pip. I don't know *how* to want Ellen, I feel so impotent . . . And I can't stand to be alone, to be stuck in the middle of it all . . . The issue is that I don't have any sexuality, that I can't imagine sex being easy or fun, it has *always* been such a battle with impotence for months now. Am I supposed to be on the floor, on the bottom, and crawl up into a relationship with a woman, deflecting myself from the pain of loving a man, and then get somewhere, allow myself to be loved, and then it falls apart because I can't make demands and then fall back to the distances with a man?

Late that night Pip called to tell me it was over between us, and I spent the next two days weeping. When I met him so we could take our keys back—in the alley behind Barney's, where Edie had gotten him a job as a cook—he told me I should feel relieved instead of sad. "I thought you understood from the beginning that it was casual," he said, "that it wasn't the point."

So what was the point? Losing Pip only seemed to intensify my divided nature. I'd spend a day or two with Ellen, pleading for wisdom, trying to stop intellectualizing my feelings. I knew she was a sanctuary, but I couldn't commit, fearful I would be using her. And then for the next couple of nights I'd be cruising at Sporter's, my bar of choice, half the time going home with someone and backing out at the last minute. Because I was as impotent with men now as with women. Or I'd go through the carnal moves with a man and flee, never staying over, running home to grab my journal so I could record the guilt and shame.

Sally told me I had to get my own place, a move that didn't surprise me. It was painful for us to face one another at breakfast, evidence of how far we'd moved apart. I signed on for another summer running the theater at Andover. That way I'd be out of Concord Avenue by the end of June but still have till the end of summer to find a new apartment—with or without Ellen. I agreed to up my reenlistment at Canton to three courses in the fall, because I wasn't exactly doing a booming business in Day-Glo bedrooms. I didn't care about work anyway, except for the poems pouring out of me about one affair and another.

But before heading up to Andover, I turned the screw of myself a further twist; I accepted Justin's invitation to spend a few days in Vermont at one of his crashed spaceships. While he laid tile in the house, I built a stone wall along the driveway. The work was profoundly satisfying, the most sweat I'd broken since riding shotgun on the coal trucks. But of course I had gone up-country for only one reason, and that was to get it on with Justin. Was it because I was angry at Sally? Or had I finally decided Justin and I were comrades under the skin, since he was embracing rather than running from his bi instincts? I didn't particularly desire him, but did get into the porno fantasy of a couple of country laborers mingling their sweat. When he fucked me, he didn't understand why I was laughing. Because we'd finally completed the twisted circle, Sally and Alida and Pip and Justin and I, and still none of us seemed to have a clue how to make love work.

I think what kept Ellen and me together that summer was the Watergate hearings. We were both Nixon haters from way back, that sweaty porkface being the perfect symbol of the lies of a dying empire. From "I am not a crook" to Erlichman's smug assertion that the Constitution was "outdated," we loved the morality play of it all, the stripping of the emperor's polyester. The hearings were replayed every night at eleven, so that after rehearsal I'd race to Newton to watch them at Ellen's house. We crowed to watch the President's men crumple and deflate, Mitchell and Haldeman and the rest. If politics is indeed an aphrodisiac, then it was Nixon's fall that got my dick hard so Ellen and I could make it. Fucking on Nixon's grave.

In July I also found out that a publisher in Boston had decided to take my manuscript of poems. A fluke of the first order, for the editor had once been a playmate of Sally's. In April he'd come for dinner to Concord Avenue, and I made sure he didn't leave without my poems under his arm. I think Sally may have even given him a wank for old times' sake. Not that my little book couldn't have made it on its own merits *eventually*, but it seemed entirely fitting that those keenings of sexual doubt should see the light of day because of a panting extramarital liaison. The editor didn't appear to understand a word of my stuff, but I didn't care. Having made it at last was all that mattered.

So I floated through that summer in a delirium of pride. In mid-July I signed a lease for an apartment at 472 Broadway in Cambridge, just behind the Fogg Museum. It was clear enough to both Ellen and me that we weren't ready to live together, even though we'd managed to achieve a workable relationship, loving and respectful if prey to those windswept distances. Saturday afternoons we'd take off for the country, out to the Berkshires or up to Crane's Beach in Ipswich. That's when we were closest, cavorting in the icy surf and hiking in the hills. We'd both grown up wanting to run away, and sometimes we brought it off, runaways in the wilderness of summer. Making love in out-of-the-way motels, lulled to sleep by the throb of crickets.

And yet the self-doubt wouldn't disappear, the sense that the love was all performance and held no desire:

7/27. Thinking about E. I think: well, perhaps I can bring it off after all, our sex life is pretty "normal" now, whatever that means. Not exciting, but that's because I don't believe in myself yet to *make* it exciting. And thinking: all right, it's a together and complete relationship, but what about my need to be alone, what about my love of the poses and smut and daring of getting a man, what about pure *desire.* . . .

It began to seem impossible, this business of trying to change. I'd see the hurt in Ellen's eyes and think I could no longer stand it. I pleaded with Cantwell to let me break up with her. But he was off for his August break and put my hysteria down to fear of shrink abandonment. Keep my life in a holding pattern, he ordered me, and we'll see what happens. I began to understand that he liked me depressed and crazy with doubt, because that way I was more honest, less full of rhetoric.

For a week over Labor Day, a client of mine let Ellen and me have her house on the dunes in Truro — a haunting fisherman's cottage that had appeared in a slew of Edward Hopper paintings. We had a glorious time there, baking out all day on the nude beach, then hunkering together on the deck to watch the sunset. We'd go nearly the whole day without talking, and yet there were no distances. I remember thinking we could make it work if we could always be on vacation. Then one afternoon, Ellen made friends on the beach with a man in his sixties, a designer from Montreal. I barely nodded hello to him, but heard later that he observed, "Your lover's a homosexual, I believe." Ellen admitted as much, saying that she loved me even though the sex wasn't very good. I was furious with betrayal when she told me this, cut to the heart, and paranoid all over again that I "looked" queer, even with a woman on my arm.

Yet we persevered, probably against our better judgment. For a while we were both too busy to have it out between us. Ellen was swamped by deadlines at *Boston 200*, and I was juggling a three-quarter schedule at Canton with the demands of several clients. Now that I had a foot in the door of Poetry, I was eager to cut free of the decorating trade. But I had these lingering commitments to get out of the way, especially my role of lay shrink to various premenopausal suburban wives. Frazzled from all the pressure, I decided I needed to work on my philosophy.

So I picked up *Walden*, one of the really glaring lacunae in my formal education. During my free periods at Canton I'd drive out into the Blue Hills, walk a ways into the woods, and strip naked, sitting in a patch of sun while I read Thoreau. I was not unaware of the pure theatricality of the gesture, but then neither was Thoreau, a pastoral drama queen if there ever was one. "I would rather sit on a pumpkin and have it all to myself," he wrote, "than be crowded on a velvet cushion." My sentiments precisely, and I was in the velvet cushion business. It would take me a year and a half to finish *Walden*, so much did I savor and brood over every line. And Thoreau would become my main man, so much so that by the next summer I'd be driving out to Walden Pond itself — to read my daily text on Henry's doorsill, all that was left of the world's most famous cabin.

Which says something about how literal I am. It also serves as a pretty accurate symbol of where I was headed in the fall of '73. I wanted to call a halt to all the demands being made on me. I was so sick of hearing myself talk about sexuality — hetero, homo, and otherwise. Maybe I was finally willing to do what Cantwell wanted: to stop grabbing at one relationship after another and get to know myself. Nothing felt right, neither my evasions of intimacy with Ellen nor my stiff sentinel pose at Sporter's, where I probably looked so fierce and self-protected that nobody dared to cruise me. I finally had an openly gay friend in Boston, when John moved to Beacon Hill after graduating Yale. But he had a lover who didn't much like me, mostly because I was still so closeted, and somehow I twisted that up into thinking I'd never fit the bourgeois restraints of a gay marriage either.

It was strange, but after fifteen months of therapy I was growing more and more inarticulate, as if I'd run out of things to say about myself. This was unnerving, but there was relief in it as well, because I was also fresh out of excuses. I only knew I had to change my life, that it wasn't enough to be naked in the woods for an hour here and there, stolen moments. I needed to steal much much more if I was ever going to make up for the years I'd thrown away in the closet.

During that Watergate summer at Andover I'd met a young poet from Yale who came up to visit some mutual friends. Sandy McClatchy was dauntingly bright, with an encyclopedic recall of everybody's work and the shrewdest analytic brain for what it all meant. I felt like a charlatan beside him, since half the poems I read went right by me. Yet Sandy was neither intimidating nor pretentious, glad to have found a kindred spirit who got off as much as he on lit'ry gossip. What was intimidating was his Black Irish good looks, though he was far too well-bred to trade on them. But I understood he'd been through an upheaval over his sexual nature that wasn't all that different from my own. Sandy was much further along in the process of self-acceptance, though he never faulted me for lagging back.

Several times during the fall, I drove to New Haven to stay overnight with Sandy, usually when some literary giant was reading at Yale. I always acted like a breathless fan, but Sandy had a capacity for deference that wasn't fawning or self-denying, so the giants tended to treat us as equals. "Well, why don't you have an affair with *him*?" Cantwell asked bluntly during one of our sessions, when I was waxing eloquent about how simpatico Sandy and I were. Out of the question, I told him. Two poets would only burn one another out. But I wasn't telling the truth, which was that I wanted Sandy yet was afraid of what would happen if it worked. For then I would have to stop this waffling — half straight, half gay, one step out of the closet, two steps back. And I would have to break up with Ellen, a prospect that left me paralyzed with cowardice.

So I played the same shell game with Sandy that I'd been playing for years with César — bonded like brothers, everything-else-but-sex. And because he was so decent, Sandy never pushed for more, though now nearly twenty years later I wish he had. As if I wouldn't have run the other way. By that point, as I began to have more contact with my gay brethren in the literary world, I was using my bisex ambiguity as a last shield. I'd stiffen at every in-joke and camp irony, fearful that if I so much as laughed, I'd be branded queer. Preferring to come off as oddly sexless, neither here nor there, and always trying to keep the conversation rigorously literary.

It's no wonder that I suffered all that autumn from a lingering neurasthenia — sleeplessness, fatigue, even hot flashes. The glands in my groin were swollen, and I had a persistent rash at the base of my dick, tiny sores. One night I woke up sweating from a dream in which my dick had come unscrewed like a light bulb, and I couldn't get it back on. My body and my unconscious knew more than I what a crisis of identity I was in. Yet doggedly Ellen and I continued giving it our best shot, driving off for weekends into the red and gold of autumn, talking it out, over and over, where we were going. It was the least I could do to try and say it, but the fact was I didn't know. It was all just words.

11/26. Heavy talks with E last night and Alida tonight, during both of which I thought I was losing my mind, going crazy, I was so incapable of knowing what to say. So I sd crazy guilt-ridden generalizations and couldn't really own them . . .

11/27. My poor rash. Cantwell says that Alida and E have a great deal invested in the old Monette and naturally (with concern, without rancor) want me to act "right" again, and I can't. But I don't know what the new Monette is and have to keep saying "I don't know." I feel fairly calm and together until I have to explain myself at all to anyone . . . Sex is more regular with E. That is, I'm not afraid I can't do it anymore, but I can't stand the intimacy of it, can't face being the man in the situation. And yet I think of Bruce on Saturday [a trick] and get pissed thinking how irrelevant I was/am in the passive role. I want to *be* the man who has me.

Two days later a doctor finally diagnosed my rash as herpes. No treatment available at that time, and the outbreak could last two years. Worse, no counseling about how not to spread it or even how contagious it was. The doctor spoke as if it was just a minor annoyance, part of the downside risk in the sexual carnival we were all living in. I didn't tell Ellen — never really confronted it till she found the first sore on the inside of her thigh, maybe a month later. It was only then, seeing the cloud of fear and betrayal in her face, that I understood it was a much more dangerous business for women. That the herpes virus might be a cofactor for certain kinds of cancer.

By then of course it was something of a last straw, proof of how destructive my waffling had been for both of us. We didn't mean to let it go on so long, except there continued to be so many occasions of grace — quiet evenings in one another's arms, the tender expressions of loyalty, and a history now as well. We were doomed, Ellen and I, but we owed some allegiance still to the honesty we managed to elicit from one another. I suppose we were really engaged in a long goodbye of our own, but we seemed determined to do it without any bitterness — to learn from this, so we would be better the next time.

Ellen decided to join her family in Paris for Christmas. This separation would mark the final divergence of our two paths, but if we knew it going in, we didn't say so. All through December Ellen was under the gun at work, and I was back and forth to Andover because my mother was in the hospital, a cancer scare that turned out to be benign. Thus Ellen and I would only meet in passing, late at night and both of us exhausted. When I left her off at the airport, over drinks in the tower lounge, I remember squeezing her hand and saying things would be different once she got back. Did I mean I would finally find the words to put an end to our misery? In any case I said *different*, not *better*.

Over New Year's I went down to New York to visit a gay couple I'd met through Sandy, a painter and a novelist. Actually I'd met only the painter, a flamboyant wit and self-proclaimed genius who knew *everybody* in the literary life. He and the novelist had been together for nearly twenty years, traveling all over, summers in the Hamptons, the whole bit. Hearing the stories, the totem names that constituted their circle of friends, I was ravenous for a taste of the high life of art. When Carl, the painter, invited me to come stay with him and Harold in the West Village, to go check out the New Year's parties, I fairly floated down on Amtrak, convinced I'd arrived at last.

What I neglected to factor in was Harold. Though he and Carl were bound at the hip and deeply loving, they were no longer much good for each other. Too much artist for one apartment. They were engaged in an even longer goodbye than Ellen and I, but they were both looking too. And indeed the excitement was palpable between Harold and me from the moment we met. His craggy intensity and the constant barrage of chain-smoking opinions. Forty-five years old — ancient to me at the time, though now that I'm forty-five myself, I feel like telling

Harold, *Oh, I get it now*. We talked till four in the morning three nights running, and I watched him fall in love with me.

But wouldn't give it back. He never actually made a pass, though I'd never felt so undressed by somebody's eyes. We tramped the city together, museums and concerts and louche cafés, laughing with giddy delight to be together. I realized this was how it must have felt to Scott when I was his poet-mentor, giving every ounce of myself the way Harold did now. I loved the feel of being taken care of. Then we'd come to the end of the night, after the theater and late supper, and Harold would get too close and talk romantic gush. And I would stiffen and stare into space, my everything-else-but pose.

"Tadzio," he would call me, clucking with irony, and tease me even harder. "Excuse me, Miss Garbo," he'd say. Or when he got angry the final night, as I turned away from a kiss that was really quite chaste: "You know what your problem is, Paul? You've seen *Queen Cristina* one too many times."

I didn't understand how truly smitten he was. To me it was only a playful brief encounter, flattering to my ego but not what I was after. Harold and I weren't in sync — I didn't want to be his boy, and that was all there was to it. Besides, I had to go home and face Ellen, a situation that was crying out for resolution. All day before her plane touched down from Paris, my mind raced: *I've got to get out of this, I can't give her what she wants*. And then she walked through the gate, sweet and easy and laughing, and I choked with relief to hold her again.

But in fact the relationship had changed. It wasn't assumed anymore that I would be staying over at her house, though I still did now and then. We no longer planned our weekends together unless at the last minute, if both of us were still free. And there was an unspoken agreement now that Ellen could date whom she liked and I could do my restless cruising, and we didn't have to talk about it. I could sense our lives grow separate, and how mournful it made us both feel, and yet how gently we went about the process of disentangling.

Carl called at the end of January, to berate me for having left Harold in the lurch. "Don't you understand how he feels about you?" demanded Carl. I dug in and got defensive, said that I'd been too overwrought with my own problems, and anyway it wasn't going to work between me and Harold. But I couldn't deny the flush of self-importance either, to think there was somebody pining for me. If only I didn't have to put out, I remember thinking fretfully, we could have a lovely time together. I don't know why sex was such an obstacle, such a non-negotiable point. Perhaps I felt frightened about having to perform in a situation where I wasn't wild with desire. I'd been in that position too often with Ellen. Or frightened of being loved again so soon. Perhaps I thought I could keep it under control if I withheld what Harold called "erotics." Unwilling to admit where the boundary lay between withholding and cockteasing.

I started calling Harold regularly, more so as I pulled further away from Ellen. The phone was always the easy part with Harold, making him laugh—a wonderful release for him, who was famous in his circle for the black hole of his chronic depression. And he seemed to love giving me advice about handling the changes with Ellen or pulling the plug on my gasping career as a decorator. I began to appreciate that Harold was the most fully evolved gay man I'd ever met—wise and yet self-mocking, secure in his manhood, a tough and brilliant judge of writing. To Harold everything was first a matter of ethics, and nothing in his life went unexamined.

Of course I also glamorized his despair, how it gave an almost Greek-tragic fire to his brooding utterances. But since I was the one who could make him laugh, I felt an implicit dare whenever we talked—that if we let it happen between us, both our lives would change forever. A mismatch of two incurable romantics, that's what Harold and I were. He'd arrived at a place in his life where he never expected to be happy again. He had a lot of money from his family which he didn't appear to touch, dressing like a peddler in moth-eaten cardigans and taking his meals in the coffee shops of lower Fifth and Sixth. Now, as we played and flirted over the phone, Harold made it clear there weren't any limits on where it went from here, so hungry was he to keep laughing. We could go to the Bahamas over my spring break, Italy for the summer, whatever struck our fancy. I saw how very taken care of I could be.

No one had ever pursued me like this. And my life otherwise was dull, in the trough of winding down with Ellen. Cantwell had begun to notice that I'd been isolating myself of late, avoiding my friends so I wouldn't have to declare myself gay or straight. I was cruising at Sporter's two or three nights a week, but mostly going home empty-handed. With my business dead in the water, I was feeling grimly out of money, and dreading the prospect of recommitting to Canton full-time for the following year. More than anything I needed some drama in my life. So why didn't I go give it another shot with Harold? Cantwell practically ordered me to.

I went down at the end of March, four days when Carl was going to be out of town. Harold was delirious to have me there. Another hurricane schedule of opera and theater and literary parties. None of which mattered to Harold, who would've gladly stayed home trying to coax me to kiss him back. He put on the carnival of events for my sake, treating me like a prince, and even as I raced about laughing on his arm I was thinking how it would be if this were a permanent thing. To be kept by Harold — no more teaching meatbrain kids, no obligations except to be a poet. Wherever we went, running into Harold's friends, I'd see the flush of pride in his face as he showed me off.

No, that's not right. I did all the showing off myself, no cuing required. I charmed the pants off Harold's brother the art dealer, his best friend the producer, anyone who might tell Harold that I was the best thing to happen to him in years. In public I was all over him, what amounted to a proclamation of being out and glad of it. But when we were alone I'd seize up again, the Queen Cristina stare, and plead that I wasn't ready yet for erotics. A saint of patience, he was content to suck my dick a little and hold me naked while we slept. "Okay, that's enough," I'd say, pushing his head from my crotch before he could really get into it. The last thing I wanted was to come, revealing myself like that. And I never touched him back, for fear he would love me even more.

It was all confusion and conflict. The more time I spent with him, the more I felt guilty, that I was doing it strictly for the princely arrangements. I suppose I made a lousy golddigger — too much Protestant training about nothing good coming so easily. But I also took a secret pleasure in playing hard to get, a histrionic uncertainty that kept all the focus on me. I needed the seventeen years' difference between us in order to put my trust in his sagacity and worldliness. But I also wanted a man my own age, to discover the world along with me. I couldn't put any of this in words, thus leaving Harold more confused than I was and aching with blue balls besides.

On the last night of my visit he shook his finger at me like a witch's curse. If I kept working this hard to avoid being loved, said Harold, I would get my wish and never have it at all. I saw how hurt and lost I'd made him. How could I tell him I was looking for the one right man and he wasn't it? Yet I wouldn't let him shut the door either. For all his frustration he sent me back to Boston with an open invitation to accompany him and Carl to Italy for the summer. I said maybe.

But I knew in my heart I wanted the summer all to myself, to finish the process of coming out — to me if not to everyone else. And to conduct the search in earnest for the one right man. Oddly, the only two people I could say that to were Alida and Ellen, to both of whom I'd decided to dedicate my book of poems. Alida didn't want to hear it that I'd finally committed to being gay. She'd just come out of an awful relationship with a Jekyll-and-Hyde doctor, and was feeling used and ugly. She decided we talked to each other too much, that we needed to establish some distance. She was thinking seriously about moving back to Texas to go to art school, where at least she might meet a good ol' boy who'd treat her right. I understood it was time for both of us to move on.

By contrast, Ellen and I somehow managed the slippery transition from lovers to friends. When I got back from New York, I found she'd left me an album of Roberta Flack, with instructions to listen to a Jimmy Webb song called "Do What

You Gotta Do." Which finally pricked the tears in me, hurting for what Ellen and I had lost, terrified of the uncertain road that lay ahead. Thank God for AM music. Two nights before, I'd sat at the Met with Harold, dutifully listening to *Der Rosenkavalier* for five hours, the point of which had gone in one tin ear and out the other. Whereas the pop song went right to my heart as I played it over and over: *I've always known you'd go and do what you gotta do, my wild sweet love . . . I had my eyes wide open from the very start . . . You never never never never lied to me . . . Find that baffled dream of yours and come on back and see me when you can . . .*

After those tears, a lightness returned to the times we spent together, Ellen and I, meeting for dinner in the Square, shrieking with delight when Nixon's thug tapes were released. It felt like brother and sister now. She'd finally said yes to a guy at work who'd been asking her out for months, and I got to be her confidant as they played the courtship game. I wasn't jealous, just a little wistful, knowing it might be years before I found a man I could love, a love that would be returned in equal measure. Meanwhile, no more falling in love *at* somebody like Pip, and no more being the passive beloved either, letting somebody get overinvolved, whose feelings I couldn't return. Ellen counseled me to be patient and trust my heart: I finally knew what I wanted, and most people never found out.

If I had any final doubts about where I was headed, it only needed the sudden arrival of Star to make me sure. She'd been in Asia for six years, writing guidebooks to Bali and Singapore — a million miles away, but we'd always kept up with letters and poems, which sometimes arrived months after being posted. And yet I'd never quite given up that fantasy of making the change to straight before Star got home, so we could be lovers. The frog would finally prove to be a prince. Happily ever after, *that* old story.

When I met her at the subway exit in the Square, lightheaded with anticipation, she was as heartstoppingly beautiful as ever. The six years' contrast was much more disorienting for her; the awkward flinching boy from Yale had vanished completely.

Not quite frog to prince perhaps, but a full-grown man at last, sexy and sure of himself — or so I appeared to Star at least. We started up again as if in mid-sentence, no walls of any kind, drunk on poems. And when it was time to go to bed that night, we gave it the old college try, a spin at lovemaking. No question about the love, but too much water had gone under the bridge in six years, under *my* bridge anyway. The last thing either of us wanted was to pretend. We would make better best friends than lovers. And so we slept all that week curled together like spoons, without any lies or expectations. Star couldn't have been more supportive about my search for the laughing man, assuring me that anyone looking as hard as I was was bound to find him.

The summer arrived, at the end of which I would be returning to Canton full-time, though refusing to live on campus. I dreaded going back, an admission of failure to make my way in the real world, but that only made the summer more urgent, a last run at freedom. To kick it off, I drove with Sandy McClatchy to Sea Island, Georgia, where friends of his had lent him a house on a tidal marsh. It was on that trip that I first began to think about writing a novel, and indeed my first big sex scene would take place there, in the wild preserve at the north end of the island. That was where Rick and David would meet, fucking on the sand before they knew each other's names — my virgin attempt at nondickless writing.

But that writing was two years away, and it definitely didn't spring from anything between me and Sandy. All the way down in the car, I told myself to go with it, not be afraid. I was beginning to worry that I didn't know how to have sex with someone I *liked*. That I was falling into the cycle of so many men I'd met at Sporter's, for whom the only hot sex was with strangers, and it never got better the second time. Maybe I hoped the tropics would free both Sandy and me. But it wasn't meant to be. No tension from Sandy's end: he said the relationship could be whatever I wanted. Yet I felt myself back off in fear — not quite Queen Cristina, since Sandy kept everything so unpressured and relaxed. I also felt this hollow dread, that I'd finally meet the laughing man and let him slip away because I didn't really believe I could bring it off. I squirmed, remembering Harold's warning, that I would run away one too many times and never have love at all.

But that week with Sandy at Sea Island marked a profoundly important advance for me. It was the most I'd ever shared with a man of my own kind. Our being gay was simply a given as Sandy and I explored our hearts and writerly visions. Should we perfect the life or perfect the work, and couldn't one have it both ways? It was the first time I'd ever considered that gay might not just be about whom we slept with but a kind of sensibility, what survived of feeling after all the fears and evasions of the closet. Sandy didn't quite buy that notion; he preferred to think of himself as a writer who happened to be gay rather than as a gay writer. But for me it was a watershed, to begin to think I could tap into that sensibility, however little I understood it yet. Certainly my writing would never be the same, from this point on. My breakthrough to my queer self happened to the writer in me as much as it happened to the man. And it would take both sides working overtime — the poet and the cruiser — to break the final bonds of self-hatred so I could begin to love.

Returning to Boston, I spent most of the next two months by myself. That is, I made a conscious effort not to fill up the empty space by entertaining my friends and being the perfect weekend guest. Several days a week I'd simply get in the car and drive. To Ipswich, to lie on the beach, reading Proust and working on a poem about Stanley and Livingston, punctuated by forays through the dunes. The latter a hotbed of male carnality, or so I'd always heard, but I must've had the wrong map or the wrong moves, because the few tank-suited beauties I spied seemed to bolt like deer at my approach. On the rare occasions when I did connect — a beachboy kneeling before me in the white glare, servicing my ambivalence — I'd be so terrified of somebody's stumbling upon us that I became my own vice squad, never letting things go too far. The most I'd have to show for one of these quickies was a mess of green-fly bites, the stinging wages of being an outlaw.

272

More often, I'd drive out to Concord and walk around Walden Pond to Thoreau's place. It was usually deserted, enough so I could skinny-dip whenever I liked. Sometimes I'd bring a radio, to follow the final crash-and-burn of Nixon, which I naively assumed would be the end of Republicans for a while. Every now and then an intrepid tourist would wander up to pace the foundations of Thoreau's cabin, and I would be there on the stoop with the book in hand, ready to lecture if they looked puzzled. Was I some sort of park ranger, they must've wondered, in my herder's hat and cutoffs? No — more the genius of the place, the very embodiment of the master's words carved on the plaque in the clearing: *I went to the woods because I wished to live deliberately, to front only the essential facts of life . . .*

I was nothing if not deliberate as I went about the business of my freedom summer. It was surely the height of self-importance, to identify myself with the sage of the Concord woods. Especially since I only took my leisure there on sunny afternoons, hurrying home by dusk so I could get ready for another night at Sporter's. In any case it wasn't the pantheism of Walden Pond that got to me, but rather the depth of consciousness. My own deliberate search was for a man — a search Thoreau himself had clearly ducked, letting the woodcutter get away with a mouthful of philosophy instead of a kiss. It was only by seeing it as a quest that I got through so many lonely nights in the bars, or the even lonelier nights of tricking with guys who weren't quite right.

When July had turned to mid-August and I was still alone, only three weeks of summer to go, I decided to take my quest on the road. I took the Friday ferry to Provincetown, a pilgrimage to Mecca. I had about forty bucks in my backpack and no reservations, determined to shack up with someone who had a room or otherwise sleep on the beach. I drifted about till I stumbled on the Boatslip, then parked myself on the beach below the pool to await a pickup. *These are your people*, I told myself, but couldn't shake the feel of disorientation, that I didn't fit in. The men all seemed to be in groups, drinking too early and loudly dishing whoever walked by on the beach. I was too self-conscious to go take a swim and thus expose myself to comment. I already had enough self-doubt as to whether I was gay enough or out enough to make it in such a Dionysian environment.

But I watched it all hungrily, missing no flex of muscles among the demigods of the Boatslip, peering over my Proust with a longing to be one of them. When night fell, I joined the restless back-and-forth among the bars and dancehalls — not quite the Age of Disco yet. At one point I even hooked up with a hot Italian from New York, jet-black hair, a tan as deep as his bones, and a butt like a couple of melons in a wet paper sack. He didn't quite believe that I was a poet but found me charming in a professorial way. *Let's go back to your place*, he said, rubbing against me shamelessly. A dream delivered on a silver platter, but alas I had no room. He shrugged, gave me a philosophical kiss, and dove back into the sea.

I ended up at last call with a sad, sad boy who looked as lost as I used to look, but at least he had a room. One of seven kids, all the Catholic hangups, lying there rigid with terror as I tried to make love to him. I spent the whole night talking him out of the guilt, realizing just how far I'd come in my own fumbling journey. The sex was at best perfunctory. I was reeling with frustration to have missed my chance with the melon Italian, but felt it a kind of duty to the tribe to take care of this kid and make it all less frightening.

I met a man from Berlin on the ferry going home to Boston, and ended up spending the night with him at his Back Bay hotel, feeling very cosmopolitan and deciding I could happily live on room service. But even with Josef's address in my pocket and a fervent invitation to visit him in Germany, I'd come up with nothing lasting from my trip to Mecca, nobody I could see again. Summer was really waning now. I was seized with the superstition that if I didn't find someone before school started, I'd be imprisoned and alone for yet another year. Something to do with growing up in a climate that kept its clothes on. Summer had always been my only chance.

My tricks accelerated. I wasn't just cruising late at night now, but stalked all afternoon the banks of the Charles, casting pregnant looks at every man with his shirt off. Yet no one I met seemed to want more than an hour's toss in bed, which only left me hungrier. Envelopes of bullshit started arriving in the mail from Canton, the knell of doom. Something had to happen fast. And that was when Harold called, back from two bad months in Italy with Carl, bickering through the Renaissance. We hadn't seen each other since April, and I don't think Harold was really planning to propose we get together. But I made him laugh, and felt once more that burning wish to be taken care of, spirited away from the looming trap of another year at school. Before either of us could raise a caution, he'd invited me down for Labor Day weekend.

One last fling, it felt like. Harold and I laughed out loud to see each other again, and went back to our old breathless pace, two romantics drunk on the city. We spent an afternoon at the Cloisters, another at the Bronx Zoo, and the pattern was just the same between us. I couldn't stop flirting, and Harold couldn't stop being mesmerized. Over dinner at '21' I leaned over and gave him a lingering tongue kiss, sending waves of outrage through the blue-haired diners on every side. I was playing the kept boy again, but mocking it as I played it, which Harold found irresistible.

And we ended up in bed, and again I was a million miles away. Nothing had really changed in the Queen Cristina department. Oh, I tried — lying there stiffly while he sucked my dick — but the trying was almost more painful than the distance. I couldn't fake a gasp of pleasure. By Saturday night Harold was pleading with me to tell him where it was going, what did I *feel* — and I answered coyly because we were safely out in a restaurant. Harold blew up; I started to sob. *I just want to be taken care of* was all I could say, but I knew I had to get out of this. Harold was letting me hurt him, powerless to avoid being burned again and again by my cold flame. And no amount of earnest trying or laughing in museums was going to make it work.

I felt drained and defeated, taking the train back to Boston. It was Sunday the third of September, and summer's lease was over. School was starting in four days. I stumbled into my apartment — it was an oven from being sealed during the dog days of the weekend, all my plants expiring. And the phone rang. It was Richard Howard, up from New York for a poetry reading and staying with Rudy Kikel, a young gay poet whom Richard was eager for me to meet. Dead from the journey home, all I wanted to do was crawl under the covers. But I owed a great deal to Richard, who'd been championing my work and getting it noticed. It was Richard in fact who'd said to me the previous autumn, hearing the tangled web of my uncertain sexuality, that it was time to "let go with your masculinity, Paul." I hadn't understood it at the time — let go *of* it or *with* it? Whatever, Richard was one of the men I counted on to show me the ropes of the tribe. Of course I was free for dinner.

I quick-showered and took the subway over to Beacon Hill. Rudy lived at 112 Revere Street, barely spitting distance from Robert Lowell's boyhood home at 91. That sort of proximity, the poets' map of Boston, made all us apprentice types feel like larger figures in a diorama. I strolled into Rudy's place, my herder's hat cocked rakishly, ready to do my Byronic thing, a poet if not a lover. And there was Roger. Smiling quietly while Richard and I exchanged florid greetings, waiting his turn as I met Rudy and Rudy's boyfriend Craig. Roger Horwitz, Paul Monette. Say hello to the rest of your life.

Seventeen years ago today, as I write this. Did I understand that I'd found the right one at last? Please — how ready can a body be? Roger didn't stand a chance against my galloping heart. He remained the quiet one among us over dinner, trying to keep up with the poetry gossip. But I made sure I sat beside him in the Chinese restaurant so as to give him a running commentary of who wrote what and who was in or out. In my journal it says he reminded me of Dustin Hoffman, but by evening's end he didn't look like anyone but himself. After dinner we all went back to Rudy's, where Richard read aloud his extravagant poem "Wildflowers," about the meeting between Whitman and Oscar Wilde. By which time I was antsy to get out of there, catching

Roger's blue eye and rolling my own impatiently, a misbehaving Philistine.

When the two of us left together at midnight, scuttling down the stairs and bursting out onto Revere Street, the laugh that erupted between us was unlike anything I'd ever felt. For we were co-conspirators already, bumping shoulders like drunken sailors as we careened down the street to Roger's car, then back to his place in Cambridge. The only time in my life, I think, that I made love all night long. But frantically talking in between kisses, trying to fill in every detail, as if now were the only chance I might get to tell him who I was. And three times during the night he shook his head with the tenderest smile and said, "You're so self-conscious. Relax."

But I couldn't relax, not then. I wanted so bad to make the right impression, to make it last beyond the morning—the only thing that shut me up was falling asleep at dawn. It's a wonder he didn't run away, I kept coming on so strong. I still don't know how we made it stick, except right from the start I was the one pushing for this to be the great love of our lives. Despite the fact that Roger was up to his tits in therapy with a Freudian, the goal of which was to straighten Roger out. Or, as he sighed a few weeks later: "Yes I'm falling in love with you, but Paul, you're a guy." Oh indeed I was. Besides which, Roger was just starting work as a lawyer on the day after Labor Day—terrified they'd all see through him, a late bloomer at thirty-two after years of teaching Comp Lit. Not exactly the ideal week to begin a romance, let alone with a breathless poet.

Myself I don't even remember school beginning, suddenly the very last thing on my mind. Making it work with Roger, seeing the world together, that's what life would be about from here on. *Not being alone.* It all seems so inevitable in hindsight, meeting the one person who would make those twenty-five years of pain bearable at last. Because if the slightest thing had happened any differently in my checkered life, I wouldn't have been there to meet Roger that Sunday night on Revere Street. That much fate I believe in, the tortuous journey that brings you to love, all the twists and near misses. Somehow it's all had a purpose, once you're finally real.

I only wish my ghosts were happier today, after seventeen years of real life. Not that the moment of our meeting ever loses its shine, or the knowledge that one will never again have to make do with shadows. But the fevers are on me now, the virus mad to ravage my last fifty T cells. It's hard to keep the memory at full dazzle, with so much loss to mock it. Roger gone, Craig gone, César gone, Stevie gone. And this feeling that I'm the last one left, in a world where only the ghosts still laugh. But at least they're the ghosts of full-grown men, proof that all of us got that far, free of the traps and the lies. And from that moment on the brink of summer's end, no one would ever tell me again that men like me couldn't love.

About the Author

PAUL MONETTE (1945–1995) is the author of seven novels, four volumes of poetry, and several highly praised nonfiction works, including *Borrowed Time: An AIDS Memoir*. He received the National Book Award for *Becoming a Man*. He died of AIDS complications.